T0095623

Wine and Dine 1-2-3

A guide to the preparation of great dishes, choosing wines/beers to "ADD" during preparation and selecting wines/beers to "PAIR" with the dishes once they are ready to serve.

Joseph Coletto

Restaurateur, Executive Chef
TV Personality;
Food Writer;
Wine/Media Food Critic

Nicholas Coletto

Primary Writer;
Chef;
Wine and Food Pairing Consultant

Joseph Kudla

International Wine Expert;
...and consultant

authorHOUSE®

AuthorHouse™
1663 Liberty Drive
Bloomington, IN 47403
www.authorhouse.com
Phone: 1-800-839-8640

First published by AuthorHouse   7/27/2011

ISBN: 978-1-4634-3021-4 (e)
ISBN: 978-1-4634-3022-1 (sc)

Library of Congress Control Number: 2011910955

Printed in the United States of America

<u>Dedications</u>

Nick: To my family with all my love: to Al,

to Kwong &Shirley and to Cameron Nicole.

Chef Joe: To Stephanie, with love and admiration

INTRODUCTION

I.   What do we hope to accomplish?

This text is meant to provide the reader with comprehensive information on the preparation of great foods and the use of wine in the preparation of foods (the **"Add"** portion). It will also provide numerous suggestions for which wines might go best with the foods you will be preparing (the **"Pair"** portions). For some of the foods we have also chosen to make suggestions for the pairing of beers with the dishes. Including variations on the recipes, there are over 350 detailed recipes and over 250 suggested variations on those recipes for a total of 600 food suggestions contained in the text. Many use wines (**Add**) in their preparation but all will compliment (**Pair**) certain wines.

In addition, each recipe is followed by detailed suggestions for specific wine and/or beer pairings to be served with the completed dish.

We hope you enjoy reading the text that will provide you information and hundreds of suggestions. Always remember that they are just that---suggestions. The use of wine and beer is subjective. I am not quite sure how we got to the point where we are being told we must use a certain wine in the preparation of a particular dish or that we must use a particular wine to pair with it. That is certainly not how it was or still is

in the towns and villages that produce wines for home consumption. In those homes, the wine of choice is the wine produced in the village or even in the home.

II.   Why have we chosen to write such a book?

There are many magazines out today that will insist there are certain food and wine pairings. We, however; will not limit our suggestions to the obvious. We will offer the unusual and the unique and in doing so we hope to expand your choices. We may offer more than one wine that can be used in the preparation of the dish and explain how each will influence the result. In addition we will offer a number of pairing suggestions for each dish.

In my job as a wine associate for a large wine and spirits store, I often hear questions and comments such as: "Please tell me what wine I should serve with this veal dish." "I need a really cheap wine to cook with." "Should I serve a Chardonnay with that fish dish?" "I really like Pinot Noir but I am serving fish, is that ok?" "Let me try that wine; if I don't like it I will use it for cooking" "Why can't I serve a nice red wine with the chicken dish I have planned?" "Should I use the same wine I deglazed the pan with to serve with the finished dish?" "I really don't like wine very much but I do like beers; what are the best beers to pair with the foods I like?" "Can you really use beer in food preparations?"

When speaking about wines, which among us has either asked or heard the above questions and comments. There is so much confusion about what wines to use when adding wine to a dish and/or what types of wine to use to pair with a particular dish.

You may not believe this but recently there was a scientific book written comparing the molecular structure of various types of wine and that of various foods. They were asking if they could find the most compatible molecular structures and then recommends the best wine food pairings. I spent over 30 years of my life teaching high school and college science and have the greatest respect for science but I really think this approach a bit ridiculous. It is like comparing the molecular structures of various color compounds to help in the decision in the creation or apparition of an artistic composition. We all believed it was time for a fairly comprehensive cookbook covering the relationship between great dishes and the wines we might choose to serve with them.

III.   What is our philosophy about wine/beer food pairings?

The selection of wine is as much an art as it is a science. It is as much a personal choice as it is the suggestion of an expert. Don't listen to some expert tell you that **you absolutely must** use this particular wine to deglaze your pan when preparing a particular dish. Don't listen to someone who tells you that you **must** serve a French Left Bank Bordeaux with that chicken dish. Don't listen to someone who tells you that you cannot serve a white wine with the dish you have prepared or that you cannot serve a red wine with the dish. When you choose a wine wisely for the dish you can choose either a red or a white that will compliment it.

In addition, it is equally correct to select one of your favorite wines and then go about planning the menu around the wine instead of planning the wine around the menu. In fact it may be easier to do so. You have a great wine you love then choose dishes around that wine.

One of the most profound relationships I have heard about great food and great wine is that it should be a marriage. You have the great flavors of the dish you have created and the great flavor of the wine you have chosen to pair with it. The two should create a third flavor that should be greater than the parts.

We hope to dispel many of the myths regarding

using wine in the preparation of foods and the pairing of wine with foods. There is a need for personal taste and a need for personal experimentation in the use of wine in cooking and the pairing of wines with foods. True, it is always nice to have the advice of someone who has made the dish. But once you have our advice and may have even tried our method of preparation and pairing there is always room for your own feelings and experimentation.

Can you serve a red wine in a fish dish? Yes, if you choose it carefully and know what you would like to express in the final dish. Can you serve a white wine with a meat dish? Yes, if you know how the wine will enhance the dish that you are presenting? Always remember that when you pair a wine flavor with a food flavor you are creating a third flavor that shares characteristic of the food and the wine. You are attempting to create something that is greater than the sum of its parts. Feel free to experiment with wine food pairings and the use of wine in food preparation.

Our team is composed of food lovers, food experts, wine lovers and wine experts. We are devoted to helping people create great dishes and select great wines. Our background is basic but extensive. We grew up loving food and loving wine. We have translated that love into our professions as recognized chefs and as recognized wine consultants. We ask you to trust us in our recommendations. We ask you to prepare the dishes offered using our suggestions and to try the wine pairings. We ask that you learn from what we have to offer and then begin to experiment on your own. Once you have mastered the dishes we present, you should feel free to experiment with them.

The use of wine in food preparation and the pairing of wines with foods has been going on for millennium. For centuries, the grapes that were available were made into the local wine and that wine was used every day in the preparation of foods and was drunk with all prepared foods.

IV.   Yes, even I was a wine maker.

As for my own family, my father and I made 50-100 gallons of red wine (mostly Primitivo) every year in our home in Brooklyn. We went to the markets and bought the grapes. My father always looked for boxes of grapes that had at least some that had dried and turned to raisins. He "knew" from generations of wine making that this would add to the fruitiness and potency of the wine we were making. We followed the age old methods handed down from his father and his father's father in the crushing (no we didn't use our feet; we used a crusher) fermentation, pressing, barreling and ageing of the wine.

This was the wine we served at all meals, meat, fish, pasta, from the start of the meal to the end. We served real homemade Italian Red wine. There was never a white wine on the table. I never thought of white wine until I was an adult and living on my own.

I would dare to say that in the homes of many other "wine makers" this was not the case. In other cultures, perhaps German, there would be only whites or homemade beers. In others there would be fruit wines or wines made from grasses such as dandelions. Some of those wines would be dry, some semi sweet and others sweet. Each would be the wine served at the family dinners. They were the wines of the culture. These were the wines produced form the local grapes.

V.   Wine as a part of the family meal

From the earliest age I was taught to respect the consumption of wine as part of the family meal. In our country it might be considered inappropriate but as I sat next to my father at the dinner table, as an older teenager I was free to take some wine from his glass during meals. I was allowed to consume a bit of the wine that I helped him produce. He very closely monitored my consumption and I didn't get my own glass until I was an adult.

I do not want to say that the pairing of wines should be that simplistic but I do want to say that the pairing of wines with foods can and should be a very personal expression of the taste of the individuals. We have become a society that demands an exact response. There can be no such thing when it comes to the discussion of what wines should be added to dishes when cooking or what wines should be served with certain dishes.

VI.   What about this cookbook or should I say wine/cookbook?

I believe that there has never been a cookbook, this comprehensive, that has been devoted exclusively to **ADD** and/or **PAIR** use of wine and beers. For this reason our team of experts offers this book on the use of wines in cooking (**ADD**) and the selection of wines to use with certain dishes (**PAIR**) with a caveat that all the wines suggested are just that, suggestions.

We will offer a number of suggested wines that you might use in each dish that is an "**ADD**" dish. What will each wine add to the dish? How will it change if you use one of the other suggested wines? Try the wines we have suggested that you add to a certain dish. Do you find it doing exactly what you want to do in the final dish? Have you tried another wine that will enhance the dish to your expectations? Never be confined by a suggested wine as you should never be confined by a suggested recipe.

You are preparing a dish and the recipe calls for a cabernet sauvignon. You check your wine rack and find you don't have one to use. What do you do? Do you abort the dinner in mid-preparation? That is not necessary. There are many red wines that would compliment any dish calling for a cabernet. One of the things we hope to do is to make you comfortable in choosing a wine that can be substituted for a particular one called for in a recipe.

In like manor we hope to be able to prepare you to select a number of wines that will compliment a particular dish. These are our **PAIR suggestions**. Which wines will best pair with the dish---compliment the flavors. Why not a nice Pinot Noir with that salmon dish or that pork dish? Why can't I use a rich white from Burgundy with that veal dish?

VII.   How should you approach our recipes and wine/beer suggestions?

As you review the recipes in the text you will find many classic recipes. Why have we included these? We have done so because we believe that you must know the basic---the classical if you are to understand the new.

If you subscribe to the many food magazines or watch the many food shows on TV you rarely see the classics. Why? We question that. These are the dishes that have stood the test of time. These are the dishes that you must know if you are to move beyond them and create new and unique dishes.

In future editions we will turn to new and unique dishes but for our initial step into the world of food/wine **ADD** and/ or **PAIR** we have chosen to devote much of the text to classic recipes.

We do suggest that you use the recipes as they are written when you first make the dishes. Also, we would ask you to use the wines suggested. But that is only for the first time you prepare the dishes. After that you should be open to experimentation. Does the dish need different herbs? Can I change it using some other wine? Can I change it from an Italian dish to a Spanish dish by changing the wine, the spices? How can I make this dish my own? What can I add or subtract to make the dish the one that will truly express my own idea of what the dish should be?

As for the wines (**PAIR**) suggested to drink with the particular dish. We will offer a number of wines for each dish. Again we ask that you try the suggested wine(s) the first time you serve the dish. After that, use your own experience and pallet. Are the suggested wines the right ones for you and the people you are serving the dish to? Are there other wines that you feel would better bring out the flavors that you are trying to express? Should you serve a number of different wines so the people have a chance to choose? Taking all of these things into consideration we encourage you to enjoy your **ADD** and/or **PAIR** experiences.

VIII.   So who are these people writing this book?

And so now, you may ask, who are these people who would pretend to advise you on the use of wine with food and the pairing of wine with food? What about this team that has gathered for this project? These are very justified questions. Why should you take advice from me and my team? I would like to give you a little background on myself and our team. Remember, we are not the stars of the food network; we are not the stars of the food magazines; we are not the stars of the cookbook world. We are a group of people with extensive backgrounds in food preparation and wine knowledge.

We have not forgotten our roots in the family meals of our youth and the basic preparations that will enable you to develop you own style of food preparation. As we lead you through this adventure you will become a better cook, chef, wine coinsure, dinner planner. We hope to lead you through this developmental experience.

While we are not in the pages of the food media, we have the knowledge and experience to present to you this great text. We, like you, are working to prefect the art and science of food preparation and wine pairings. We, like you are still developing. We, like you are not jaded by the media. We, like you are ready to try new things without giving up the classics. From our humble but very expert backgrounds we offer you an introduction to Great Foods and Great Wines. So who are we? Let me begin with myself the primary writer of this text.

Nicholas Coletto:

I am the primary writer for the team. I was born into an immigrant Italian family where home cooking was the only way. I don't remember going to a restaurant until I was an adult. Everything was homemade—pasta—sauce—sausage—etc—etc.

Every September we turned 20-30 bushels of tomatoes into jarred whole tomatoes with basil, tomato puree and tomato paste. And we made 50-100 gallons of homemade red wine.

My father had a huge vegetable garden and we ate fresh grown vegetables all summer long. We then preserved all the excess produce. I must admit that while living at home I never cooked but I ate wonderful food all the time thanks to Mom.

I loved to eat fresh foods and when I left home to live on my own I had to learn to cook. I was a high school teacher, assistant principal, principal and superintendent in the New York City educational system for over 30 years.

I lived most of my life in the most ethnically diverse neighborhood in New York City (Jackson Heights, Queens). Within walking distance of our home we could eat in a restaurant specializing in the food of countries that most could only dream about---Italy, France, Spain, Germany, India, Chile, Argentina, Uruguay, Thailand, China (all areas you could think of), Viet Nam, Tibet, Malaysia, Ethiopia. Not only could we eat in this wide variety of restaurants but we could also shop in specialty shops and supermarkets that would provide all the fresh ingredients and sauces necessity to cook all of these ethnic foods at home.

One of my greatest joys was to eat in one of these ethnic restaurants, savor the foods and then try to duplicate the dishes at home. I pride myself with the ability to duplicate dishes at home using the ingredients available.

As with any food, fresh ingredients are the most important. I lived in a neighborhood that had unlimited selections. I rarely had very much in my refrigerator. Since I was a teacher most of my life, I could come home after school and walk down to the avenue and select the best of the best to use in dinner that evening. There were four fruit/vegetable markets, two supermarkets, 2 butcher shops and untold specialty shops within a two to three block walk from our home. You may say that I was able to use the European method of shopping for dinner, plan your meal by what is fresh in the market that day.

It is more important to select the freshest of ingredients for dinner than it is to plan a specific dinner menu. The menu should be driven by the ingredients available. If you have the time and ability to plan your menu as you shop, that will be the best way to provide the great meals. Fresh ingredients made simply will always provide you and your family with an outstanding dinner.

Once you have chosen the freshest and best ingredients for your meal it is then and only then that you can select the best wine to **add** and/or **pair** with those ingredients. Do not fall victim to the fact that you have a particular wine you would like to serve with dinner. It may not be possible to plan a dinner around a particular wine when you are unable to find ingredients to use in the preparation of dinner that will compliment or be complimented by the wine. Always be prepared with a number of alternatives for the dishes to be prepared and/or the wine to be served.

As for my background in wine, I have prided myself in the ability to select wines to go with the dishes I have created. I have never been confined by the white with this dish and the red with this mentality that many others have. I have always experimented with wines and have chosen the wines that I feel best compliment the dishes I serve.

As for the "add" aspect of wine, I have also experimented with various wines with various dishes. I have used sweet vermouth or sherry in dishes that called for Marsala. I have also used sweet sherry in these dishes. As for dishes that require a dry white wine, I have used dry vermouth (thank you Julia Childs) to deglaze a pan when making a wonderful veal Franchise.

My background in wine does not end with the simple trying of wines and experimentation with wines and food. For the last three years I have been employed by a national chain of wine, beer and spirits superstores. Over the past 2 years I have had the opportunity to taste over 1,500 wines.

In addition, I have been the wine/food pairing expect in the store where I have worked. I have been responsible for the selection and preparation of foods for all of the classes offered throughout the year. I have been responsible for the preparation of foods using the wines selected for the classes and for the pairing of foods with other wines used in the classes.

Joseph Coletto:

The major food contributor, in addition to me, is my nephew Joseph Coletto. He is one of the primer chefs in South Florida having grown up in the restaurant industry. After years in a family owned restaurant he spent time as a chef with **Legal Seafood**. From there he moved into an executive position with **Cheesecake Factory** and was responsible for opening new location around the country. He is now the chef in a private country club restaurant in Boca Raton Florida. Joseph, please tell our readers a little about yourself:

With over 30 years of experience in the food and hospitality industry, I like to think that the knowledge I've accumulated over that span will provide me with the knowledge and insight necessary for the many recipes I've created for this cookbook. Currently a Chef at the #1 Private Country Club in the State of Florida, and the #1 Residential Country Club in the United States, I like to think that at my current professional level, I've developed the understanding of people's likes and dislikes; and part of that understanding is the matching of food with other food; and food with wine and other spirits.

Having worked for some of the leading restaurant companies in the industry, holding positions in everything from a line cook, to kitchen manager, to restaurant manager, to general manager, to executive chef, to culinary area director; and having also been a proprietor of a very successful family owned restaurant in Boca Raton, Florida, my passion for food and drink is limitless.

Coming from a very close family, where Sunday dinner was a celebration of the family, the food became an important part of the celebration. Later, in college, when I met my wife to be, I learned a whole new level of appreciation from her large Italian family. Having owned restaurants in Manhattan for many years, they gave me a whole new perspective about the love of food, wine, and family. I like to think that my level of passion for what I do has been greatly influenced from both my family and my wife's family.

Some of my accomplishments and recognitions over the years have included; Chef Chairman of Boca Bacchanal Food & Wine Festival in Boca Raton, Florida in 2003 & 2004; Featured Chef at the Creative Cooking Expo at City Place, West Palm Beach in 2004; appearing on WPTV Channel 5 News as the "South Florida Sea Food Authority", with a number of featured television series such as: "Fearless Fish Cookery", and "Cool Cookin' in Hot Weather".

I've been awarded the "Best of the Palm Beaches" award in 2003 from the Palm Beach Post for "Best Sea Food" restaurant in Palm Beach County. I've also had a number of recipes published in all areas of print, and earned the opportunity to be flown to Hollywood, California to cook for the cast of the Emmy-Award winning show, "The West Wing" when they craved some east coast style seafood cooking.

Some of my other accomplishments include volunteer work for local charities and a participant of the "Taste of the Nation" fundraiser to feed the homeless. I've also participated in the "Principal for a Day" program in Palm Beach County where I had the opportunity to go to area high schools to teach students about the culinary and hospitality industries.

By far, though, my proudest accomplishment is being married to my wife Stephanie for 20 years, and watching my son Joey's performances on the drums. I currently reside in Lake Worth, Florida; previously in Boca Raton, Florida and Brooklyn, New York.

Joseph Kudla:

The other team member and the one responsible for bringing untold wine expertise to the team is Joseph Kudla. He has years in the wine business and has been trained in wine tasting and selection. He has visited over 100 vineyards in the U.S. and Europe and by his own conservative estimates has tested and evaluated in excess of 4,500 wines from around the world. In addition to his expertise in the selection of wines and evaluating he is an avid chef who loves to experiment with food and wine. Many of the recipes offered in this text will be ones he has experimented with and offers to you. I would now ask Joseph to introduce himself to you and present what he hopes to bring to this effort.

Hi, my name is Joseph Kudla and it seems that throughout my life wine has played a role even when I was too young to appreciate it at the time. I grew up in a predominately Italian neighborhood

where it was commonplace for everyone to save their empty 3 and 4 liter jugs for filling with your own homemade concoction we dared to call wine.

I moved to Florida in 1999. At the time I was 23 years old with a Bachelor's Degree in economics and psychology and having a career in the wine industry was not even thought of as plausible. I began working in a clearing house of a brokerage firm in Boca Raton. I was in charge of selling out accounts that were below the required margin equity for clients who were, for lack of a better phrase, playing with house money. After about a year, the firm was bought out and I was given a very generous severance package to "go away".

My two passions have always been sports and wine. In my married days, it was pretty much a ritual every Sunday for us to select 2 wines we had never tried before and drinks them with dinner and while watching television that evening. This was prior to my working in retail where Saturday and Sunday were days of the week when I didn't have to work. Ahh the memories

I used to do this thing where I wanted to prolong the weekend so I would wait to open the second bottle of wine and also prepare a special dish to go with it. The rules were that I had to keep the selection of wines and dishes new and not repeat myself as much as was possible. Keep in mind that this was several years before joining the company I now work for. Over the years I studied wines and tried to increase my knowledge by attending wine classes and tastings. I read much and visited wineries.

I find that the thing that has changed in the last few years since is there once was a time when I would think to myself I am preparing a certain dish for dinner so what wine should I pair with it. Now I decide what wine I want and then build a meal around it.

Over the past years working for a national chain of wine superstores, I have had an extensive education in wines from around the world. The company's classes have been extensive. They have sent me to California, Spain and France to visit and taste at all the major and many minor wineries in the world. I would compare my knowledge to wine to the most experienced in the industry.

One thing I can say after having tasted an average of 1,550 wines a year over the past 3.5 years is that pairing the right wine and food together is as close to achieving perfection that a person can do in their everyday life. The right pairing adds so much to the meal that it is almost indescribable. The intent of this book and what I hope to bring to it is to help each of you capture these brief moments of perfection in tonight's dinner.

IX.   Let the adventure begin:

As a team devoted to the enjoyment of wines and beers in the preparation of foods and in pairing the right wine, beer or spirit with foods we hope you enjoy the journey you are about to enter. Above all remember that recipes, wine suggestions, beer selection etc are just that.

We always suggest that you try the recipes as written the first time you prepare the dish. After that you should feel to experiment. Likewise feel free to experiment with the wines suggested in food preparation and pairing. Beers and spirits should be treated likewise. Above all remember the sky's the limit and your imagination and pallet should be your guide.

So now let's enter into our wine food adventure together. We will begin with a brief chapter on the major grape varietals. We believe that it would benefit the reader to know a little about the types of grapes used in the production of wine and their characteristics.

Then we will enter into the meat and bones and of course wine (pardon the pun) of the book. In each section we will offer a number of recipes some of which use wine in their preparation others that don't. For the ones that use wines, we will offer suggestions of wine(s) to use and for all dishes we will offer a number of suggestions for which wines would pair well with the finished dishes.

There was much discussion on how we should organize the book and present the recipes. Should we do it by country or region? Should we group dishes by the wines suggested? How would we best serve you the reader?

One thing we agreed upon immediately was the necessity of offering a huge variety of both traditional recipes and new recipes. We agreed that we should offer recipes that would enable you to be successful in their preparation and also enable you to experiment in variations.

For this reason we have chosen to use an eclectic approach in organizing the book. You will find sections on **"Chickens and their Wings From Around the World"** or **"Tapas---Tapas---Tapas"**. In addition you will find chapters on **"Classic and Not so Classic Italian Dishes"**. One of the most interesting chapters, we hope, will be **"From the Heart"** where members of the team present dishes that are very traditional in their families or that they have personally developed and their suggestions for add and/or pair of wine and/or beers.

Once we have presented a recipe for a particular dish we will introduce our discussion of wines by the statement, **"Let's talk about wine."** We will then offer a number of suggestions for wines to ADD and/or PAIR with the dish. We may also offer beer suggestions if we feel beer would best compliment the dish under discussion. Our suggestions will be specific and not just a statement like "choose a dry red wine". We will be offering you suggestions as to the type of wine we believe best, the vintner and the style.

In some cases we will group recipes, such as in desserts, and then speak in both general and specific terms about suggested wines for the dishes.

By the end of the book we will have offered many hundreds of wine suggestions in to hope to expand your knowledge in the selection of wines. In most cases, if the dish suggested is ethnic, we will present wine suggestions from the same region (country) as well as complimentary wines from other regions.

After you have absorbed all the information contained in this book, you still may have questions relating to food preparation or the pairing of foods with wine, beer or spirits. Don't hesitate to follow up on those questions. We would welcome hearing from you with these questions or other comments about the book.

X.   www.wineanddine123.com

The site www.wineanddine123.com is presently under construction and we expect it to be an interactive site. In addition to being able to email us with you questions and comments we hope you will provide us feedback on this and future editions. We promise to get back to you as soon as possible.

In addition we will be posting new recipes and variations on old recipes on a regular basis. We will also bring you news about our appearances at book signings and other special events. We look forward to a long and productive relationship with our new Wine and Dine family.

Contents

Chapter 1:

An Introduction to Grapes and the Wines They Become

Since this is one of the first of hopefully many comprehensive guides to the preparation of great food paired with wine, we thought it might be informative to present you with a little introduction to the various types of grapes and the wines they produce. While this introduction will not list every wine grape, we hope we will cover the most popular. Many of us believe that white wines are limited to chardonnay, pinot Grigio and sauvignon blanc and that red wines are limited to Chianti, merlot, pinot noir and cabernet. We hope to dispel this belief with the introduction of the many white and red grape varietals and the great wines they produce.

As we present the grapes, we will also provide a brief description of the characteristic flavors of the wines. Many of those characteristics will vary depending on variations in the soil and climate of the different areas in which they are grown. For example, the sauvignon Blanc from New Zealand will be very different from the ones from Napa Valley. Likewise, the Rieslings from Alsace will be totally different than those from Germany or from Washington State.

All too often, we in the industry are asked to suggest a wine to pair with a particular dish or series of dishes. When asked this question, I always ask in return: "What herbs will you be using in the dish?" "What side dishes will you be serving?" "Will most of your guests like white or red wines?" In addition, I always find out what types of wines the person likes? Once I have all the information, I will always offer 2 or 3 suggestions pointing out the qualities that each wine will bring to the dish.

Sometimes, when people are looking for a wine to add during the cooking process, they may ask us to suggest a really "cheap" wine to cook with. Occasionally people will say "don't worry, if the wine isn't that good, I will just be using it for cooking." When this occurs, I always try to convince that person that it is always better to cook with a wine that you would like to drink. Any wine you hate that remains in a bottle should be discarded; it should not be used for cooking because it will not compliment the dish being prepared.

As we suggest wines to "ADD" or "PAIR" in the following recipes, be sure to check back here in this chapter to review the flavor profiles and the characteristics of the wines we are suggesting. Knowing the characteristics of the wines and their taste profiles, will help you make the correct choice for the wines to ADD to the foods you are preparing, and to PAIR with those foods when you eat them. For this reason, we hope you find this brief introduction to grapes and the wines they produce informative. Enjoy your adventure in wine exploration. We trust that you will be able to use our suggestions with some expertise.

Some of the Most Popular White Grape Varietals

Chardonnay:

There are more chardonnay grapes planted throughout the world than any other white grape. From California to Burgundy to South America to Australia, chardonnay reigns supreme among the white grape varietals. That said, there are marked differences in the wines that this most popular grape varietal produces. The wines of Burgundy are vastly different from the wines of California because of the use of oak in the aging process of the wines.

Chardonnays can be one of three styles. They can be unoaked where the wine is crisp and clean without the woodiness of some California chardonnays. The wonderful chardonnays of Burgundy provide you with rich flavorful wines with a complexity of flavors. These are among the best of the chardonnays in the world.

As we move to California, we experience the introduction of oak in the aging of chardonnay, which adds woodiness to the flavor profile, as well as butter and vanilla flavor to the fruit flavors that are characteristic of chardonnay. The longer the wine spends in the oak barrel, the heaver the oak flavors of the final product. Chardonnay is one of the most diverse grapes, and in order to choose a chardonnay best suited to your taste and to the dishes you are preparing,

you must try the various styles with different profiles and taste characteristics.

Sauvignon Blanc:

Here is a wine where I could give you two glasses of the two different styles, and you would think that they are two totally different wines. Sauvignon Blanc has been a Bordeaux, France grape for untold years. The Bordeaux Blanc wines that it produces are crisp and clean with a bit of citrus. They lend themselves to fish and mushroom dishes. When the grape is exported to New Zealand, it will go from a light citrus to a very heavy grapefruit citrus. The second style is the "grassy" style that is a product of California. This grape produces wine that is crisp and clean with a sense of new mown grass and an apple/pear flavor profile. The two styles are very different, and will add much to dishes as an ADD or PAIR wine, depending on the style used.

Pinot Grigio/Pinot Gris:

These are one and the same grape but they can produce very different wines depending on the place that they are grown and produced. This is the number one white grape in Italy. The vast majority is grown in the Veneto Region of northern Italy. The wine produced is light, crisp and clean. It is not very complex and lends itself to drinking by itself on a hot summer day or with very light foods. The Pinot Gris' from Alsace and California are a bit more complex, elegant, aromatic and fuller bodied. These wines can range from light crisp and clean to complex, elegant and full.

Gewürztraminer:

This wonderful, complex, and wide-ranging wine is probably one of the most difficult to pronounce and to spell. Given that, this grape produces some of the best white wines in the world. From Alsace, to Germany to the Pacific Northwest, there are a vast number of gewürztraminers produced. The term itself means "spicy grape." It produces fruity, elegant, semi sweet, refreshing wines. The wines from Alsace are some of the best in the world. They are rich and elegant with a long and soft spicy finish. German gewürztraminers are crisper and cleaner with a slight sweetness and a crisp finish. Wines from the new world tend to be sweeter and less elegant and less spicy.

Riesling:

Considered one of the "Noble Grapes" Riesling makes some of the best and most versatile white wines. They can range from fruity and dry to very sweet dessert type wines. The three major areas where they are grown are Germany, Alsace, in France and in the Pacific Northwest. Riesling is the most widely grown grape in Germany and range in sweetness from the most dry (Kabinett) to slightly sweet (Spatlese) to sweet (Auslese). Late harvest wines, such as the Beerenauslese and Trockenbeerenauslese are even sweeter. It is light in style and usually unoaked. Some of the higher quality Rieslings lend themselves to some ageing and will improve with age.

Chenin Blanc:

This is a light, crisp wine that will have a very slight sweetness. Many come from France (the Loire Valley) and make excellent "Vouvray." They are also produced in the Pacific Northwest and some of the best come from South Africa. Their wonderful floral notes, slight citrus and melon/pear flavors, make them a welcome alternative for lovers of Rieslings.

Viognier:

What a wonderful alternative to chardonnay. This grape is rich and often full-bodied and has wonderful fruit tones. There are great types produced in the Rhone Valley of France and in the Pacific Northwest. It also has exploded in the Virginia vineyards and is producing many wonderful wines there. If you like gewürztraminers, I am sure you will love this wine also. They range from light and fruity flavors, to wonderfully rich, complex and dense wines that stand up to rich foods.

Pinot Blanc:

A grape that does very well in Alsace this is a grape that is a descendent from Pinot Noir and Pinot Gris. It is crisp and clean in nature with hints of pear and citric but has a low acid level that tends to make it gentle on the pallet.

Ribolla:

Planted in both Italy and Greece it is a grape that produces a wine that is very dry with citric hints.

Albarino:

An up and coming grape varietal that is used in the production of Vinho Verde in Portugal and some more rich and full wines from Spain.

The "Vinho Verde" wines are very light and slightly effervescent. Crisp, with the slightest hint of citrus, they are very easy drinking wines with very low alcohol content. The wines from Spain are richer and fuller bodied. They have more complex fruit flavors with that same hint of citrus. You should certainly look to these wines as part of your white wine experience.

Cortese:

Known in the Piedmont and Lombard regions, this grape produces the light and elegant Gavi and Gavi di Gavi wines. They are acidic yet delicate wines.

Furmint:

The great "Tokays" of Hungary are produced from these grapes. Many would say that they rival the sauternes of France in their complex sweet flavors. While they also can produce dry whites, they are best known for the sweet dessert wines. These wines have a high alcohol content and complex sweet flavor, to be enjoyed alone or with rich liver dishes or desserts.

Garganega:

Along with Pinot Grigio, this is the great white grape of the Veneto region of Italy. It produces one of the very light wines of the region—"Soave." These are very light wines.

Grechetto:

The wonderful light whites of Orvieto are from this grape. This is yet another of the light Italian whites.

Gruner Veltliner:

This is the great white grape of Austria. It produces a crisp wine with some citrus hints that are medium bodied and slightly spicy. It is a nice alternative to sauvignon blanc.

Malvasia:

This is a grape whose existence can be traced back for at least two thousand years. Although it is grown in Greece, this grape is very well known in southern Italy, because they were Greek provinces for millennia. Puglia, (the heel of the boot) produces a wonderful white. In Spain, the grape produces a sweet wine known as "Madeira," the favorite wine of Thomas Jefferson. It is a low yielding grape and may soon be replaced by higher yielding varietals.

Muscadet:

Famous for wines from the Loire Valley in France, it produces dry white wines with a hint of citrus and some minerality. Like sauvignon Blanc, they are crisp and fresh.

Some of the Most Popular Red Grape Varietals

Cabernet Sauvignon:

This grape is the most revered of the red grapes. It is used in blending in Bordeaux and as a standalone grape in all parts of the world. Its styles vary from the easy drinking to the big and bold. Cabernet sauvignon can be rich in tannins that range from soft to intense. It can produce wine that is ready to drink soon after production; to wine that should be laid down for 5—10—15 years.

The easy drinking style is made for everyday consumption; the more intense tannin style offers the ripe fruit and the tannins to offset them. The more elegant style will show softer tannins and ripe fruit flavors, and the most intense, will offer very concentrated flavors with tannins that are harder. Regarding "tannins" they are naturally occurring in red grapes and can be soft or hard. We refer to them sometimes as the "pucker power" of the wine---that dry feeling in your mouth after sipping a red wine. When robust reds are young

they often have harder tannins and as they age in the barrel and finally in the bottle they soften.

Cabernet Franc:

This is a wonderful grape that produces wine with light tannins and a floral berry undertone. It is blended into wines in France but is also produced as a standalone grape in California. Cabernet franc is one of the most common red grapes in the vineyards of Virginia. It is a great alternative to the cabernet sauvignons.

Carmenere:

Another of the traditional blending grapes in France, it has found a home as a wonderful standalone grape in Chili and now in other parts of the world. It is a big, bold red that has light tannins.

Corvina:

This is the grape that produces Valpolicella and its great partner Amarone. The lighter Valpolicella is soft and fresh with hints of cherry. The deeply flavored Amarone is elegant with deep fig highlights.

Gamay:

The light fresh grape of Beaujolais it is soft and easy drinking with light hints of cherry and plumb.

Grenache:

One of the blending grapes of the Rhone in France, Grenache has become a wonderful standalone grape in Spain and in Australia. It produces a light to medium wine with soft fruit flavors and tannins.

Malbec:

Originally one of the lesser blending grapes of Bordeaux, it has become the major red grape of

Argentina. It produces wines from the soft and easy, to the rich full-bodied reds. The tannins are soft and it lends well to blending with merlot and other grapes.

Merlot:

This is one of the more popular grapes for the general public. It offers a more fruit forward wine with softer tannins. Merlot is used as a blending grape in Bordeaux, and as a standalone grape in most of the world. Its major fruit flavors are cherry and currant, but can express other red fruit flavors as well. It can be light and easy drinking or more intense and rich.

Petite Sirah:

Although related to syrah, it produces a more intense red wine with a rich full body and ripe tannins. Aging adds greatly to the quality of this wine. It is a great wine alone, but is also sometimes blended.

Pinotage: The red grape of South Africa, it is a cross between a pinot noir and Cinsault. It can range from a light easy drinking wine similar to a pinot noir, to rich full-bodied wine with rich flavors and light tannins.

Sangiovese:

Throughout Italy, this is the red grape grown the most. It can produce widely different styles depending on the areas where it is grown. Sangiovese can produce the light easy drinking Chianti, the more intense Chianti, the rich full-bodied "Brunello", and the wide variety of local wines that have made Italy famous.

Zinfandel (in Italy Primitivo):

The great Primitivo grape of Italy, it was transported to this country by Italian immigrants and established as one of the premier grapes. It produces rich fruit forward wines that can be light and fruity or full-bodied and rich.

Pinot Noir:

This is sometimes considered the most elegant and velvety of the red grapes. It is difficult to grow, but it produces one of the most delightful wines of the reds. It can be very light with hints of cherry or strawberry, or more complex with a rich, inviting and even seductive velvety richness. It is the red of Burgundy, and now the red of the Pacific Northwest, in particular Oregon.

Shiraz or Syrah:

A wonderful blending grape in France, it was transported to Australia and became the dominant red grape there. It is one of the major grapes in the Rhone blends, and provides a richness and smoothness to their blends. The wines from Australia can range from a light and easy drinking table wine, to a rich and full-bodied wine with soft tannins and a peppery finish. The Pacific Northwest has now adopted the grape, and is producing some wines of great quality.

Barbara:

This Italian grape that is now being raised in other areas including California is a rich yet smooth grape that produces wine with soft tannins and rich flavors. It can be full bodied and can be a wonderful addition to rich Italian foods.

Gamay:

This is a very light red grape that produces the light and fruity Beaujolais.

Pinotage:

The wonderful grape of South Africa, it can produce light to full bodied wines that range in flavors form the elegant to the intense.

"Opening the Wine"

As a final note in this red wine section we would like to take a brief moment to speak with you about the fact that some red wines may be "too young to drink" and about the necessity of allowing some wines time to open.

Many of the richer reds such as the Bordeaux Blends from France; Deep reds from Italy or Spain as well as many Cabernets from California and other parts of the world may need anywhere from 1-5 or six++ hours to open.

That means that you will have to plan your day accordingly. You will have to open the bottle and decant it into a decanter and allow the wine to sit for 3---4---6---8 hours to allow it time to reach its full drinking potential. On last Christmas Day I opened two of the wines (one from Italy and one from California) when I got up in the morning so they would be ready to drink that evening with dinner.

We have made suggested notes after many of the wines we have suggested for pairing with the foods we have presented to you. The times suggested are minimum and may be shortened a bit if you pass the wine through an aerator when you decant it.

When you purchase such a wine ask you wine specialist how long it will take the wine to open and follow their suggestions.

How are Wines Rated?

For many, one of the mysteries of the wine industry is how are wines rated. One wine is rated 90 pts. From **Wine Spectator,** another rated 88 pts from **Wine Advocate.** Then there are ratings from **Wine Enthusiast** or **International Wine Cellar** or from other organizations. Why are there different ratings from different people? Whose ratings can you trust? Do they all use the same criteria when rating wines?

Everything about wine rating is somewhat subjective. While all rating agencies use the same criteria and the same rating sheets when they judge a wine, the judging is subjective. There is a person or group of people in the organization who sit down, taste and evaluate the wines. They score the wines in each of the listed criteria and then add up the score to generate a score of up to 100 points. The higher the score the better they think the wine is.

As you taste and even rate more and more wines you may find that your pallet is similar to one of the rating agencies/people but not to another. I have found this to be true of myself. In cases like this you may be more comfortable choosing a new wine to bring home when that agency/person has given it a good rating.

Regardless of who has rated the wine, a score above 90pts is considered exceptional. Scores above 95 points are rare and few wines have ever scored 100 points. A score of 85-90 is granted a wine that is excellent but may have one or more minor faults; 80-85 points a wine that is very good but does not reach the level of other wines. Wines given a score below 80 points are considered inferior.

You can evaluate wine yourself. As you evaluate each aspect of the wine use the clues along the way that are provided. When you judge color you might want to hold a blank sheet of white paper behind the glass.

Before you judge the aroma, swirled the wine in the glass and then smell the aroma. Breathe deeply and concentrate on the various aromas you detect in the wine. Are there many or few---are the aromas simple or complex. Can you detect different aromas?

Take a sip of the wine and move it about in your mouth before swallowing. How does it taste? As you swallow are there changes in the wine's taste? What are the characteristics of the wine from the time it enters your mouth until you swallow it and beyond?

Concentrate on the "Beginning" "Middle" "Finish". Some wines may start out fine but have no or little middle or finish. Others may be lacking in some other area. Never judge on only one sip of the wine. Smell and taste a number of times as you rate the wine.

As you taste a new wine you may want to make notes as to its characteristic, aromas, flavors, etc. You may also want to think of foods you would want to eat with the wine you taste.

1. What is the color of the wine? How aromatic is it? How would you judge the color—the aroma? Were you able to identify specific aromas? Is it very strong—pleasant—nice—not strong at all—little or none?

   Rate up to 5 points _____

2. How was the flavor of the wine? Was it enjoyable? Can you list the various flavors you have experienced? How did they all add to your enjoyment of the wine? Was flavor very strong to just there?

   Rate up to 25 points_____

3. What is the style of the wine? If white, is it crisp and clean---full bodied---oaky? If red is it intense, concentrated, or elegant? Does the style enhance the wine? Is the wine a good example of the type of wine? Is the style of the wine what I expected?

   Rate up to 10 points_____

4. How would you rate the complexity of the wine? Is it light, medium or full bodied? What about acidity? Were the flavors simple or complex? Did the flavors seem in balance? Is it food friendly? What about the sweetness? Was the wine dry—off-dry---semi-sweet—sweet? How did this affect your enjoyment of the wine?

   Rate up to 5 points_____

5. Does the wine finish well? Is it a complex or simple wine? Does it leave an appealing taste? How long does the finish last? Does it ask for more?

   Rate up to 5 points_____

6. Add up all the above ratings and then add 50 points to the total to arrive at your

   Final Rating:_____

Congratulations, you are now a wine evaluator!

As you sample more and more wines you will begin to develop some expertise in your ability to detect the subtle aromas and tastes that wine experts speak of when they evaluate wines. Remember that these are most often very subtle with just hints of the flavors identified.

The following are briefs list of some hints of aroma and/or flavors that you might experience with each of the types of wines. As you smell and taste the wine see if you can detect them. Remember there may be one or two or three such hints. Don't look for everyone listed.

Types of Wines and aromas/flavors to look for when evaluating:

1. **RED WINE**: Some of the aromas/tastes you might detect are:

   Fruit: Cherry, strawberry, current, blackberry, cassis, plum, resin

   Wood: oak, cedar, spice, smoke, butter, vanilla, pepper

   Others: dark chocolate, espresso, petroleum, barn yard, leather, earth, various herbs

2. **WHITE WINES:** some of the aromas/flavors you might experience are:

   Fruit: general citrus or specific citrus

fruits, apple, pineapple, peach, apricot, banana, various melons

Wood: oak, vanilla, butter, butterscotch, pepper, various spices

Other: various nut flavors, hay or grass, various herbs and/or minerals

3. **ROSE WINE:** When smelling/tasting Rose Wines look for the same aromas/flavors as white wine with very subtle flavors/aromas of the lighter berry aromas/flavors of red wines.

4. **DESSERT—PORT—SHERRY:** Here again you may detect the aromas/flavors of both whites and reds.

   Additional aromas/flavors: almonds, Pecans, walnuts; honey, maple, toffee, caramel

5. **SPARKLING WINES:** Since sparkling wines can be made from white grapes, red grapes or may be rose, the flavors/aromas will be dependent on the type of wine you taste. Look to the above sections for white, red or rose to assist you.

We encourage you to visit our website often **wineanddine123.com**. We welcome your evaluation of new wines you have tasted and we will be offering our own evaluations of wines that we have tasted along with suggestions for their pairings with foods.

Chapter 2:

A LITTLE BIT OF EVERYTHING

A Little Bit of Everything

Even though most cookbooks will be organized in a progression where the chapters flow from appetizers to first courses, then main courses and finally desserts, I have chosen to begin our effort with this chapter. After this chapter the progression will be more formal.

As we spoke about in the introduction, one of the major inspirations for the development of this cookbook were the wine classes we've conducted as part of our wine advisory positions in the past. In the beginning, food was ordered in for the participants and it usually had little or no bearing on the wines that were to be tasted that evening. Often the food that was ordered was in conflict with the wine.

When I first started going to the classes as one of the "pourers" for the wines being tasted, I realized that much more could be done to relate the food to the wines and at a much reduced cost.

I volunteered to do the food preparation and thus the whole thing began. For each class, I would research the foods from the wine applications we were to feature and created recipes that would complement the wines. Yes, the recipes were created by me and not just copied from the research I did.

As the classes flowed, I would present foods to compliment individual wines. We would then discuss both the wines and the wine/food pairings.

And so, this section is devoted to a hodgepodge of recipes developed and served in those wine tasting classes. We have decided to add a number of additional pairing suggestions to the ones that were originally paired with the dish during the classes. We hope you enjoy these foods as much as the class participants did.

For this section we have suggested some of the wines that were originally paired with the dishes as well as additional ones we feel would also compliment them.

Wine Bloody Mary/Gazpacho

4 large shallots, minced
4 stalks celery, sliced very thin
6-8 radishes, cut in half and sliced thin
4 ripe tomatoes, large chop
1 clove garlic, minced
2 tablespoons extra virgin olive oil
Juice of 3 lemons
2 limes sliced very thin and cut into small sections
3 liters tomato juice
1-750ml bottle white wine
3 teaspoons bitters
6-8 teaspoons creamy horseradish
12+ dashes Worcestershire
3+ dashes hot sauce
Salt and pepper to taste

Place the shallots, celery, radishes, tomatoes, garlic, limes and extra virgin olive oil in a bowl and mix together. Combine the tomato juice, lemon juice, wine, bitters, horseradish, Worcestershire, and hot sauce and adjust the flavor with salt and pepper. Chill the tomato juice mixture and vegetable mixture.

When ready to serve, add a spoonful of the vegetable mixture to a small glass and then fill with the tomato juice mixture. Serve.

Let's talk about wine: There is no other ADD & PAIR wine that fits as well with this dish as a *Vinho Verdi* **Gazella** or **Nobilus** from Portugal. To ADD/PAIR a little sparkle you might want to try a Prosecco such as **Botter** or even slightly sweet sparkler such as **San Orsola Asti**. If you wanted to use a dry sparkler you might want to try the Rondel Cava from Spain. Enjoy!

Tangy Citrus Shrimp

2 pounds 21/25 count deveined, cooked shrimp
1 fennel bulb, cut in quarters and sliced very thin
1 small yellow onion, julienned
¾ cup prepared cocktail sauce
2 tablespoon orange juice
1 ½ tablespoons lemon juice
1 tablespoon grated orange peel
2 teaspoons grated lemon peel
¼ teaspoon lemon pepper
¼ teaspoon white pepper
¼ teaspoon black pepper
¼ teaspoon cayenne pepper

Combine all the ingredients in a large bowl, except the shrimp and blend well. Add the shrimp and toss to blend well. Refrigerate 8 hours or overnight and then serve at room temperature.

Variation #1: Instead of shrimp, try using cooked lobster tail meat cut into chunks.

Variation #2: Grill 2-1 pound tuna steaks that were lightly seasoned with salt and pepper. Allow them to cool then cut them into bite size pieces and use them as the fish in the dish.

Let's talk about wine: To slightly offset the tang of the citrus in this dish, you might try a *Vouvray* from the Loire valley such as **"V"**. You also might try a *Pinot Grigio* such as **Santa Margarita, Kupelwieser** or **Kris**. A sparkler such as **Piper Heidsiech Extra Dry** would also compliment the tanginess of this dish. A crisp chardonnay such as **Edna Valley** or **Gumdale** would also compliment the dish. You could even add a bit of sweetness by using a Chenin Blanc such as **Mulderbosch Chenin Blanc.**

Roasted Mushrooms with Shallots and Fresh Herbs served with Basmati Rice

5 tablespoons sesame oil
8 cloves garlic, minced
6 tablespoons fresh ginger, minced
3 tablespoons dark soy sauce
1 pound shiitake mushrooms, stems removed and quartered
1 pound medium button mushrooms, quartered
1 pound medium Crimini mushrooms, quartered
8 large shallots, cut in half and sliced thin
½ cup fresh mint, chopped
½ cup fresh parsley, chopped
2 tablespoons fresh dill, chopped
2 tablespoons black and white sesame seeds
Sea Salt to taste
Ground black pepper to taste

Basmati Rice:

2 cups basmati rice
4 cups water or chicken stock
Sea salt to taste

In a large bowl, combine the sesame oil with the garlic, ginger, soy sauce, and the mushrooms. Toss the mushrooms to coat well. Spread the mushrooms on a baking sheet and roast in a preheated 400° oven for about 25-30 minutes, turning once. Scrape the mushrooms into a large bowl and add the fresh herbs and sesame seeds.

In 4 cups water or chicken stock, boil the basmati rice 20 minutes. When I cook rice, I like to use low fat/low sodium chicken broth. It adds much in the way of flavor and richness to all rice dishes.

Mix mushroom mixture with 2 cups basmati rice and serve warm or at room temperature.

Let's talk about wine: While this dish would most likely be a side dish for something else it could also be a brunch dish or main course like a risotto. If a side dish you will have to choose a wine that best Pairs with the combined flavors of the entire dish. If eaten alone the dish would pair well with a *dry rose* such as **Sobon; Dom Fontanel, Mulderbosch** or **Muga.** It would also pair well with an *Albarino f*rom Spain such as the **Rio Braxis**. A BRUT Rose such as **Taittinger Prestige Rose** would add a nice sparkle (pardon the pun) to the dish.

Cheddar, Bacon and Scallion Biscuits

(Yields 12 biscuits)
6 thick cut apple wood bacon slices
3 ¾ cups bread flour
1 ½ tablespoons baking powder
1 ½ teaspoons baking soda
1 ¼ teaspoons sea salt
½ cup (1 stick) unsalted butter, cubed
Melted butter for brushing
2 ½ cups grated cheddar cheese
1/3 cup scallions, chopped
1 ¾ cups buttermilk very cold

Position the rack in the oven just above the center and heat to 425°. Line a heavy baking sheet with parchment paper. Lay bacon on parchment and cook bacon until crisp; drain bacon fat and chop bacon coarsely; set bacon aside until ready to use.

Combine flour, baking powder, baking soda and salt in a processor and blend 5 seconds. Add butter cubes and blend until a coarse grain mixture forms, about 30 seconds. Transfer to a large bowl. Add cheese, bacon and scallions and mix well. Incorporate the buttermilk slowly to the flour blend. (The dough will be sticky.) Using lightly floured hands, drop one generous ½ cup of the biscuit mixture onto the baking sheet. Space about 2 inches apart. Bake the biscuits until golden brown, about 18-20 minutes. Brush lightly with melted butter and let cool.

Let's talk about wine: While this would almost always be served with another main dish, I could see serving these as a savory dessert with honey or maple syrup and butter. In that case, the **Bellini VIN Santo** or **Villa Lanata Muscotto de Asti**, or **Osborne Cream Sherry** or **Harvey's.** It would all go very well. In addition it would pair well with extra dry champagne such as **Martell Extra Dry** or a cava such as **Rondel Semi Seco. Martini & Rossi Asti** or **San Orsola Asti** would also add a nice touch of sweetness to the dish.

Pasta and Vegetable Salad with Soppressata

1 pound dry small pasta like Orecchiette
½ pound fresh mozzarella, cut into ½ inch cubes
6 ounces snow peas cut in thirds
1 small jar marinated artichoke hearts, cut in half
1-8 oz jar roasted sweet peppers (red/yellow), sliced thin
½ pound baby arugula, washed
1 small head cauliflower, broken in florets
1 pint cherry tomatoes cut in half
3 scallions cut into ½ inch slices, on the bias
¼ cup grated Romano cheese
1tablespoon fresh basil, chopped
½ cup extra virgin olive oil
2teaspoon grated lemon zest
4 tablespoons fresh lemon juice
½ pound Soppressata (sweet or hot), cut into ¼ inch cubes
Sea salt to taste

Ground black pepper to taste

Break the Cauliflower head into small florets. Toss with 3-4 tablespoons of extra virgin olive oil, salt and pepper. Spread the cauliflower in a single layer on a cookie sheet and bake in oven at 350° until just starting to turn golden (about 15 minutes). Turn at least once during the baking. Allow to cool.

Cook the pasta in salted water until al dente. Drain. Spread evenly on a cookie sheet and allow cooling.

Assemble all ingredients in a large bowl. Adjust the flavor with salt and pepper. May be refrigerated until ready to use, but remove at least an hour before serving. Red wine vinegar may be substituted for the fresh lemon juice.

Variation #1: Use sweet or hot capicola instead of the Soppressata.

Let's talk about wine: If serving this recipe as a brunch dish, a nice light sparkler would go well. You don't have to go over the top and one of the

Cook's or Andre sparklers would be just fine. A nice *cava* from Spain **Rondel** or dry *Prosecco* from Italy **Santi Nello** would also go well. If it is a special occasion than by all means bring out a bottle of **Montaudon Brut Rose** or the **MUMM Napa Brute Rose.**

Chicken Meatballs (with pork) in Light Gravy

1½ pounds ground chicken
½ pounds ground pork
1 small yellow onion, minced
3 cloves garlic, minced
1 tablespoon fresh basil, chopped
1 tablespoon fresh oregano, chopped
1 tablespoon flat leaf parsley, chopped
½ cup dry breadcrumbs
½ cup Romano cheese
2 Eggs
Canola Oil to fry

Gravy:

2 tablespoons extra virgin olive oil
1 small sweet onion, minced
1 clove garlic, minced
½ pound Crimini mushrooms, sliced
1 teaspoon fresh thyme, chopped
½ cup dry white wine
1-12 ounce jar of good quality chicken gravy
½ cup chicken stock
Sea Salt to taste
Ground black pepper to taste

In a large bowl, combine all the ingredients for the meatballs and mix very well. Form the meat into meatballs about 2 inches in diameter. In a large frying pan, over medium high heat, fry the meatballs in batches in the canola oil until golden.

For the gravy, in a large pot, over medium heat, add the extra virgin olive oil and sauté the onion until soft. Add the garlic and sauté another 30 seconds. Add the mushrooms and cook briefly. Add the wine and bring to a boil. Reduce the liquid by ¼. Add the gravy and chicken stock.

Bring to a slow boil. Add the meatballs and slowly simmer for about 30 minutes. (It may be necessary to add some additional chicken stock or water so that the meatballs are covered.) Serve as an appetizer or as a main course over rice or egg noodles.

Let's talk about wine: OK---your turn. Along our journey we will ask you to choose the wine to serve with the dish we are presenting. You may hesitate at first but as you try more and more of the suggested pairings and learn more about wine, it will become easy. Remember the flavors of the food plus the flavors of the wine should equal a third taste and that combined taste should be greater than the sum of its parts. Have Fun!

Rice & Ham Croquettes

1 cup day old cooked rice
½ cup finely chopped Virginia ham steak
1 green onion, chopped fine
½ teaspoon garlic powder
1 tablespoon onion powder
¼ cup frozen sweet peas (small)
½ tablespoon flat leaf parsley, chopped fine
¼ cup Romano
3 large eggs, divided
1 cup dry breadcrumbs (plain, herbed or Italian)
Oil for deep frying
Sea salt to taste
Ground black pepper to taste

Honey Mustard Dipping Sauce:

½ cup good quality Dijon mustard
¼ cup honey
2 tablespoons soy sauce
Freshly ground black pepper

Cook the rice the day before and refrigerate. I like to cook my rice with chicken broth instead of water, but you may also use beef, or vegetable stock as well.

Mix together the rice, ham, green onions, garlic, peas, parsley, Romano and 1 egg in a large bowl. Adjust the flavor with salt and pepper. Place the remaining eggs (beaten) in another bowl and the breadcrumbs in a third.

Heat 1 ½ inches of oil in a deep frying pan to heated to 350°. With dampened hands, make small cakes of the rice mixture. Lightly coat the cakes with the egg, and then coat with the breadcrumbs. Fry in small batches until golden.

Mix all the ingredients for the honey mustard sauce and serve the croquettes.

Let's talk about wine: The complexity of the tastes in the dish call for a rich white such as a full bodied *California chardonnay*: **Muirwood**, **Newton Unfiltered**, **Mer Soleil Silver or Gold**, **DuMOL,** or **Patz & Hall** that would all add much to the enjoyment of this dish and pair their complexity to the complexity of the dish. A blend such as **Conundrum** would also add excellent notes.

Bread Rolls with Soy Ginger Dipping Sauce

12 slices of a firm, sliced bread (white, whole wheat, sour dough etc. can be substituted); crust removed and rolled thin with a rolling pin.
1 cup mashed potatoes, whipped smooth
1/8 cup half and half
1 shallot, minced
2 tablespoons extra virgin olive oil
¼ teaspoon Sambal or other Asian chili sauce
½ tablespoon garlic powder
2 eggs mixed with 2 Tbs water in a dish
Oil for frying
Sea salt to taste
Ground black pepper to taste

Soy Ginger Dipping Sauce:

¼ cup good quality soy sauce
1 tablespoon seasoned rice vinegar
¼ teaspoon freshly ground ginger

1 green onion, cut in half lengthwise and sliced thin

Sauté the shallot in the extra virgin olive oil until tender. Mix it together with the potatoes, half & half, Sambal and garlic powder. Roll each slice of bread into a thin dough layer. Brush the edges with the egg/water mixture. Place about 1 teaspoon or more of the potato mixture in the center of the bread roll. Press the edges to seal. Fry the rolls in the oil until golden and serve with the dipping sauce. These rolls can be served with a variety of dipping sauces. Feel free to experiment.

Let's talk about wine or maybe beer: This appetizer could easily fall into the tapas/ Bruschetta category. If served as one of many "small bites" at a cocktail party, the wines chosen or beers chosen should be of a wide enough range so your guests can make their own choices. If it is the appetizer first course for a dinner or even a side dish for some entrée it may compliment then choose a wine or beer that will compliment the entire experience. Are you serving it alone as an afternoon snack? Try serving it with a nice cold beer such as **Land shark or Bass Ale**. An IPA such as **Pikes IPA** would also go well.

Chicken Tetrazzini

2-3 pound roasting chickens, skin removed and meat cut into ½ inch pieces.
1 pound elbow or bow tie pasta
4 ounces unsalted butter
¼ cup extra virgin olive oil
1 large yellow onion, diced
2 stalks celery, cut in half lengthwise, sliced thin
1 carrot cut in half lengthwise, sliced thin
4 cloves garlic, minced
½ pound button mushroom, sliced
½ pound Crimini mushroom, sliced
1 teaspoon flat leaf parsley, chopped fine
1 teaspoon fresh sage, chopped fine
1 teaspoon fresh thyme, chopped fine
1 cup dry white wine

½ cup flour
6 cups low sodium chicken stock
½ cup heavy cream

Coating:

2 cups fresh breadcrumbs
1 cup Romano cheese
5 tablespoons extra virgin olive oil

Boil the pasta in a large pot of salted water until al dente. Drain well and set aside for later use.

Remove the skin and bones from the whole roasting chickens. Cut the meat into 1 inch pieces. In a large pan or pot over medium high heat, melt the butter and the extra virgin olive oil. Carefully add the chicken parts to the oil, and cook on all sides. Remove the chicken from the oil and set aside for later.

Drain about half the oil from the pot and discard. Using the same large pot used for cooking the chicken, over medium heat, add the onions, celery and carrots and cook until tender. Add the garlic and cook an additional minute. Add the mushrooms and continue to cook for 2 additional minutes. Add the parsley, sage, and thyme. Deglaze the pot with the wine. Bring to a boil and reduce the liquid by about half. Add the flour and cook for 1 minute over medium high heat, stirring constantly to form a roux. Add the chicken stock and bring to a boil. Lower heat and cook until slightly thickened. Return the chicken to the pot, along with the pasta and cream. Remove the pot from the heat.

Place the ingredients in a baking dish. Combine the fresh breadcrumbs, cheese and extra virgin olive oil and season with salt and pepper. Spread the crumbs over the chicken and pasta dish, and bake in a 350° oven until the crumbs are golden.

Let's talk about wine: This is a very rich and creamy chicken dish. As with other recipes in this category, the team thinks a sparkler would be an excellent choice. They tend to cut through the heaviness of the cream and still stand up on their own. Try: **Martell Prestige**, **Rondel Cava**, **Montaudon Brut or Rose**, **Krug Brut** all excellent choices. If you wish a "still: wine we suggest a full bodied *chardonnay* such as **Mer Soleil Gold**, **Lloyd**, **Chalk Hill** or **Sonoma Loeb Reserve.** Of course the ever popular **Kendall Jackson Chardonnay** could also be your choice.

Shepard's Pie

¾ cup flour
2 tablespoons paprika
1 tablespoon onion powder
1 tablespoon garlic powder
3 teaspoons sea salt
1 head garlic, sliced thin
2 leeks (white & light green parts only), sliced thin
3 teaspoons ground pepper
Extra virgin olive oil
5 pounds chuck roast, cut into 1 inch cubes
1 pound thick cut bacon, cut into ½ inch slices
1 tablespoon anchovy filets, chopped
2 cups yellow onion, coarse chop
1 cup carrot, coarse chop
1 cup celery, coarse chop
1 bottle of dry red wine
5 cups low sodium chicken broth
1-28 ounce can whole tomatoes, hand crushed
8 ounces tomato paste
2 tablespoons herb de province, crushed
1 teaspoon dry sage
1 teaspoon dry marjoram
1 pound pearl onions
1 pound baby carrots
1 pound parsnip, ½ inch dice
1 pound Crimini mushrooms, cut into quarters
1 pound button mushrooms
2 large portabella mushrooms, stem and gills removed, 1 inch dice
Mashed potato crust:
5 pounds Yukon Gold potatoes, peeled and diced
1 cup heavy cream
2 sticks unsalted butter

Sea salt to taste
Ground black pepper to taste
2 large eggs, beaten
½ cup pecorino Romano
1 cup pecorino Romano

Combine the flour, paprika, onion powder, garlic powder, salt and pepper in a bag and mix well. In a large pot over medium high heat, add 3-4 teaspoons extra virgin olive oil. Add the bacon and cook until crisp; then remove the bacon and reserve. Lightly dust the beef in flour and cook in the oil until brown on all sides. Remove and reserve for later use.

In the same pot over medium heat, add the anchovy to the pot and melt. Add onions, celery, leeks and garlic to the pot and cook until soft. Add the wine to deglaze. Add tomatoes, tomato paste, chicken broth, reserved bacon and all the herbs. Return the beef to the pot. Reduce heat to low, cover and simmer until the beef is tender (about 1-2 hours). Add the onions, baby carrots, parsnips and mushrooms to the pot and cook until tender (10 min). Adjust the flavor with salt and pepper. Place mixture into a large baking pan.

Potato Garnish:

In a large pot, boil the peeled potatoes until tender. Drain. Mash the potatoes until smooth. Add the half & half, melted butter, salt and pepper, eggs and ½ cup cheese.

Smooth the potatoes over the baking dish with the beef. Smooth and sprinkle the remaining cheese over the top. Bake the completed dish at 350° for 30-40 minutes. Let the dish rest at least 20 minutes before serving.

Let's talk about wine: Another rich comfort food dish that needs a wine that will add to the comfort. A bolder *merlot* such as **Courtney Benham**, **T-Vine**, **Pahlmeyer**, **and Duckhorn Estate** would be perfect. For the *cabernet lovers*, you might think of: **Jordan, Rudy, Martin Ray Stags Leap District; Caymus Special Select**, or **Edgewood.**

Mushroom & Pork Ragu Pasta

3 pounds Bucatini pasta, cooked al dente
8 ounces button mushroom, sliced
8 ounces Crimini mushrooms, sliced
8 ounces of assorted wild mushrooms, sliced
5-6 cloves garlic, minced
2 pounds boneless pork shoulder with some fat, cut into ½ inch pieces
8 ounces capicola, chopped
5 links of sweet Italian sausage with fennel, casings removed
1 bottle dry white wine
2 large yellow onions, chopped fine
2 carrots, chopped fine
2 stalks celery, chopped fine
1-28 ounce can whole tomatoes, hand crushed
8 ounces tomato paste
2-3 cups low sodium pork or veal stock (chicken stock can be substituted)
2 tablespoons fresh basil, chopped
¾ cup grated pecorino Romano cheese
1 teaspoon fresh oregano, chopped
Extra virgin olive oil
Grated pecorino Romano cheese for garnish
Crushed red pepper flakes for garnish
Sea salt to taste
Ground black pepper to taste

Heat 2-3 tablespoons extra virgin olive oil in a large frying pan over medium high heat. Add the garlic and half the onions to the pan. Cook until the onions start to brown a little. Then add the button and Crimini mushrooms to the pan. Cook the mushrooms just until they begin to soften, adding 3-4 grinds of pepper while they cook. Deglaze pan with about 1/3 of the bottle of wine, cook an additional 2-3 minutes and set aside.

In a large pot, heat 2-3 tablespoons of extra virgin olive oil over high heat. Season the pork with some salt and pepper and cook in the oil until just browned on all sides. Remove pork from pot and lower heat to medium. Add the Capicola and start to render out the fat, about 1 minute. Add the sausage and cook until brown. Add the remaining onions, carrots, and celery, and cook until soft. Add remaining wine and cook until it is almost absorbed. Add tomatoes, tomato paste, 1½ cups of stock, reserved pork, basil, oregano, cheese, and additional pepper. Bring to a boil. Then, reduce heat to a simmer.

Simmer until pork is tender (about 1 hour). Add additional stock along the way if the "ragu" starts to get dry. Add the mushroom mixture after the hour and warm through. Adjust flavor with salt and pepper. The amount of sauce suggested here can easily accommodate 3+pounds of pasta, but you can adjust the recipe to make less, or you can use what you need for the day, and freeze the remainder in portions for future use.

Let's talk about wine: This may sound strange, but for this dish, we are suggesting a white to ADD and a series of reds to PAIR. The entire team believes this make sense from a culinary point of view. For the ADD wine we suggest the **Mulderbosch Chenin Blanc**, or from France **Rothschild's Bordeaux Blanc**. As for wine to PAIR, we believe a nice *Valpolicella* would work well, Try **Montresor**, or **Bolla.** You might want to try a new wine out of California that uses an "Italian" grape: **Macchia Barbara** or if you wanted to go high end try the **Zenato Amarone.** If you wanted a touch of sweetness in a red that can be chilled then try a "real" Dornfelder from Germany such as the **Dr. Heidemanns RED.**

Mongolian Beef Wraps

1 tablespoon canola oil
1 teaspoon sesame oil
2 pounds "coarse ground" sirloin
4 ounces shiitake mushroom, stems removed, thinly sliced
4 ounces bamboo shoots, coarse chop
4 ounces water chestnuts, coarse chop
4 cloves garlic, minced
2 tablespoons fresh ginger, minced

12ounces prepared oyster-sherry sauce*
2 green onions, chopped
¼ cup unsalted peanuts, chopped

*Oyster-Sherry sauce:

½ cup Hoisin sauce
½ cup sweet sherry
1 cup oyster sauce
¾ cup water
½ cup soy sauce
2½ tablespoon sesame oil
2½ tablespoon sugar, granulated
5½ tablespoon corn starch

Remove stems from shiitake mushrooms; slice ¼ inch thick. Remove bamboo shoots and water chestnuts from packing liquid, and rinse. Coarsely chop both and combine with shiitakes. Set aside for later use.

Using a wok or very large frying pan over very high heat, add the canola and sesame oils. Add the ground beef to the pan and sear meat quickly, browning all sides. Immediately add the garlic and ginger. Cook for another 30 seconds, then add the shiitakes, bamboo shoots, and water chestnuts, continuously tossing all ingredients to prevent burning. After one minute, lower the heat to medium, and add the Oyster-Sherry sauce. Allow pan to come to a simmer. Continue to cook until the sauce begins to thicken and becomes "glazed" to the meat.

Plate in a large rimmed bowl and garnish with chopped green onion and chopped peanuts. Serve with rice noodles on side. Serve with lettuce cups such as iceberg or Bibb lettuce.

Oyster-Sherry Sauce:

In a blender, combine the Hoisin, sherry, oyster sauce, water, soy sauce, sugar and cornstarch.

Pulse blender to combine all ingredients. Once ingredients are incorporated, set blender on high and add sesame oil slowly to blend thoroughly.

Let's talk about wine: There are a number of *sweet Sherries* that can be used to ADD and PAIR. Serve the PAIR wine chilled or over ice. The classic "Cream" of course is **Harvey's** but other excellent ones are **Osborne** or **Graham's**. As a variation, you could try using a nice tawny port instead of a sherry the **10 year old Illaparra** from Australia would be outstanding. You might also pair the dish with a red such as **Ch. Chamirey Mercurey Rouge 2005.** A Cabernet such as the Marten Ray 2007 would add to the complexity of the dish and is worth a try.

Grilled Tarragon Shrimp Salad

2 pounds 21/25 shrimp, peeled and deveined, tail off
1 small yellow onion, sliced thin
2 ribs celery, cut thin on the bias
2 heads romaine hearts, quartered and sliced thin
2 plum tomatoes, diced
1-8 ounce jar marinated artichoke hearts, rinsed and sliced thin
½ pound fresh French green beans, snipped and blanched

Marinade & Dressing:

½ cup fresh basil, chopped
1 cup fresh tarragon, chopped
½ cup fresh chives, chopped
2 tablespoons shallots, chopped
2 tablespoons garlic, chopped
2 ounces lemon juice
Zest of 1 lemon
1 teaspoon chili flake
1½ cups blended olive oil
½ cup extra virgin olive oil
Sea salt to taste
Ground black pepper to taste

In a large mixing bowl, combine the onion, celery, romaine, green bean, tomato, and artichoke hearts. Set aside under refrigeration for later use.

To make the marinade; in a blender add the basil, tarragon, chives, shallots, garlic, lemon juice, lemon zest, and chili flake. Turn blender on high, and slowly add both oils to emulsify the dressing.

In a separate bowl, place the cleaned shrimp; add about half the marinade to the shrimp. Mix well and allow the shrimp to marinate for at least one hour.

Preheat a grill to a high temperature. Grill shrimp on both sides for about 3 minutes each, or until opaque.

Serve the shrimp over the salad mix; add some additional marinade/dressing over the salad. Toss well and enjoy.

Let's talk about wine: OK, here's another one for you. You have a grilled shrimp in a tangy marinade/dressing. What type of wine will play off the tanginess? What will add to the flavors? MMMMM maybe we should choose a beer to pair. If so what type will compliment the flavors?

"Broken" or "Deconstructed" Stuffed Mushrooms with Pasta

30 large button mushrooms
2 cups Panko breadcrumbs
8 cloves garlic, minced
6 green onions, chop fine
2 tablespoons flat leaf parsley, chopped
½ cup grated Romano cheese
½ cup+ extra virgin olive oil
½ cup dry white wine
2 pounds pasta, cooked al dente
Pasta water as needed
Sea salt to taste
Ground black pepper to taste

Remove the stems from the mushrooms and chop fine. Place them in a large mixing bowl. Add the Panko, garlic, green onion, parsley and cheese to the bowl and blend well. Add the olive oil and blend again. Adjust the flavor with salt and pepper. Stuff the mushroom caps loosely with the stuffing and place in a large baking dish. Add the wine to the bottom of the dish. Bake in a 350° oven for 30 minutes.

Remove mushrooms from the pan and cut into large pieces allowing the stuffing to blend with the mushrooms. Mix together.

Cook 2 pounds of your favorite pasta al dente and reserve one cup of the pasta water. Blend the broken mushroom mixture with the pasta and add pasta water as necessary. Drizzle with additional extra virgin olive oil and serve. Offer crushed red pepper flakes as a garnish along with additional grated Romano cheese.

Let's talk about wine: As the *ADD wine* you should use a California style *sauvignon Blanc* such as; **Groth; Adler Fels;** or **Amici**. You could use a lighter on the citrus one from elsewhere such as **Anekena** but try to stay away from the intense grapefruit ones from New Zealand for this dish. Here is one of the few dishes that we unanimously agreed on one wine to *PAIR*. We suggest the **Zenato Amarone**. But feel free to choose another rich red wine that you might want to PAIR with this dish.

Shrimp BLT

½ pound pancetta cut in small ¼ inch chunks
1 tablespoon extra virgin olive oil
2 pounds 21/25 shrimp, peeled and deveined, tail off
½ cup good quality mayonnaise
½ tablespoon fresh basil, chopped
½ tablespoon fresh tarragon, chopped
½ tablespoon fresh parsley, chopped
2 heads romaine lettuce, shredded thin
2 pints cherry tomatoes, chunked
1 small red onion, sliced thin
3 tablespoons extra virgin olive oil
Sea salt to taste
Ground black pepper to taste

In a pan over medium high heat, add the olive oil. Render the pancetta until just crisp. Remove from pan and reserve.

Cook the shrimp in the same pan with the pancetta fat and cook until done, about 3-5 minutes or until opaque. Remove and reserve. Cool the shrimp to room temperature.

Blend with the mayonnaise, basil, tarragon, parsley and the pancetta. Add the shrimp and fold together.

In a separate bowl, blend the romaine lettuce, tomatoes, red onion and olive oil. Adjust the flavor with salt and pepper. Serve the shrimp over the salad blend.

Let's talk about wine: This would make a great summer brunch dish and as such would be paired well with a lighter summer type white or rose. First think of a nice sparkler such as **Santi Nello Prosecco** or **Botter Prosecco Spumonti**. A light *Vinho Verdi* such as **Nobilus** would go well, as would a rose such as **Dom Fontanel** or **Muga**. Think light and chilled. You could also choose a sparkler such as: **Louis Bouillet Roes** of the **Montaudon Brut Rose**. **MUMM Napa Brut or Rose** would add much to the dish.

Thai Chicken with Basil

2 pounds boneless, skinless chicken breast cut into thin 2 inch slices
Peanut oil to fry
2 tablespoons peanut oil
2 large shallots, sliced thin
4 cloves garlic, minced
3 tablespoons fresh ginger, minced
1 large sweet onion, sliced thin
3 tablespoons good quality soy sauce
2 tablespoons Nam Pla
1 large bunch Thai basil, stems removed, coarse chop
Juice of 2 limes
½ cup chicken broth
Sambal to taste

In a large wok over high heat, add the peanut oil. Quickly fry the chicken slices, browning all sides and remove. Reduce heat to medium.

Add the shallot, ginger and garlic to the wok and cook for 1 minute, or until a light golden color. Add the onion and cook an additional 2 minutes, being sure to stir continuously. Add the soy, Nam Pla and basil. Stir and return the chicken to the wok. Add the lime juice and Sambal. Add the chicken broth and heat through. Serve over some Jasmine rice if you like.

Let's talk about wine/beer: The last ingredient Sambal will be definitive in your choice of wine. Sambal is an extremely spicy sauce. Remember when you pair spicy food there is a good general rule to take into consideration: "the more heat— the more sweet" regarding wines: try **Washington Hills Riesling** or **Botter Prosecco Spumonti**. On the other hand, you might choose to go with a nice yeasty beer like **Pikes IPA** or **Singha** that will bring out the tastes and spices of the dish.

Calabrese String Bean Salad

1 pound fresh haricot verts (French green beans), blanched and cooled
1 pound wax beans, blanched and cooled
1-8 ounce can white beans, rinsed well
1 medium red onion, sliced very thin
6 ounces thick cut apple wood smoked bacon, cut into ¼ inch cubes
8 ounces oven roasted plum tomato in olive oil
¼ cup extra virgin olive oil
1½ ounces sherry vinegar
1 tablespoon fresh oregano, minced
1 tablespoon fresh basil, chiffonade
Sea salt to taste
Ground black pepper to taste

Prepare an ice bath for blanching of the beans.

In a large pot, with a colander insert, blanch the haricot verts in rapidly boiling salted water for about 2-3 minutes. Immediately, plunge the beans into the ice bath and cool completely. Remove beans from ice bath and drain well. Repeat the process with the wax beans. They will take about 4-5 minutes to blanch.

In a sauté pan, over medium high heat, render the bacon until very crispy. Remove from heat and allow bacon and fat to cool completely. Set aside. Place the blanched beans in a large mixing bowl. Add the white beans, red onion and plum tomato. Add the bacon and fat to the bowl, along with the olive oil, sherry vinegar, basil and oregano. Adjust the flavor with salt and pepper. Toss well and refrigerate for at least 2 hours before serving.

Let's talk about wine: This is really a standalone salad or side dish and the wine you choose will be very dependent upon what you serve with the dish. This would make a great side to a BBQ steak and as such a nice *Rhone blend* would pair well as well as a Rich *Cabernet* or *Merlot:* **Robert Mondavi Napa Cabernet** or **T-Vine Merlot** are wonderful. The dish would also go well with a roast leg of lamb and then you might want to choose a *Pinot Noir* such as **La Crema Pinot Noir** or **Angelene RRV**. . Finally, you could pair the dish with a roasted chicken and then serve a full bodied *Macon Village* from Burgundy or a full bodied *chardonnay* from California such as **Ch. La Tour** or **Chalk Hill Chardonnay**. In each case, the side dish adds to the flavors of the entrée and combines to pair with very different wines all providing that third layer of flavor we have mentioned.

French Beef Stew

6 pounds boneless chuck roasts, cut into 1 inch pieces
1 cup flour
4 tablespoon extra virgin olive oil
2 cups carrots, 1 inch dice
2 cups celery with leaves, 1 inch dice
4 large shallots, minced
2 cloves garlic, minced
2 bottles red Bordeaux wine
2 quarts beef stock
4 large russet potatoes, peeled, 1 inch dice
2-1 pound packages of frozen pearl onions
2 tablespoons "herbs de Provence"

A "Bouquet Garni" wrapped in a cheese cloth (2 bay leaves, 2 sprigs fresh thyme, 10 whole black pepper corns, 4 whole cloves, large sprig of fresh basil, sprig of fresh Rosemary)

2 pounds frozen peas
Sea salt to taste
Ground black pepper to taste

Season the beef with salt and pepper. Dredge the beef chunks in the flour. Add the olive oil to a large pot over medium high heat, and cook the beef in small batch until brown in color on all sides. Remove and reserve.

After frying the beef, drain a bit of the oil from the pot. Turn the heat down to medium and add the carrot and celery to the pot and sauté for 3-4 minutes. Add the shallots and garlic to the pan and sauté one more minute. Deglaze the pot with the wine, making sure to scrape up the brown bits on the bottom of the pot. Bring the pot to a simmer and reduce by 1/3. Return the meat to the pot along with the pearl onions, potatoes, herbs de Provence, the "bouquet garnie", and the beef stock. Bring pot to a simmer and cook for one hour until the meat is cooked and the vegetables are tender. During the last 5 minutes, add the peas. Remove the "Bouquet Garnie" and serve.

Let's talk about wine: Here the ADD/PAIR wine should come from Bordeaux. You will want to ADD/PAIR a Pauillac such as **Ch Lynch Maussas Pauillac 2003 or 2005** (4-6 hours to open) or perhaps a Margaux such as **Ch Baron de Brane 2005 or 2006** (4-6 hours to open). The problem is these are expensive and adding such an expensive wine might not be too wise. We still want to add a wine that is "drinkable" so you may wish to choose less expensive Bordeaux (choose one in the $15-$20 range) and choose the more expensive one to pair. Remember, Bordeaux wine needs decanting and aeration in order for the flavors to "open." You should plan on at least 3-5 hours or more for the pair wine to open. The most approachable of the Bordeaux are the Margaux and you might want to try one of these.

Roasted Vegetable Caponata

¼ cup extra virgin olive oil
1 cup zucchini, ½ inch dice
1cup yellow squash, ½ inch dice
1 cup eggplant, ½ inch dice
½ cup red pepper, ½ inch dice
½ cup yellow onion, ½ inch dice
6 garlic cloves, chopped
¼" cup red wine vinegar
1-28 o ounce can San Marzano plum tomatoes, hand crushed
¼ cup Calamata olives, quartered
2 tablespoons small capers
2 tablespoons fresh basil, chopped
Sea salt to taste
Ground black pepper to taste

Add the extra virgin olive oil to a large saucepot over high heat. Add onion and red pepper and sauté for one minute. Add the zucchini, squash, and eggplant, and sauté for 2 minutes more. Add the garlic and sauté until garlic starts to become a light golden color. Deglaze the pot with the vinegar.

Reduce the pot to medium high heat and add the tomatoes to the pot. Bring pot to simmer for 10 minutes. Remove from heat. Add the basil, olives, and capers to the pot. Fold ingredients together. Adjust flavor with the salt and pepper.

Can be served either hot as a side, or room temperature as a condiment with some crusty Italian bread.

Let's talk about wine: Here again we have a side dish that can be served with a wide variety of entrees. Review the discussion after recipe

#17 in this chapter.

Best Damn Meatballs

Sauce:

1 medium yellow onion, minced
5 cloves garlic, minced
½ cup extra virgin olive oil
3-28 ounce cans San Marzano style crushed
   tomatoes
8 ounces tomato paste
2 tablespoons fresh basil, chopped
1 teaspoon fresh oregano, chopped
¾ cup grated Romano cheese
Sea salt to taste
Ground black pepper to taste

Meatballs:

1 pound ground chuck
1 pound ground pork
1 pound ground veal
1 small yellow onion, minced
3 cloves garlic, minced
1 tablespoon fresh ground black pepper
1 tablespoon fresh basil, chopped
1 tablespoon fresh parsley, chopped
1 teaspoon fresh oregano, chopped
½ cup dry seasoned breadcrumbs
½ cup Panko breadcrumbs
1½ cups grated Romano cheese
3 eggs, scrambled
Olive oil for frying
½ bottle dry red wine

In a large pot over medium heat, sauté the onion in the olive oil until tender. Add the garlic and sauté an additional 30 seconds. Add the tomatoes, tomato paste, basil, oregano, and cheese, and stir well. Bring to a simmer while you prepare the meatballs.

In a large bowl, combine all the ingredients for the meatballs and mix well without over working the meat. Roll the mixture into balls of a desired size. In a sauté pan over medium high heat, add the olive oil and cook the meatballs to a deep golden color. Add them to the saucepot as they are finished cooking. When finished cooking the meatballs, carefully drain the oil from the pan.

Deglaze the pan with the wine, scraping the pan with a wooden spoon to remove all the brown bits from the pan. Reduce the wine by half, and add to the saucepot and stir well. Allow the sauce and meatballs to cook at a low simmer for at least 1 hour, but optimal flavor will be at least 4 hours.

Let's talk about wine: Need I say Italian red? But remember that there are some great "Italian" reds produced in California such as the following: **Macchia Barbera**, **Macchia Sangiovese**; **Sobon Sangiovese,** and then from Italy: **Ruffino Chianti**, **Trecciano Chianti**, **Scavino Barolo 2005** (4+ hours to open), **Vasco Sassetti Brunello 2003** (2+ hours to open)**, San Guido 2005 or 2006** (5+ hours to open)**.**

Paella

1 large red onion, coarse chop
8 cloves garlic, sliced thin
4 tablespoons extra virgin olive oil
1 large red pepper, sliced thin
1 large yellow pepper, sliced thin
2 cups dry weight rice
1 cup dry white Spanish wine
4 cups low sodium chicken broth
1 large pinch saffron
1 tablespoon Spanish paprika
1 1/2 tablespoons skinless, boneless chicken
   breasts cut into 2 inch chunks
1 pound Spanish Chorizo, cut into 1"chunks
1 pound 13/15 shrimp, peel and deveined
Sea Salt to taste
Ground black pepper to taste

In a large pot, over medium heat, sauté the onion in the olive oil until tender and translucent. Add the garlic and sauté an additional 45 seconds. Add the peppers and sauté an additional minute. Add the dry rice and stir until fully coated with the oil. Add the wine to the pot and allow to completely evaporating.

In a separate pot, heat the chicken broth with

the pinch of saffron and bring to a simmer. Add the saffron chicken broth to the rice and return to a simmer. Add the chunks of chicken and the chorizo. Cover pot with a lid and allow pot to come to a simmer. Stir once or twice until *almost* all the liquid is absorbed. Add the shrimp and cover pot tightly to finish the cooking process. Adjust flavor with the salt and pepper and serve.

Let's talk about wine: In keeping with the Spanish nature of the dish, you should choose an *Albarino* or *Rueda* as your ADD/PAIR wine: **Monticello**; **Nora**; **Val Do Sesego** or the **Palma Rueda**. You could also pair a lighter Spanish red such as the **El Pardo Tempranillio/Cabernet**. One of the great Spanish wines that would go well is **Cleo** and you should give it a try.

Chapter 3:

Tapas—Tapas—Tapas

NOTE: Be sure to review the entire Wine/Tapas ADD and PAIR discussion in the Chapter Introduction and at the end of the chapter.

1. **Squid Rings Salad**

   And 1 variation

2. **Squid Rings Salad**

   And 1 variation

3. **Stuffed Mushrooms**

   And 2 variations

4. **Stuffed Peppers**

   And 1 variation)

5. **Asparagus & Serrano Ham**

6. **Shrimp with Garlic Sauce**

   And 2 variations

7. **Warm Mixed Spanish Olives**

8. **Cod with Tomatoes & Olives**

9. **Fried Breaded Cod**

10. **Chorizo**

    And 1 variation

11. **String bean Salad**

12. **Chicken Livers in a Sherry Sauce**

13. **Spanish Tapas Frittata**

14. **Mussels in a White Wine Sauce**

    And 3 variations

15. **Shrimp & Serrano Ham**

    And 2 variations

16. **Lamb Meatballs in Tomato Sauce**

    And 1 variation

17. **Clams with Crimini Mushroom and Serrano**

    And 2 variation

18. **Clams Valencia**

    And 1 variation

19. **Orange Chicken**

20. **Andalusian Mushrooms**

21. **Asparagus, Shrimp, & Mushroom Salad**

22. **Fried Peas and Eggs**

    And 1 variation)

23. **Seville Cauliflower**

24. **Galician Scallops**

25. **Fried Fingerling Potatoes in Aioli**

26. **Summer Rice Salad**

Tapas—Tapas—Tapas

If you have ever been to Europe and lived on the schedule of the natives, you know that in many countries "lunch" is usually the main meal of the day. It may be followed by a 1-3 hour break before returning to work and then "dinner" is eaten late in the evening. My experience in Spain was that they are perhaps the latest dinner eaters in Europe. I remember my first time in Barcelona, arriving a little after 8:00 PM for a "late" dinner at a very fine restaurant. We literally opened the place. The staff was still setting up and gave us very strange looks until they realized---Ah Tourists. By the time we left around 10:30, after enjoying our leisurely dinner, the place was packed and people were still coming in. So, what do people in Spain do to tide themselves over from lunch at noon until diner at 9:30 or even later? **Tapas---Tapas---Tapas!!**

Tapas are small 3-4 bite dishes meant to be eaten alone, or shared with others over a glass of wine or sherry. They are served in tapas bars all over the cities and the entire experience is intended to be a journey from bar to bar in search of the tapas you love with the friends you cherish. It goes like this: find a tapas place---eat 2-3 dishes with wine---walk and talk. Find another place and do the same. Enjoy the journey and remember that the journey is meant to be shared.

When thinking about preparing a tapas experience for your family or friends, remember that variety is key. Many different dishes are preferable to a huge platter of one particular "Tapas." When shopping for ingredients think small amounts, or think foods that can be used for a main dish and a portion turned into some special small tapas. Consider using the livers from that chicken you are planning to roast to prepare tapas. Use a few shrimp from that pound of shrimp you bought.

When shopping for ingredients, think FRESH-garlic, shallots, cilantro, tomatoes, wines including sherry and the best Spanish olive oil

you can buy. Think easy preparation-in the same small crocks (ovenware or casserole dish) that are used for service. Think finger foods and tooth picks as utensils. Think great Spanish breads to accompany your tapas.

Plan your dishes, so that they are all complimented by one or two wines, or plan a series of dishes and a series of complimentary wines to go with them.

For six people, you might want to prepare 3 portions (4 bites per portion) of each type of tapas you decide to prepare. If you prepare 4-5 different tapas, each person will get 8-10 small bites of food. Depending on what you wish the experience to be, you can adjust the number and/or types of tapas you prepare.

In this section, we have provided you with recipes for 30 tapas dishes along with many suggestions for the wines to use in their preparation and to be paired with them. I'm sure, once you start exploring the world of tapas, you will think of many more tapas dishes and other wines to use. Have fun experimenting.

Since Tapas are meant to be enjoyed in groupings of dishes it is very difficult to recommend a specific wine for each dish. There are many wines we could offer as suggestions to enhance your tapas selections. Many will be Spanish. The selection of excellent Spanish wine is extensive in every price range. The wines from Spain are sort of a hidden treasure, but once you discover them you will find some of the best wines at the best value in the store. Begin with the ones offered here and then branch out to others of the same varietals or from the same or different regions of Spain. There are also wines from other regions.

Let's talk about wine and Tapas

Instead of offering specific wines for each dish we have chosen to present to you a general discussion at the end of the recipe section of **TAPAS—TAPAS—TAPAS**. In this way we hope to educate you more on wine selection when you might have conflicting dishes presented to you or when you have a number of small dishes. There are also considerations when you might be using a "Small Bite" menu for a cocktail party or buffet.

You might want to read that section at the end of the chapter first before you begin experimenting with the recipes provided and then read it a second or third time as you try preparing these wonderful little bites.

Many of the dishes could be expanded to 2-3 times and be served as an appetizer. For some of these we will offer a wine suggestion to pair with the dish.

We will offer specific wines for some or the dished but we also would encourage you to read and react to the general discussion at the end.

Squid Rings Salad

½ pound squid, cleaned, cut into ½ inch rings
¼ cup green pepper, small dice
¼ cup plum tomato, small dice
1 each green onion, ¼" dice
1 clove garlic, minced
¼ cup Spanish onions, thinly sliced
2 tablespoons cured black olives, sliced
1 tablespoon fresh dill, chopped

Vinaigrette:

2 tablespoons Spanish, extra virgin olive oil
1 tablespoon fresh lemon juice
¼ teaspoon Dijon mustard
Sea salt to taste
Fresh ground pepper to taste

Clean and slice squid into ½" rings. Combine remaining salad ingredients with squid in a bowl. Add vinaigrette to salad, toss well and chill. Allow salad to macerate for at least 2-3 hours. Serve with fresh bread.

Variation #1: Try a simpler version of this salad using only the tentacles of the squid cut in half and marinated with fresh lemon juice, extra

virgin olive oil and salt and freshly ground black pepper.

***Palma Real Reuda**

Marinated Stuffed Squid

1-2 large squid bodies (use tentacles for above)
2-3 teaspoons fresh breadcrumbs
Pinch of Spanish paprika
1/8 teaspoon ground cumin
1/8 teaspoon ground cinnamon
1 teaspoon Serrano ham, chopped
¼ teaspoon garlic, minced
¼ teaspoon shallots, minced
Sea salt to taste
Fresh ground pepper to taste
1 teaspoon fresh cilantro, minced
3 tablespoons Spanish, extra virgin olive oil
Splash of Spanish sherry

Combine breadcrumbs, ham, garlic, shallots, olive oil, salt and pepper, and half the cilantro. Mix well. Loosely stuff the squid with the mixture. Add remaining olive oil to the tapas crock. Add the stuffed squid. Bake at 400 degrees for 2-4 minutes, turning once. Remove from the heat; cut into pieces; add the splash of sherry and remaining cilantro and serve.

Variation #1: add ¼ cup golden raisins to the stuffing.

***Sterling Vineyards Chardonnay**

Stuffed Mushrooms

12 medium size mushrooms, stems removed and washed
2 tablespoons melted, unsalted pepper
2-3 teaspoons fresh breadcrumbs
Pinch of Spanish paprika
1/8 teaspoon ground cumin
1/8 teaspoon ground cinnamon
1 teaspoon Serrano ham, chopped
¼ teaspoon garlic, minced
¼ teaspoon shallots, minced
Sea salt to taste

Fresh ground pepper
1 teaspoon fresh cilantro, minced
3 tablespoons Spanish, extra virgin olive oil
Splash of Spanish sherry
1 tablespoon fresh cilantro leaf

Combine breadcrumbs, ham, garlic, shallots, olive oil, salt, pepper and half the cilantro. Mix well. Stuff the mushrooms with the mixture. Add remaining olive oil to the tapas crock. Bake at 350 degrees for 8-10 minutes. Remove from oven and add a splash of sherry and remaining cilantro and serve.

Variation #1: Instead of Serrano Ham try using ground Spanish Charizo as the meat in the dish.

Variation #2: try making the dish without a meat ingredient.

*****Rothschild Blanc Bordeaux**

Stuffed Small Sweet Cherry Peppers

12 sweet cherry peppers, stems and seeds removed
2-3 teaspoons fresh breadcrumbs
3 tablespoons Spanish, extra virgin olive oil
Pinch of Spanish paprika
1/8 teaspoon ground cumin
1/8 teaspoon ground cinnamon
1 teaspoon Serrano ham, chopped
¼ teaspoon garlic, minced
¼ teaspoons shallots, minced
1 anchovy, minced
1 teaspoon fresh cilantro, minced
Splash of Spanish sherry

Carefully remove the stem and seeds from the cherry peppers, being careful not to tear the peppers. Set aside.

In a sauté pan over medium high heat, add the olive oil. Add garlic, shallots, ham, and anchovy to oil and cook until golden, about one minute. Add a splash of sherry to the pan and reduce by half. Remove the pan from heat, and add breadcrumbs, salt, pepper and half the cilantro.

Mix well. Stuff the peppers with the mixture. Add remaining olive oil to the tapas crock. Bake at 350 degrees for 8-10 minutes. Remove from oven, add a splash of sherry and remaining cilantro and serve.

Variation #1: Use hot cherry peppers or jalapenos instead of sweet peppers.

Variation #2: Use jalapeño peppers.

Variation #3: increase the amount of filling and use halved sweet red or orange peppers.

*****Nora Albarino**

Asparagus & Serrano Ham

4 pencil thin asparagus spears, ends trimmed
Chicken broth
4 slices of Serrano ham, sliced very thin
1 tablespoon Spanish, extra virgin olive oil
Sea salt
Fresh, ground black pepper

Steam the asparagus in chicken broth until tender and allow cooling. (About one minute.) Wrap each spear in a slice of Serrano ham, drizzle with olive oil and fresh ground pepper. Serve.

*****Muga Rose**

Shrimp with Garlic Sauce

½ pound 21/25 size shrimp, shelled and deveined
4 tablespoons Spanish, extra virgin olive oil
2 tablespoons unsalted butter
3 cloves garlic, coarsely chopped
1 dried red chili pepper, stem and seeds removed, split in half
½ teaspoon Spanish style paprika
1 tablespoon minced parsley
Sea salt to taste
Ground black pepper to taste
Fresh cilantro leaves

Dry shrimp well and season with sea salt. Let shrimp sit at room temperature for ten minutes.

Combine oil and butter in preheated 8" casserole dish. Add garlic and chili pepper. When the garlic starts to turn golden, add the shrimp. Cook the shrimp over medium-high heat, stirring for 2 minutes, or until the shrimp are opaque.

Sprinkle with paprika and parsley. Adjust flavor. Finish with fresh cilantro leaves. Serve immediately, right in the cooking dish if possible. Provide lots of good, crisp bread for dunking.

Variation #1: Remove the meat from a large lobster tail; cut it into bite size pieces and use that instead of the shrimp.

Variation #2: use large but bite size chunks of Halibut instead of the shrimp.

***Barone Fine Pinot Grigio

Note: Be sure to review the entire wine/tapas discussion in the chapter introduction and at the end of the chapter.

Warm Mixed Spanish Olives

1 cup green Spanish olives
1 cup black Spanish olives
1 rib celery, sliced thinly
1 small carrot, cut in half & sliced thinly
2 cloves garlic, minced
1 small shallot, minced
Zest of ¼ lemon
Zest of ¼ orange
¼ teaspoon black pepper
Pinch of red pepper flakes
1 bay leaf
½ cup Spanish, extra virgin olive oil
½ tablespoons cilantro, minced

In a pan over medium heat, add the oil. Once the oil is hot, add the garlic, shallots, lemon zest, orange zest, bay leaf and cilantro. Sauté the ingredients for one minute, or until the garlic is a light, golden brown.

In a bowl, combine the olives and remaining ingredients. Pour the oil mixture over the olive mixture and mix well. Allow the olives to macerate. Olives may sit for about 7 days in the refrigerator.

To serve, remove the bay leaf; place mixture in a pan and reheat so that the olives are warm. Drizzle with fresh olive oil and cilantro and serve. This will make 4 or more tapas servings.

***Alder Fels Sauvignon Blanc

Cod with Tomatoes & Olives

4 chunks of salted cod that have been rehydrated and desalinated
½ small Spanish onion, sliced thinly
1 clove garlic, sliced thinly
1 plum tomato, chopped
1/8 teaspoon Spanish paprika
Fresh ground black pepper to taste
Pinch of red pepper flakes
1/8 teaspoon ground cumin
¼ tablespoon fresh cilantro
1-2 tablespoons Spanish, extra virgin olive oil
4+ Spanish green olives
2-3 tablespoons white wine

To desalinate the cod, soak in cold water under refrigeration for 24-36 hours, changing the water occasionally. Drain water when ready for preparation and dry with paper towel.

In a tapas crock over medium heat, place 1 tablespoon of oil along with the onions and garlic. Sauté until tender. Add the wine and reduce by half. Add the tomatoes, pepper, red pepper flakes, cumin and cilantro. Mix and heat through. Add the cod and olives and bake at 400 degrees until the cod is cooked, about 10-15 minutes. Serve with bread.

***Montebuena Rejoa

Fried Breaded Cod

4 chunks of cod that has been rehydrated and
 desalinated
2 tablespoons all purpose flour
Freshly ground black pepper to taste
¼ teaspoon Spanish paprika
1 egg, beaten
4 tablespoons Panko breadcrumbs
3-4 tablespoons Spanish extra virgin olive oil
Pinch red pepper flakes
Fresh cilantro for garnish

To desalinate the cod, soak in cold water under
refrigeration for 24-36 hours, changing the
water occasionally. Drain water when ready for
preparation and dry with paper towel. Blend the
flour, black pepper and paprika. Dredge the pieces
of cod in the flour and shake off excess. Dip cod
in the egg and then coat with the breadcrumbs.
Fry gently in 2 tablespoons of oil until the cod is
cooked through and the breadcrumbs are golden.
Remove and drain on paper towels.

Plate the cod, then drizzle with olive oil and
sprinkle with red pepper and cilantro. Serve with
a wedge of lemon, if desired.

***Il Ginepro e**

Chorizo

4 ¼ inch thick slices of Spanish chorizo, sliced
 on the bias
2 tablespoons Spanish, extra virgin olive oil
1 tablespoon dry white or red wine
Crusty French bread

Place the oil in a tapas crock over medium-high
heat. Add the chorizo and cook until brown on
all sides. Deglaze the pan with the wine and let
it evaporate. Garnish with flat leaf parsley, and
serve with crusty bread.

Variation #1: use Serrano ham instead of
chorizo.

**Although a bit upscale try the great Spanish
red Cleo with this Tapas**

Note: be sure to review the entire wine/tapas

*discussion in the chapter introduction and at
the end of the chapter.*

String Bean Salad

12 oz haricots verts (or other green beans),
ends snipped
4 cured black olives, sliced
1 medium tomato, small dice
1 hard-boiled egg, diced
1 small Spanish onion, sliced thin
1 tablespoon fresh oregano, minced
4 tablespoons Spanish, extra virgin olive oil
1-2 tablespoons good quality Spanish sherry
 vinegar
Sea salt to taste
Fresh ground pepper to taste

Blanch beans in boiling water for 2-3 minutes.
Place beans into ice water bath immediately.
Remove beans from water and drain thoroughly.
Place beans in mixing bowl with remaining
ingredients and mix well. Refrigerate for 30
minutes to 2 hours. Serve with bread. (Makes
3-4 tapas size servings.)

***Amici Sauvignon Blanc**

Chicken Livers in a Sherry Sauce

1 pound chicken livers, cleaned and dried
2 tablespoons Spanish extra virgin olive oil
1 tablespoon unsalted butter
2 green onions, chopped (green part only)
2 cloves garlic, minced
6 medium mushrooms, quartered
4 teaspoons flour (optional)
2 ounces Spanish sherry
6 ounces chicken broth
1 tablespoon white truffle oil (optional)
Fresh ground pepper to taste
1 tablespoon Spanish olives, minced
1 tablespoon hardboiled egg (yolk only), minced
Fresh cilantro leaf for garnish

Dust chicken livers with a bit of flour, and sauté
in oil over medium-high heat. Brown livers on
all sides, cooked about half way, and remove

from casserole dish. Add butter to casserole over medium heat. Add green onions and garlic. Sauté for one minute, and then add mushrooms. Cook for two minutes and then add the sherry to "deglaze" the casserole dish. Reduce liquid by half, and add chicken broth and truffle. Return chicken livers to casserole. Cover and simmer for about 4 minutes. Adjust seasoning. Garnish with minced olives, eggs, and cilantro. Serve with toast.

***ADD/PAIR **Cockburn's Dry or Medium Dry Sherry.**

Spanish Tapas Frittata

3 eggs
1 tablespoon heavy cream
½ tablespoon fresh oregano, minced
¼ teaspoon Spanish paprika
1/8 teaspoon cinnamon
2 tablespoon shaved Manchego or Tetilla cheese
2 tablespoons Spanish extra virgin olive oil
1-2 slices Serrano ham, coarsely chopped
1 green onion, minced
¼ cup frozen or fresh peas
Sea salt to taste
Fresh ground pepper

Spray a tapas casserole dish with cooking spray. Parboil the peas for 30 seconds in salted water and drain. Into the baking dish, sprinkle in the ham, onion and peas. In a separate bowl, whisk together the eggs, cream, oregano, paprika, cinnamon, cheese salt, and pepper. Pour into the baking dish. Bake at 350 degrees until the eggs are set, about 15-20 minutes. It may need an additional 15-20 seconds under the broiler to set and brown the top. Serve with toast.

*****Sandemans Dry Sherry**

Mussels in a White Wine Sauce

2 dozen Prince Edward Island mussels, cleaned
4 tablespoons Spanish extra virgin olive oil
2 cloves garlic, minced

1 small shallot, minced
2 teaspoons flour (optional)
2 plum tomatoes, seeded and chopped
Pinch of red pepper flakes
2 tablespoons lemon juice
½ cup white wine
1 bay leaf
Fresh flat leaf parsley for garnish

Heat the oil over medium heat. Add garlic and shallot, and cook slowly until the garlic is a very golden color. Add the tomatoes and sauté together. Then, add the pepper flakes, wine, lemon juice, bay leaf and flour. Cook 2-3 minutes more until slightly thickened. Add the mussels, cover and cook until all the mussels are opened. Discard any mussels that fail to open. Garnish with parsley and serve with crusty bread for dipping.

Variation #1: Use little neck or other small clams instead of mussels.

Variation #2: Add 2 tablespoons of cream instead of lemon juice.

Variation #3: Add 1-2 tablespoons unsalted butter to the steaming liquid.

ADD & PAIR*****Mendoza Station Torrentes**

Shrimp & Serrano Ham

4 large 13/15 shrimp, peeled and deveined, tail on
4 thin slices of Serrano ham
2 tablespoons Spanish extra virgin olive oil
Wedge of fresh lemon
Flat leaf parsley for garnish

Place the oil in a tapas casserole dish. Wrap each shrimp with a slice of Serrano ham. Place the wrapped shrimp in the dish and bake at 400 degrees for about 5 minutes, turning once. Garnish with a squeeze of fresh lemon and flat leaf parsley and serve.

Variation #1: use chunks of lobster tail meat instead of the shrimp.

Variation #2: use chunks of Halibut instead of the shrimp.

***Ch. Montet Blanc**

Lamb Meatballs in Tomato Sauce

12 ounces ground lamb
4 ounces ground sirloin
1 whole egg
2 cloves garlic, mashed
2 tablespoons parsley, chopped
2 shallots, minced
Sea salt to taste
Fresh ground pepper
½ cup seasoned breadcrumbs
2 tablespoons red wine
1 tablespoon Spanish olive oil
2 tablespoons Spanish brandy
2 ounces prepared tomato sauce
½ cup beef or lamb broth

Combine the lamb, beef, egg, garlic, shallots, parsley, salt, and pepper. In a separate bowl, soften breadcrumbs with red wine. Add crumbs to meat mixture. Mix well. Form lamb mix into approximately 30 bite-size meatballs. Heat oil in large casserole and cook meatballs, browning them on all sides. After browning, deglaze casserole dish with brandy. Carefully, ignite liquid to burn off alcohol. Add tomato sauce and broth. Cover casserole, reduce heat to medium-low, and allow simmering for 45 minutes.

Variation #1: use ground pork instead of the lamb.

***El Prado Cabernet Norton Malbec** would also go well

Clams with Crimini Mushroom and Serrano

4 tablespoons Spanish extra virgin olive oil
1 tablespoon unsalted butter
3 cloves garlic, sliced
¼ pound Crimini mushroom, quartered
12 each littleneck clams
4 tablespoons diced Serrano ham (cut from a 1/8 inch thick slice)
6 ounces chicken broth
1 green onion, minced
¼ teaspoon crushed red pepper
1 bay leaf
1 teaspoon flat leaf parsley, minced
Sea salt to taste

Heat the oil and butter in a shallow casserole dish over medium-high heat. Add garlic, and cook to a light golden color. Add ham to pan, and cook for 30 seconds. Immediately add the mushrooms, and cook for two minutes. Then, add the clams, broth, chili flake, bay leaf, and green onion, and place lid on top of casserole dish. Steam until clams are open. Sprinkle with parsley and serve in same dish.

Variation #1: Use Spanish Chorizo instead of the ham.

Variation #2: use 20 mussels instead of clams in either of the recipes.

***Mulderbosch Chenin Blanc**

Clams Valencia

12 littleneck clams, rinsed
¼ cup Spanish, extra virgin olive oil
1 ripe tomato, finely chopped
1 dried chile pepper, stem and seeds removed, cut into two pieces
1 clove garlic, sliced
¼ cup white wine
1 teaspoon fresh parsley, chopped
Sea salt to taste
Fresh ground pepper to taste

Place oil in tapas casserole dish over medium heat. Add the tomato and Chile pepper. Allow tomatoes to come to a simmer. Add wine, and clams. Cover casserole dish with lid and cook until all clams have opened. Stir in the garlic and parsley. Serve with bread for dipping.

Variation #1: use 20 mussels instead of clams.

***<u>Nora Albarino</u>**

<u>Orange Chicken</u>

2 tablespoons Spanish sherry
½ cup fresh squeezed orange juice
1 tablespoon orange zest
1 teaspoon fresh ground cumin
4 tablespoons Spanish, extra virgin olive oil
Sea salt to taste
Fresh ground pepper to taste
1 pound chicken breast cutlets, cut into 1 oz. strips

<u>Orange Walnut Sauce:</u>
1 ½ cups orange marmalade
3 tablespoons raisins
½ cup walnuts, chopped
3 ounces fresh squeezed orange juice
2 tablespoons water

In a bowl, combine sherry, orange juice, orange zest, cumin and half the olive oil. Add chicken strips and macerate in the refrigerator for two hours. Remove chicken from marinade and pat dry.

Sauté chicken in remaining olive oil over medium-high heat. Remove chicken from casserole dish. Drain off all oil. To prepare Orange sauce, combine all ingredients, and allow sauce to simmer for 10 minutes. Return chicken to sauce. Heat through and serve.

***ADD/PAIR <u>Don Benigno Cream Sherry</u>**

<u>Andalusian Mushrooms</u>

1 tablespoon Spanish extra virgin olive oil
2 ounces slab bacon, cut into half inch cubes
12 medium size button or Crimini mushrooms, cleaned
¼ cup white wine
1 tablespoon fresh lemon juice
Sea salt to taste
Fresh ground pepper to taste
½ teaspoon ground cumin

½ teaspoon Spanish paprika
Pinch of cayenne

<u>Aioli Sauce:</u>
4 cloves garlic, mashed
1 cup good quality mayonnaise
Pinch sea salt
Pinch fresh ground pepper
½ teaspoon lemon juice

In a sauté pan, cook the bacon/pancetta until crisp to render out the fat and flavor. Chop and reserve the meat. Add the mushrooms and remaining ingredients and cook until almost all the juices have evaporated.

To prepare Aioli sauce, blend all ingredients well and allow the flavors to meld for about 1 hour. Serve with toast.

***<u>Amici or Duckhorn Sauvignon Blanc</u>**

<u>Asparagus, Shrimp, & Mushroom Salad</u>

½ pound medium shrimp, par cooked
1 plum tomato, small dice
½ pound very thin asparagus ends snipped
Chicken broth
1 green onion, sliced thinly on the bias
3 medium mushrooms, cleaned and thinly sliced

<u>Vinaigrette:</u>
4 tablespoon Spanish, extra virgin olive oil
2 tablespoon Spanish sherry vinegar
¼ teaspoon Sea salt
¼ teaspoon Fresh ground black pepper
1 teaspoon parsley, chopped
1/8 teaspoon fresh thyme

Poach asparagus in chicken broth for about one minute. Place asparagus in ice bath to cool quickly, and to retain the color of the asparagus. In a bowl, combine shrimp, tomato, asparagus, green onion, and mushroom.

To prepare Vinaigrette, combine the sherry vinegar, salt, pepper, parsley, and thyme in a separate bowl. With a wire whisk, slowly add olive oil to vinegar mix, whisking vigorously to emulsify the dressing. Taste to adjust seasoning.

Add the vinaigrette to the shrimp salad. Toss well. Chill for 2 hours. Serve. Will make up to 4 Tapas servings.

***Harvey's Cream Sherry (ADD/PAIR)**

Fried Peas and Eggs

½ cup frozen sweet peas
3 tablespoons Spanish extra virgin olive oil
½ small sweet onion, minced
1 clove garlic, minced
½ cup white wine
Sea salt to taste
Fresh ground pepper
2 fresh eggs
Fresh cilantro for garnish

Boil the peas in salted water until tender. In separate Tapas pan, sauté the onion and garlic until tender, careful not to burn the garlic. Add the white wine and cook an additional minute. Add the peas and mix. Adjust flavor with salt and pepper. Crack the eggs into the pan, cover and bake until the whites of the eggs set, but the yolks are still loose. Serve with crusty bread.

Variation #1: add ¼ cup Serrano ham or Spanish chorizo.

***Freixenet Cava Brut**

Seville Cauliflower

1 head cauliflower, cut into florets
2 teaspoons lemon juice

Vinaigrette:

¼ cup Spanish extra virgin olive oil
2 tablespoons Spanish sherry vinegar
1 clove garlic, minced
1 tablespoon capers, coarsely chopped
1 teaspoon Spanish paprika
Pinch of cayenne pepper
Pinch of Sea salt
1 hard cooked egg, chopped
1 tablespoon parsley, minced

Boil the cauliflower in salted water, with lemon juice added, until tender. Cool the cauliflower in ice bath; the drain well.

To make the vinaigrette, in a separate bowl, combine the vinegar, garlic, capers, paprika, cayenne and salt. Using a wire whisk, slowly add the olive oil to the bowl, at the same time whisking vigorously to emulsify the dressing. Add cauliflower to vinaigrette, toss, and allow to stand 10 minutes. Sprinkle the chopped egg and parsley over the cauliflower and serve.

***Osborne Fino Sherry**

Galician Scallops

6 large sea scallops
3 strips of bacon, pancetta or pork belly cut in half
1 ½ tablespoon Spanish, extra virgin olive oil
2 green onions, sliced thinly on the bias
3 tablespoons white wine
½ teaspoon saffron threads
½ teaspoon Spanish paprika
Pinch of cayenne
¼ teaspoon flat leaf parsley
Sea salt to taste
Juice of ¼ lemon
1 tablespoon Panko breadcrumbs

Wrap each scallop with half a slice of bacon or pancetta, and secure with a toothpick. In a casserole dish, over medium heat, quickly sear the scallops on all sides in the oil. Remove and reserve.

Add the onion to the pan and cook until tender. Add the wine and reduce by half. Then, add paprika and cayenne. Adjust flavor with salt. Turn off heat. Return scallops to casserole dish, along with some lemon juice. Sprinkle the Panko over the scallops and bake at 400 degrees for 1-2 minutes then broil for 20 seconds. Serve with bread.

NOTE: *Be sure to read the entire wine/Tapas discussion at the beginning and end of the chapter.*

Fried Fingerling Potatoes in Aioli

16 very small fingerling potatoes, skin on
Oil for frying
Sea salt

Aioli Sauce:

4 cloves garlic, mashed
1 cup good quality mayonnaise
½ teaspoon lemon juice
Pinch Sea salt
Pinch fresh ground black pepper

To prepare Aioli sauce, blend all ingredients well and allow the flavors to meld for about 1 hour. Boil the potatoes in salted water until tender. Drain water and allow potatoes to dry. Fry in the olive oil until crisp. Mix with the Aioli and serve.

***Mer Sole Silver Chardonnay**

Summer Rice Salad

2 tablespoon Spanish olive oil
1 cup short grain rice
¾ cup boiling water
¾ cup boiling chicken broth
¼ teaspoon thyme
1/8 teaspoon tarragon
Sea salt to taste
1 anchovy fillet, chopped
1 slice Serrano ham, chopped well
1 thin slice of Spanish chorizo, chopped
1 green onion, chopped well
1 clove garlic, minced
¼ rib celery, chopped well
1 ½ teaspoon flat leaf parsley, chopped
1 ½ teaspoon cilantro, chopped
Fresh ground pepper

For the sauce:

2 tablespoons Spanish extra virgin olive oil
1 clove garlic, minced
1 shallot, minced
1/3 cup Spanish sherry
1 tablespoon unsalted butter
Sea salt to taste
Fresh ground pepper

In a deep casserole dish, add the rice, stir the rice to coat with oil and then add the water, broth, thyme, tarragon, and the salt. Bring casserole to a boil, cover tightly and cook for 5 minutes. Remove from heat. Let rice steep until all liquid is evaporated. Remove rice from dish, and allow the rice to cool completely.

In a large bowl, combine anchovy, Serrano, chorizo, green onion, garlic, celery, and parsley. Add the cooled rice to bowl, and combine well. Using your hands, press and roll the mixture into about 12-16 equal sized balls and place on a sheet in a single layer. Allow rice balls to chill for about 2 hours.

To prepare Sauce, combine the garlic and shallot in the olive oil in a pan, and cook gently until they are a light, golden brown. Add the sherry. Remove from the heat and allow the pan to cool 2-3 minutes. Add the butter and swirl the pan to incorporate it. Adjust flavor with salt and pepper. Keep the sauce warm enough so that the butter does not coagulate, but not too warm that the sauce would "break". Spoon one generous tablespoon of the sauce over each rice ball serving.

***Muga Rose**

Some Notes about the "Spanish Ingredients"

While you should feel free to experiment and substitute other than the suggested "Spanish" ingredients such as olive oil, we strongly suggest that you to pay particular attention to trying to secure Spanish paprika and Spanish chorizo for the dishes that call for one or both of these ingredients. They are sweeter and less spicy than other types and substitutions would change the dishes substantially. In addition Spain is noted worldwide for its excellent hams and we would strongly suggest you try to secure the best quality Serrano or other Spanish hams for your preparations.

Let's Talk About Wines and Tapas

It is very difficult to speak about particular wine suggestions for individual tapas dishes since in most cases the individual or more likely group of people will be sampling a variety of dishes. It is equally difficult to speak about a particular wine for use in the preparation of a particular tapas dish since experimentation here can lead the same dish into a variety of directions depending on the wine chosen. For that reason, we would like to offer some general suggestions and discuss how each of the suggestions might help affect the overall enjoyment of the dish.

"PAIR WINES":

As with all other dishes, it is fine to "pair" the wine used in cooking with the dish itself.

However, with tapas we will again face the problem of the variety of dishes. By all means, stay with one of the sherries or whites used in cooking, or if you want to explore other options we would like to suggest some of the following:

This is a wonderful place to experiment with one of the great "Cavas" from Spain or elsewhere. The **Rondel Cava** can be bought in dry, semi seco or rose and all would pair wonderfully with an array of tapas dishes. Another *Cava* to consider is **Freixenet**. You could move beyond Spain to *Champagne* from France such as: **Montaudon Brut or Brut Rose, Martel Prestige,** or **Moet.**

A *Dry Rose* such as the Spanish **Muga** or **Nostrada** would be able to stand up to all of the tapas dishes listed here and many others. For those

who like reds, a *Rioja* such as **LAN** or **Muga** or **Montebuena** are suggested.

We have stayed mostly in Spain with our wine suggestions because there are so many great wines from there. You can explore wines from other areas in addition to the ones suggested here.

When reviewing the recipes that call for the addition of wine we would offer the following:

"ADD" Wines:

Many of the dishes call for a splash of sherry. Since there are so many types of *Sherries* how will each affect the dish?

"Fino" or the driest of the group will be like a dry white wine that adds a slight crispness to the dish with a very slight hint of nuttiness.

"Amontillado" *Sherries* will be slightly sweet and acidic. They will add these qualities to the dish. *Cream Sherries* will be sweet and will add a richness and sweetness to the dish.

"Ximenez" *Sherries* are almost syrup-like in sweetness and consistency. I would not recommend using these in most dishes.

We encourage you to start with the "Fino" types, the first few times you make the dish, and then experiment with the others as you prepare the dishes for the second or third time. Taste the wine before adding it so you can be sure you wish to add its profile to the dish.

Some brands we strongly recommend are: **Taylor, Osborne** and **Don Benigno.** All are of high quality and reasonably priced.

As for dry whites we will stay here in Spain with our recommendations. You want to stay light in most cases and a nice place to start is with an *Albarino* such as **Val Do Sosego** or a *Rueda* such as **Palma Real Rueda.**

Chapter 4:

CAN YOU TOP THIS? BRUSCHETTTA

NOTE: Be sure to review the entire wine/ Bruschetta discussion in the introduction to the chapter.

1. **Classic Chopped Tomatoes**

   And 7 variations

2. **Roasted Peppers**

   And 5 variations

3. **Cheeses & Sun Dried Tomatoes**

4. **Balsamic Onions**

   And 3 Variations

5. **Buffalo Mozzarella**

   And 4 variations)

6. **Zucchini**

   And 4 variations

7. **Mushrooms**

   And 5 variations

8. **Olives**

And 3 variations

9. **Italian Tuna**

10. **Hot Peppers**

    And 3 variations

11. **Cannellini Beans & Pancetta**

    And 2 variations

12. **Peppers & Eggs**

    And 2 variations

13. **Potatoes & Eggs**

    And 3 variations

14. **Spanish**

    And 2 variations

15. **Shrimp**

    And 2 variations

16. **Crabmeat Spread**

17. **Artichoke Spread**

18. **Eggplant**

    And 3 variations

19. **Grilled Steak**

    And 2 variations

20. **Italian Sausage**

    And 5 variations

21. **Chopped Broccoli Rabe**

    And 2 variations

22. **Mashed Cauliflower**

    And 2 variations

23. **Cannellini Beans Bacon/Onions**

24. **Ricotta**

    And 5 variations

Can You Top This? Bruschetta

In our last chapter, we offered you many suggestions for Spanish "small bites" dishes known as tapas that people snack on between lunch and dinner. In our second chapter, we move to Italy and again offer you suggestions for the Italian version of "small bites" known as Bruschetta.

Here again, they are used as a small snack between lunch and dinner or as appetizers before dinner. Just as with tapas, Bruschetta is an excellent selection for a cocktail party. Bruschetta is a finger food where the utensil is always bread. True you may need a fork or spoon to get the topping onto the bread, but once there, that's it.

In general, you can use any good quality Italian bread to make the "crostini" slices. Thick crusted breads make an exceptional choice for Bruschetta. Baguettes also make an excellent "crostini". Simply slice the bread thinly, brush lightly with extra virgin olive oil and bake, in a single layer, on a cookie sheet until just crisp. When you remove the bread from the oven, rub the slices with a cut clove of garlic and they're ready to go.

Although this is the traditional way, we think an excellent alternative is to chop 2-3 cloves of garlic very finely and blend them with ½ cup extra virgin olive oil. Allow maceration for an hour or more and use this to brush the bread before baking.

An alternative to using store bought breads is to make your own bread for the Bruschetta. (see Potato Pizza Dough section in the "From the Heart" Chapter) To one portion of the dough, you can add herbs and spices to add to the flavor. Some of the combinations we like are:

1. 1 tablespoon black pepper and 1 tablespoon fresh chopped rosemary.

2. 2 tablespoons finely chopped shallots and 3 tablespoons chopped sun dried tomatoes

3. 1 teaspoon fresh ground black pepper and one head mashed, roasted garlic

4. 1 head mashed, roasted garlic and 1/3 cup Romano cheese

5. 2 tablespoons fresh pesto

6. ½ cup chopped Calamata olives

Add any one of these combinations to the dough when you first mix it for rising. Spread the dough out in a baking pan and bake until done. It can then be sliced into thin slices and used for the Bruschetta.

There are also some commercially produced toasted rounds for Bruschetta that you might choose to use in order to skip the baking part. Some are excellent, but some are full of salt and other flavors that may distract from the toppings you might be offering. Try a few and choose the one you like.

You might see some similarities between these toppings, and the" tapas" dishes offered. We thought of making this a combined chapter called "small bites" but decided to keep the chapters separate.

We did so to preserve the peace between Spain and Italy, for neither would admit that there is any similarity between tapas and Bruschetta. So, for the sake of peace in Europe, we've kept them separate.

With all of the variations in the recipes, we have offered in excess of 80 suggestions for Bruschetta. Enjoy the recipes we have offered and we hope you experiment with these suggestions and invent toppings of your own.

Let's Talk About Wines Now

As you will see in this chapter, there are many variations to Bruschetta. These suggestions are really only a jumping off point for you to use in the development of you own toppings. When we titled the chapter, "Can You Top This?" we meant to inspire you to create more of your own toppings than the ones we have suggested. Likewise, as we offer wine suggestions we offer them with the full expectation that you will use them as a jumping off point for your own wine selections.

If you choose to serve one or two of the toppings as a first course for dinner, you may want to choose your toppings so that the wine chosen can also be used for the first main course of the dinner.

"PAIR Wines

Let's say you will be offering a light pasta course such as spaghetti with garlic and oil or a light fish dish. You might want to choose toppings such as the spinach spread or the shrimp scampi. In that case, you could choose wines such as a dry Prosecco, like **Nino Franco**; a Pinot Grigio such as **Poderi di Carlo, Friuli;** or a Sauvignon Blanc such as **Courtney Benham,** Napa.

If you are having heavy pasta or meat course to follow the Bruschetta such as Pasta Putanesca or a veal dish, you might want to choose toppings such as the grilled flank steak or the sausage. In that case, you could serve a nice *Brunello* such as **Vasco Sassetti,** or **Vecchia Cantina Rosso di Montepulciano**.

As with tapas, it is difficult to suggest specific wines for pairing with Bruschetta. You usually would serve a number of them at a party or before dinner. In addition, you could always host a "small bites" party that features a number of types of Bruschetta and a number of tapas dishes.

A great way to have a party might be to offer six, eight, ten or more toppings with the bread on the side and people can choose their own toppings. In that case, you might want to offer a number of choices of wine or perhaps a choice of a dry, off dry and sweet *Prosecco*; or other sparkling wine or champagne. Offer a *Brut Champagne* like **Montaudon Classe M** and a

Rose **Bullecourt- Salome Rose**. The combination will score a hit with family and friends. Sparkling wine can always be paired with foods; it goes well with a variety of "small bite" types of dishes.

When reviewing the recipes that call for the addition of wine we would offer the following:

"ADD" Wines:

For a good cooking white wine, try a *unoaked chardonnay* such as **Dominican Oaks** or **La Vuelta.** A crisp *Pinot Grigio* such as **Cavit, Barone Fini,** or **Oak Grove** would also go well.

As for a *tawny port* or *sherry,* we would suggest **Osborne.**

A nice red to cook with would be Chianti, such as **Bolla, San Andrea,** or a nice **Nero d' Avola** from Southern Italy.

You could also add a high quality *Marsala* to these dishes such as **Colombo** or **Florio.**

Remember, they come in dry and sweet and each will add different characteristics to the dishes you are preparing.

Please try to avoid those vile jugs of wine that cost $4.00 a gallon. Always remember if it tastes cheap out of the bottle, it will add that same cheap taste to your food. If you wouldn't drink it by itself, don't cook with it.

As with Tapas for a few of the suggested Bruschetta we will off a particular wine should you choose to serve it as a standalone course for a dinner progression>

Classic Chopped Tomatoes

4 plum tomatoes, coarsely chopped
1 clove garlic, minced
1 scallion minced
1 teaspoon fresh basil, minced
3 tablespoons extra virgin olive oil
Salt and fresh ground pepper to taste

In a bowl, combine all of the ingredients and mix. Adjust the flavor with salt and pepper. Allow the tomatoes to macerate for at least 5-10 minutes before serving.

Variation #1: add 2 teaspoons red wine or balsamic vinegar.

Variation #2: Use oregano instead of basil.

Variation #3: Add 1 teaspoon grated Romano cheese.

Variation#4: Add 2 tablespoons crumbled Feta cheese.

Variation #5: Add ¼ teaspoon cracked red pepper flakes.

Variation #6: Add ¼ cup chopped walnuts or pine nuts.

Variation #7: Add one seeded and chopped hot pickled cherry pepper.

Use your imagination and make any number of variations that add to or combine the suggestions offered above.

Roasted Peppers

1 pound red bell peppers
2 cloves garlic, minced
1 shallot, minced
6 tablespoons extra virgin olive oil
Sea salt to taste
Fresh ground pepper to taste

Over an open flame, blister the peppers on all sides until charred. Immediately place the peppers in a container with a lid and close tightly. Allow the peppers to "steam" the charred skin away from the meat of the pepper. Remove the peppers from the container and clean the peppers of the charred skin, the stem and the seeds, and discard. Slice the peppers into thin strips.

In a bowl, combine them with the garlic, shallots and olive oil. Adjust the flavor with salt and pepper. Allow to stand for 10 minutes before serving.

Variation #1: Add 1 teaspoon minced capers.
Variation #2: Add 2 chopped anchovy fillets.

Variation #3: Add one seeded and chopped hot cherry pepper.

Variation #4: Add 1 tablespoon red or white wine vinegar.

Variation #5: Use roasted banana peppers or some other hot pepper instead of the sweet peppers in any of the variations.

***Ruffino Chianti Gold

Cheeses & Sun Dried Tomatoes

1 cup fresh Ricotta
1/4 cup grated Romano
¼ cup grated ricotta Salada cheese
2 tablespoons extra virgin olive oil
Fresh ground pepper to taste
¼ cup oil cured sun dried tomatoes, sliced thin

In a bowl, combine the cheeses and olive oil and blend well. Adjust the flavor with pepper. Add the sun dried tomato. Spread some of the cheese mixture on the crostini and top with a few small slices of the tomatoes.

***T-Vine Petite Syrah

Balsamic Onions

1 medium red onion, sliced very thin
3 scallions, sliced thin on the bias
3 tablespoons extra virgin olive oil
1 tablespoon balsamic vinegar
Sea salt to taste
Fresh ground black pepper to taste

Slice the red onion and scallions very thin. In a pan, heat the oil over medium heat and add the onion and scallions. Sauté the mixture slowly until very wilted and carmelization starts to begin. Add the Balsamic and cook an additional minute. Adjust the flavor with salt and pepper. Serve warm or at room temperature.

Variation #1: Instead of balsamic vinegar, use sweet Marsala wine.

Variation #2: Add 2 cloves of chopped garlic to the sautéed onions just before adding the vinegar or the wine.

Variation #3: Use some other variety of onions such as Vidalia or Cipollini instead of the red onions.

*****San Andria Chianti Reserva**

Buffalo Mozzarella

½ pound fresh buffalo mozzarella
2 tablespoons extra virgin olive oil
2 teaspoons fresh basil, chiffonade
Sea salt to taste
Fresh ground pepper to taste

Slice the mozzarella thin, and then slice each slice into thin strips. In a bowl, mix the cheese with the olive oil and basil. Adjust the flavor with salt and pepper and serve.

Variation #1: Add a thin slice of tomato and some chopped fresh basil for a Caprese.

Variation #2: Add an anchovy filet to variation #1.

Variation #3: Add a few chopped capers to any of the above.

Variation #4: Assemble any of the above variations and place them on a cookie sheet; place under the broiler for 1-2 minutes to melt the cheese and serve.

*****Bella Sera Pinot Grigio**

Zucchini

1 medium zucchini

3 tablespoons extra virgin olive oil
1 clove garlic, minced
1 tablespoon fresh mint, minced
Sea salt to taste
Fresh ground pepper to taste

Slice the zucchini into thin discs; about 1/8th of an inch thick. In a sauté pan over medium high heat, sauté the zucchini in olive oil until tender; about 3 minutes. Add the mint and sauté an additional minute. Season with the salt and pepper and serve.

Variation #1: Add 2 tablespoons red wine vinegar to the mixture when frying.

Variation #2: In addition to the vinegar, add one seeded and chopped hot cherry pepper.

Variation #3: To any of the above add one scrambled egg and cook until done.

Variation #4: Instead of ovals, slice the zucchini into thin slices lengthwise and then into thin strips making spaghetti like pieces then sauté quickly in the olive oil. Replace the mint with garlic. Sprinkle with ¼ cup grated Romano cheese and serve.

*****Ch. Montet Bordeaux Blanc**

Mushrooms

½ pound button or Crimini mushrooms, sliced thin
3 tablespoons extra virgin olive oil
2 cloves garlic, minced
½ teaspoon fresh oregano, chopped fine
2 tablespoons dry white wine
Sea salt to taste
Fresh ground black pepper to taste
Shaved Romano cheese for garnish

In a pan over high heat, sauté the sliced mushrooms in the olive oil for 2 minutes. Do not shake the pan too much to start. This will allow the mushrooms to sear on the outside. After the 2 minutes, gentle turn over the mushrooms, the best you can, to finish the searing process on the other side; another 2-3 minutes. Add the garlic and sauté an additional minute. Add the oregano and the wine. Adjust the flavor with salt and pepper. Continue to sauté until almost all the liquid in the pan has evaporated. Garnish with some shaved Romano cheese and serve.

Variation #1: Instead of dry white wine, use a dry or sweet masala.

Variation #2: Instead of dry white wine, use a tawny port.

Variation #3: Instead of dry white wine, use a dry or cream sherry.

Variation #4: instead of dry white wine, use a hardy red.

Variation #5: add ¼ cup chopped prosciutto, hot or sweet copra salami to any of the above.

*****Saluda White Label Gavi de Gavi**

Olives

¼ cup oil cured olives, pitted
¼ cup Sicilian green olives, pitted
¼ cup black olives, pitted
¼ cup Calamata olives, pitted
¼ cup extra virgin olive oil
2 cloves garlic, minced

Cut the olives into small slices. Combine them in a bowl with the garlic and the olive oil and serve.

Variation #1: Add 1 teaspoon cracked red pepper flakes to the mixture.

Variation #2: Place the mixture of sliced olives and garlic in a food processor and blend until almost smooth. Add an additional ¼ cup of olive oil while blending.

Variation #3: After making the olive tapenade in variation #2, spread a thin layer on the bread and top with any of the toppings in this section.

NOTE: Be sure to review the entire wine/ Bruschetta discussion in the introduction to the chapter.

*****Paulo Scavino Borolo**

Italian Tuna

1 can Italian style tuna, packed in olive oil
1 small shallot, minced
1 small garlic clove, minced
1 tablespoon Italian parsley, chopped
1 teaspoon capers, chopped
Sea salt to taste
Fresh ground black pepper to taste

Place the tuna with the oil from the can into a bowl. Add the shallot, garlic and capers and blend well. Adjust the flavor with salt and pepper. Serve chilled or room temperature.

*****Bell Gloss Meiomi Pinot Noir**

Hot Peppers

4 long fresh Italian hot peppers
4 tablespoons extra virgin olive oil
2 cloves garlic, sliced thin
2 shallots, sliced thin
Sea salt to taste
Fresh ground black pepper to taste

In a pan over medium heat, gently sauté the whole peppers in the olive oil until soft and slightly charred. Remove from the pan and seed the peppers. Slice the peppers into chunks and return to the pan. Add the garlic and the shallots and sauté 2-3 minutes. Adjust the flavor with salt and pepper and serve.

Variation #1: Instead of fresh peppers, use pickled hot cherry peppers.

Variation #2: Instead of hot peppers, use sweet red and or yellow peppers.

Variation #3: To any of the above, add 3 chopped anchovies to the mixture either when frying or after.

*****Ch Saint Michel Riesling**

Cannellini Beans & Pancetta

¼ pound pancetta, cut into small chunks
2 tablespoons extra virgin olive oil
1 small sweet onion, chopped
2 cloves garlic, minced
8 ounces can cannellini beans, rinsed & drained
Sea salt to taste
Fresh ground pepper to taste

In a pan over medium high heat, sauté the chunked pancetta in the olive oil until just crisp. Add the onions and sauté until tender. Add the garlic and sauté an additional minute. In a bowl, combine the beans with the pancetta mixture. Adjust the flavor with salt and pepper and serve.

Variation #1: Add 2 chopped anchovies to the mixture before serving.

Variation #2: use garbanzo beans instead of cannellini.

***Dr. Heidemanns QBA

Peppers & Eggs

5 sweet Italian frying peppers
4 tablespoons extra virgin olive oil
1 shallot, minced
1 clove garlic, minced
3 eggs
Sea salt to taste
Fresh ground pepper to taste

Seed the peppers; cut into 2 inch by 2 inch pieces. In a pan over medium high heat, sauté the peppers in the olive oil until tender. Add the shallot and garlic and sauté an additional minute. Slightly scramble the eggs and add them to the pan. Cook, stirring until the eggs are done; adjust the flavor with salt and pepper and serve.

Variation #1: Add ¼ teaspoon crushed red pepper flakes to the mixture before serving.

Variation #2: Add ¼ cup grated Romano cheese to the mixture before serving.

***Bella Sera Pnot Grigio

Potatoes & Eggs

1 large Idaho potato, peeled and sliced
4 tablespoons extra virgin olive oil
1 shallot, minced
1 clove garlic, minced
3 eggs
Sea salt to taste
Fresh ground pepper to taste

Slice the potato into ¼"rounds, and then slice the rounds into thin ¼" strips. In a pan over medium high heat, sauté the potato strips in the olive oil until golden and almost done, stirring all the time. Towards the end of the cooking, add the shallots and then the garlic. Be careful not to burn the garlic. Lightly scramble the eggs and add them to the potatoes. Cook and stir until the eggs are done. Adjust the flavor with salt and pepper and serve.

Variation #1: Add ¼ teaspoon of dry red pepper flakes to the mixture before serving.

Variation #2: Add ¼ cup grated Romano cheese to the mixture before serving.

Variation#3: Instead of a raw potato, try using a baked potato.

***Luna de Luna Pinot Grigio

Spinach Crostini

1 package frozen chopped spinach
1 shallot, minced
1 cup sour cream
¼ cup grated Romano
Sea salt to taste
Fresh ground pepper to taste

Thaw the spinach and squeeze as much of the water out of the spinach as possible. Combine it with the shallot, sour cream and Romano. Adjust the flavor with salt and pepper.

Variation #1: Add 1 finely minced garlic clove to the mixture.

Variation #2: Add ½ teaspoon of hot red pepper flakes to the mixture.

***Ruffino Orvieto Classico**

Shrimp Scampi Crostini

6 large shrimp, 16/20 size, peeled and deveined, tail off
1 tablespoon extra virgin olive oil
1 tablespoon unsalted butter
3 cloves garlic, minced
1 shallot, minced
1 tablespoon dry white wine
Sea salt to taste
Fresh ground pepper to taste

In a pan over medium high heat, add the oil and the butter. Add the garlic and shallot and cook until tender. Be careful not to burn the garlic. Add the wine and cook 30 seconds. Add the shrimp and cook until opaque, about 2-3 minutes. Remove from the heat and coarsely chop the shrimp. Combine with the remaining pan juices, garlic and shallots and serve.

Variation #1: instead of large shrimp, use smaller shrimp (21-25 or 51/60) and serve them whole.

Variation #2: instead of shrimp, use the meat from one large lobster tail coarsely chopped.

***Bolla Orvieto Classico**

Crabmeat Crostini

16 ounces jumbo lump crabmeat
1 small shallot, minced
½ stalk celery, minced
1 teaspoon extra virgin olive oil
2 tablespoon good quality mayonnaise
½ teaspoon dry mustard
½ teaspoon lemon juice
Sea salt to taste

Fresh ground pepper to taste

Inspect the crabmeat and remove any shell fragments that may be present. Combine the crabmeat with the shallot, celery, olive oil and mayonnaise. Blend well. Adjust the flavor with salt and pepper and serve.

Variation #1: use lobster tail meat instead of crab.

Variation #2: use cut shrimp instead of crab.

***Moet Imperial Rose**

Fried Eggplant

2 each Japanese eggplants, cut into ¼" ovals
½ cup flour
Sea salt to taste
Fresh ground pepper to taste
2 eggs, scrambled
½ cup Panko breadcrumbs combined with ½ cup grated Romano
Olive oil for frying
Shredded Regianno cheese as garnish

Slice the eggplant into ovals. Set up a breading station with the flour, (seasoned with salt and pepper) in one dish, the scrambled eggs in a second and the Panko/Romano mixture in a third. Dredge the eggplant slices in the flour, shaking off the excess. Then, dip in the egg mixture and finally coat with the bread crumbs. Allow the breaded eggplant slices to sit for 5 minutes.

Fry in the oil until golden and drain on paper towels. Salt lightly as the slices are removed from the frying pan. Sprinkle the fried eggplant with some shredded Regianno and serve.

Variation #1: Serve with a small plate of your favorite marinara sauce on the side.

Variation #2: Add 1/8 tsp each of dried basil, dried oregano, garlic powder and onion powder to the Panko/Romano mixture.

Variation #3: add one chopped seeded cherry pepper to the mix while frying.

Masi Valpolicella Classico

Grilled Flank Steak

1 pound flank steak
2 cloves garlic, minced
1 small onion, minced
1 cup dry red wine
½ teaspoon fresh basil, minced
½ teaspoon fresh oregano, minced
Sea salt to taste
Fresh ground pepper to taste

In a non-reactive bowl, combine all the ingredients. Allow the steak to marinate for at least 4 hours or overnight. Remove the steak from the marinade and discard the marinade. Grill the steak to the desired doneness. Allow

the steak to "rest" before cutting into thin slices. Slice the steak so each slice will fit on the crostini. Serve warm or at room temperature.

Variation #1: Serve with good quality Dijon mustard and/or good quality mayonnaise on the side.

Variation #2: Serve with a sauce made of ½ cup sour cream mixed with 1 tablespoon of prepared horseradish, ½ teaspoon of Worcestershire sauce, and a pinch of salt and white pepper.

Montresor Valpolicella Repasso

Italian Sausage

2 each sweet Italian sausages, meat removed from the casing
1 medium onion, sliced thin
1 clove garlic, minced
2 tablespoons extra virgin olive oil

In a pan over medium high heat, add the olive oil and add the crumbled sausage meat; cook until done. Remove the sausage from the pan and reserve. In the same pan, sauté the onion until

tender. Add the garlic, and sauté an additional 30 seconds, being careful not to burn the garlic. Return the sausage meat to the pan and heat through. Serve.

Variation #1: Use some other favorite type of sausage meat—hot, parsley/cheese, turkey, etc.

Variation #2: Add a dollop or two of your favorite marinara sauce to the mixture when you return the sausage meat to the pan.

Variation #3: Instead of sauce, add a well beaten egg to the mixture during the final stage of cooking and cook until done.

Variation #4: Instead of sausage meat use the equivalent amount of ground beef, chicken or pork as the meat in any of the above variations.

Variation #5: When you remove the sausage meat from the pan, add one chopper russet potato and cook until just tender before adding the onion.

Chopped Broccoli Rabe

1 head broccoli Rabe, leaves and soft tops only
3 tablespoons extra virgin olive oil
3 cloves garlic, minced
½ cup water or low sodium chicken stock
Sea salt to taste
Ground black pepper to taste

In a pan over medium high heat, sauté the garlic in the olive oil until a light golden color. Immediately add the broccoli rabe, the water or chicken stock, and a pinch of salt and pepper. Mix together, cover and cook until soft. Adjust the flavor again with the salt and pepper; add 2-3 tablespoons fresh extra virgin olive oil and serve.

Variation #1: Add 2 anchovy filets to the garlic and allow them to melt before adding the broccoli Rabe.

Variation #2: After being cooked, add ¼ tsp crushed red pepper flakes and serve.

NOTE: Be sure to review the entire wine/

Bruschetta discussion in the chapter introduction.

Mashed Cauliflower

1 head cauliflower florets
3 tablespoons extra virgin olive oil
4 cloves garlic, minced
½ cup water or low sodium chicken stock
Sea salt to taste
Ground black pepper to taste

Cut the cauliflower florets into very small pieces. In a pan over medium high heat, add the olive oil and the garlic. Cook the garlic to a light, golden color; then add the cauliflower and the water. Add a pinch of salt and cook covered until the cauliflower is very soft. Mash the cauliflower with a potato masher. Adjust the flavor with salt and pepper. Add 2-3 tablespoons fresh extra virgin olive oil. Stir and serve warm or at room temperature.

Variation #1: when you add the garlic, add 2 anchovy filets and allow them to melt as the garlic cooks.

Variation #2: before serving add ¼ tsp red pepper flakes and mix well.

***Edna Valley Chardonnay

Cannellini Beans with Bacon and Onion

3 slices of bacon or pancetta
1 small sweet onion, minced
1 clove garlic, minced
1 can cannellini beans, drained and rinsed
Sea salt to taste
Ground black pepper to taste
2 tablespoons extra virgin olive oil

In a pan over medium heat, fry the bacon or pancetta until crisp. Remove, chop and reserve.

Add the onion to the bacon drippings and sauté until tender. Add the garlic and sauté an additional minute being careful not to burn the garlic. Add the beans and blend well. Return the chopped bacon or pancetta to the pan. Adjust the flavor with the salt and pepper. Add the olive oil and mix together. Serve.

Variation #1: Mash the mixture with a potato masher and serve as a spread.

Variation #2: Before serving add ¼ tsp red pepper flakes and mix together with the whole bean or mashed bean mixture.

***Billecart-salmon Rose

Ricotta

1 lb fresh or homemade Ricotta
½ cup grated Romano
½ cup grated fresh mozzarella
1 Tbs flat leaf parsley chopper finely
Salt and fresh grated black pepper to taste

Combine all the ingredients in a bowl and spread on freshly baked and garlic rubbed crostini.

Variation #1: top the Bruschetta with oil cured sun dried tomatoes.

Variation #2: top with marinated artichoke hearts

Variation #3: top with sliced sautéed or marinated mushrooms.

Variation #4: add chopped fresh Basil instead of parsley and proceed with any of the variations.

Variation #5: drizzle the top with extra virgin olive oil.

***JJ Prum Riesling

Chapter 5:

America the Beautiful and Bountiful

1. **Southern Fried Chicken**

   And 4 variations

2. **All American Hot Dog Toppings**

   And 10 variations

3. **Chicken Fried Steak in Country Gravy**

4. **Chicago Deep Dish Pizza**

5. **Nick's Chili**

6. **Philly Cheese Steak**

7. **Long Island "On the Half Shell"**

   And 7 variations

8. **New Jersey Tomato Tart**

   3 variations

9. **Cedar Glazed Cedar-Planked Alaskan Salmon**

10. **New Orleans Chicken and Sausage Jambalaya**

    And 2 variations

11. **San Francisco Ciopino**

12. **Boston Corned Beef and Cabbage**

13. **New England Clam Chowder**

14. **Manhattan Clam Chowder**

15. **Maine Lobster Rolls**

16. **Baked Virginia Ham**

17. **Mom's Midwest Meatloaf**

    And 2 variation

18. **Texas Style Beef Ribs**

19. **Chesapeake Bay Crab Cakes**

20. **Key West Shrimp**

21. **Gulf Shrimp Bisque**

22. **Mississippi River Fried Catfish**

23. **Great Lakes Roasted Duck**

    And 2 variations

America the Beautiful and Bountiful

When we think of uniquely American dishes, we really must think of dishes that have been influenced by the ethnic make-up of the people who immigrated to the various parts of our country. Most of the dishes that we think of as American are the result of the ethnic background of these individuals and the local products that were available.

In this section, we hope to offer you a wide range of foods that are famous for their local development and popularity. Others will be the unique development of American sensibilities. All will be uniquely American.

Some of the recipes in this section are from particular cities or states. Others recipes can be identified by the region of America from which they originate. Some are traditional and others are influenced by the background of our chef.

My background from New York City and Brooklyn, will bring certain prejudices to the dishes from that area. Joseph will offer his own interpretation to many of the dishes offered in the chapter.

We have tried to present as many recipes as possible in this cookbook, from all parts of our wonderful country for all to enjoy. We hope in future editions of this cookbook, to continue to offer other regional dishes.

Southern Fried Chicken

4 pound whole chicken
4 cups buttermilk
1 tablespoon coarse salt
1 tablespoon freshly ground black pepper
2 cloves garlic, minced
2 large shallots, minced
4 teaspoons Tabasco
4 pounds chicken, cut into 10 pieces

Flour Coating:
2 cups flour
1 tablespoon onion powder
1 tablespoon garlic powder
1 teaspoon sea salt
1 teaspoon ground black pepper
1 teaspoon white pepper
1 teaspoons cayenne pepper
Canola oil for frying

Completely wash and pat dry with paper towel one 4 pound chicken. Cut bird into 10 pieces resulting in 2 legs, 2 wings, 2 thighs, and splitting the breasts pieces in half, resulting in a total of ten pieces of chicken. (The breast is cut in half to equalize the cook time of all pieces of chicken). In a large bowl combine buttermilk, salt, pepper, garlic, shallots, and Tabasco. Add chicken to the marinade, toss well, cover, and allow marinating overnight in the refrigerator.

Combine all ingredients of the flour coating and mix well. Remove the chicken from the refrigerator and allow chicken to come to room temperature. Heat the oil in a cast iron or other heavy frying pan to 350 degrees. Dredge the chicken pieces in the flour and fry in the oil a few at a time until chicken is golden brown. Internal temperature of the chicken should be 165 degrees.

Variation#1: Instead of 2 cups of flour use one cup flour and one cup fine corn meal.

Variation #2: Add 2 tablespoons of good quality curry powder to the flour for curried southern Fried chicken.

Variation #3 Add 2 tablespoons Cajon Seasoning to the flour to make Cajon Fried Chicken

Variation #4: To make a pan gravy, remove all but 2 Tbs of the oil from the frying pan leaving all the brown bits behind. Add 1 Tbs of flour and cook stirring until the Rue is very light golden. Add 2-3 cups liquid (water, milk, chicken broth) and return to a boil. Adjust the salt and pepper and serve alongside the chicken.

Let's talk about wine: We'll start off with a shocker. Why not pair this first dish we are presenting with a *sparkling wine*? Many don't think of pairing food with champagne or other sparklers, but they go great together. You will be seeing this recommendation often in this text. Some that would "pair" well might be: **Louis Bouillet Brut Rose, Moet, Soria Asti, Nino Franco Prosecco**, and **Rondel Cava.** White Wines such as: **Albrecht Gewürztraminer** or **Titus Chardonnay** would stand up to the dish. Try *reds* such as **Angeline Merlot or Pinot Noir, Kunde Merlot, Blackstone Merlot, 7 Deadly Zins**, or **Sobon Hillside Zin** would complement the dish. And don't forget a good *Beer* such as **Pikes IPA Ale or Sam Adams Larger.**

All American Hot Dog Toppings

All Americans love hot dogs. After the usual mustard or ketchup, sauerkraut, relish and/or onions, there are many additional options that will compliment the all American hot dog. We have provided you with a number of toppings to compliment this uniquely American dish. Each of the following should supply enough topping for 4 Hot Dogs:

Chili: use one of the chili's suggested

Cherry Pepper Relish: Chop 2-3 pickled cherry peppers. Add one clove chopped garlic, 1 tablespoon olive oil and one shallot, chopped.

Mushrooms: Chop one clove garlic and 4-5 mushrooms in a pan with 1 teaspoon olive oil. Add salt and pepper and 2 Tbs cream sherry. Cook until dry and top the hot dogs.

Tomatoes: Chop two plum tomatoes and blend with one clove chopped garlic and 1 tablespoon olive oil and salt and pepper to taste.

Artichokes: Drain one small jar of marinated artichokes, and then chop them. Mix in one clove garlic minced and 1 tablespoon olive oil.

Roasted Peppers: Chop one small jar of roasted peppers with one clove garlic chopped and 1 tablespoon olive oil.

Onions/peppers/garlic with 3 Condiments: In a bowl, combine one small chopped sweet pepper, one chopped yellow onion, 1 chopped clove, salt and pepper and 2 tablespoons olive oil. To the dog, add a small stream each of mustard, ketchup and mayonnaise. Top with the pepper mixture.

Cheese: Melt 4 ounces of Velveeta cheese and 1 ounce of Swiss cheese in 3 tablespoons dry white wine. Add a dash of your favorite hot sauce and salt and pepper to taste.

Sautéed Onions: Sauté one sliced medium yellow onion in 1 tablespoon extra virgin olive oil with salt and pepper to taste. Add ¼ teaspoon cracked red pepper flakes and blend.

Peppers & Onions: Sauté one yellow onion and one small sweet pepper, both sliced, in 2 tablespoons of olive oil along with one clove of garlic that's also sliced. Add salt and pepper to taste and serve.

Sausage Topping: Remove the meat of one sweet (or hot) sausage from the casing. Sauté the sausage in little a olive oil until almost done. Add 1 clove chopped garlic and one small chopped shallot and cook an additional 30 seconds. Add one chopped plum tomato and cook and additional minute. Serve.

These are but a few of the possible toppings for the world famous hot dog. Please use these suggestions for your own experimentation in the world of hot dog toppings.

Let's talk about beers and wines: Hot Dogs cry out for an ice cold beer. You can bring out the **Bud or the Coors** or try one like **Dogfish Head,** or **Land shark**. Additionally, you might want to try the beer from the oldest American brewery **Yuengling Lager.** The **Pikes IPA** would be a rich addition. For a rich addition you might try **Murphy's Stout** or the wonderful **Smiths Oatmeal Stout** from England. **Wine to Pair:** As you choose a wine remember the phrase: **"The more heat---the more sweet."** When a food is very spicy, a sweeter wine such as a

Riesling will stand up well. **Fetzer Riesling or Gewürztraminer** makes a nice dryer one and their **Late Harvest (LH)** is way up there on the sweetness level. You could also try a *sweet red* such as a **Dr. Heidemanns Dornfelder** from Germany. For a red you could try the **Dr. Heidemanns RED** Dornfelder and a nice Shiraz called **Jam Jar.**

Chicken Fried Steak in Country Gravy

(4) 6 oz pieces of sirloin steak pounded ¼" thick
1 cup seasoned flour
4 eggs scrambled
Sea salt to taste
Fresh ground pepper to taste
½ cup canola oil, adjust amount as needed

Gravy:

2 tablespoons unsalted butter
1 teaspoon garlic, chopped
2 tablespoons flour
¼ cup fresh, brewed coffee
2 cups whole milk
¼ teaspoon thyme, fresh chopped
Sea salt to taste
Ground black pepper to taste

Dredge the steak in the seasoned flour, dip in the egg wash and then the seasoned flour for a second time. Fry in the oil at 325 degrees until done. Remove the steaks from pan and reserve.

Remove the oil from pan. Reduce heat to medium and add the butter. Melt butter completely and add the garlic. Cook garlic until a light golden brown; then add the flour, a little at a time, to prevent lumps to form a roux. Cook until a light golden brown. Add ¼ cup of coffee and stir to smooth consistency. Add the milk and bring to a light simmer, to thicken. Season the gravy with the thyme, salt, and pepper. Return the steaks to the pan for 30 seconds and then serve with the pan gravy.

Let's talk about wine: Because of the creamy gravy and the beef inside, this dish can take

a number of whites, roses or reds. The white should be rich such as a *Viognier* like **Gassier Les Piliers**, **Sobon** or **Bridgeman**. A rich *Rose* such as **Mulderbosch**, or **Muga** would pair well. A *GSM from the Rhone* would be an excellent red to pair such as **Rasteau Cotes-du-Rhone Prestige** or one of the excellent **Domaine de la Presidente** wines. An *alternative red* that would pair well might be the **Phebus MMC** from Argentina or the **Alamos Malbec**.

Chicago Deep Dish Pizza

1 portion pizza dough
2 tablespoons extra virgin olive oil
¼ pound slices salami
¼ pound grated mozzarella
½ cup of pizza sauce
½ pound button mushrooms, sliced
¼ pound ricotta
2-3 meatballs, sliced
½ cup sauce
¼ pound sliced pepperoni
¼ pound sliced mozzarella
½ cup sauce
1/3 cup grated cheese

Purchase a 10-12oz pizza dough portion, usually found in the freezer section of your local market. Most commercial pizza dough products are decent enough so you don't have to necessarily make the dough when you're short on time.

Allow dough to thaw under refrigeration for at least 24 hours before use. Once thawed, dust the dough with some all purpose flour, and press it flat by hand. Place dough in a large bowl, and cover with a towel to allow the dough to rise. About one hour.

Conversely, most important to any pizza is the sauce. To buy a ready-made pizza sauce would be sacrilegious according to my Grandmother. This is how I make my sauce:

Pizza Sauce:

12 ounce can San Marzano tomatoes, whole and
  peeled
4 ounce can tomato puree
¼ cup basil, fresh
1 tablespoon oregano, fresh
2 teaspoons thyme, fresh
1 tablespoon sea salt
2 teaspoon ground black pepper
1 tablespoon granulated sugar

Puree the tomatoes in a blender until smooth.
Place the puree in a large bowl, and add remaining
ingredients to the puree. Mix well.

Grease a deep 12 inch round baking dish with
the olive oil. Spread the dough in the dish so
that it covers the bottom and up the sides. Evenly
distribute the remaining ingredients in the order
listed above. Bake at 350 degrees until golden
on the bottom. Approximately 20-25 minutes.
Feel free to experiment with your own list of
ingredients.

Let's talk about wine: We suggest that you stick
with reds on this one. A Sangiovese: **Macchia** from
California or **Vasco Sassetti** from Italy would
be great. A *cabernet* such as **Dominican Oaks
Napa, Charles Krug, Santa Ema, Edgewood,
or Bridgeman** would all go well. Try *Zins* such
as **Sobon Old Vines, Rosenblum,** or a *Malbec*
such as **Cupcake, Flichman Gestos** or **Norton.**
Don't forget the jug wine" although you may
not think it great some are nice party wines, in
particular the **Opici Homemade** is s nice red for
a big pizza party.

Nick's Chili

3 tablespoons olive oil
1 large yellow onion, chopped
1 sweet red pepper, chopped
1 stalk celery with leaves, chopped
5 cloves garlic, chopped
2 jalapeños with seeds, chopped
1 pound boneless country style pork ribs,
cut into ½" chunks.
1 pound ground beef

28 ounce can plum tomatoes, hand crushed
8 ounce can tomato paste
16 ounce can tomato sauce
¼ cup cilantro, chopped
¼ cup flat leaf parsley, chopped
3 teaspoons ground cumin
2 teaspoons chili powder
3 tablespoons soy sauce
3 tablespoons fish sauce
12 ounce can pinto beans (optional)

In a large pot, heat 2 tablespoons of oil over
medium high heat. Add onion and sauté until
tender. Add the pepper, celery, and jalapeño,
and sauté the vegetables until tender. Add the
garlic and cook an additional minute. Remove
all the vegetables from the pot and reserve. Add
the remaining oil. Add the pork and sauté until
browned on all sides. Add the ground beef, and
continue to cook until meat is done. Return the
vegetables to the pot along with the plum tomato,
tomato paste and sauce. Stir pot well, then add
the cilantro, parsley, cumin, chili powder, soy
and fish sauce. Bring to a simmer and cook for
30 minutes. Add one can of beans and reheat.
Serve with grated cheddar cheese, sour cream and
chopped raw onion as toppings.

Let's talk about wine and beer: Once again, a
great choice for this dish is one of the *sparkling
wines* mentioned in the previous recipes. "The
more heat—the more sweet, applies to this dish
as well." *Beer* is also a good choice for this recipe.
Singha from Thailand is great with spicy foods
as well as **Negro Mondello** from Mexico. Two
others you might try would be **Pikes IPA** and
Arrogant Bastard. Another great beer would be
Monk in a Trunk or **Dogfish Head.**

Philly Cheese Steak

1 pound rib eye or top round roast, shaved very
  thin
3 tablespoons extra virgin olive oil
2 yellow onions, sliced thinly
3 cloves garlic, sliced thinly
1 teaspoon ground black pepper

Good quality beef broth
Italian bread, 8 inches long
½ cup dry white wine
½ cup chicken stock
2 cups *Cheese Whiz or Velveeta*
½ teaspoon fresh ground black pepper

Place the rib-eye or roast in the freezer for 45 minutes. This will assist you in slicing the meat as thin as possible.

In a sauté pan over medium high heat, place the olive oil and add the onions. Cook the onions until the onions start in brown. Add the garlic and cook an additional minute. Remove from the pan and keep warm. In a separate pot, add the wine and the chicken stock. Add the cheese and pepper and melt. In the used oil, sear pieces of the beef until done. Add a sprinkle of the broth to moisten the meat.

Place the cooked meat in Italian bread that has been moistened with some of the broth. Add some of the onion/garlic mixture and top with the melted cheese.

Let's talk about wine: Note the suggestions under Chicken Fried Steak, recipe # 3 above.

Long Island "On the Half Shell"

(Littleneck Clams & Blue Point Oysters)

Open the clams or oysters, leaving as much of the juices as possible. Serve cold with your choice of sauce. The following are a list of sauces that you might use to enjoy these little gems from the ocean. Each recipe should be enough to sauce 6-12 clams depending on size and how much sauce you like with your clams.

Sauce 1:
¼ cup ketchup
1 tablespoon horseradish
Juice of ¼ lemon
Dash hot sauce
Dash fish sauce
1 tablespoon fish sauce

2 tablespoons apple cider vinegar
1 scallion chopped finely

Sauce 2:
2 tablespoons soy sauce
1 tsp seasoned rice wine vinegar
1/8 teaspoon fresh ground ginger
1 scallion, chopped

Sauce 3:
1 plum tomato, chopped
1 tablespoon extra virgin olive oil
1 clove garlic, minced
Sea salt to taste
Fresh ground pepper to taste

Sauce 4:
¼ cup mayonnaise
1 teaspoon Dijon mustard
Fresh ground pepper to taste

Sauce 5:
2 tablespoons extra virgin olive oil
1 teaspoon red wine vinegar
Sea salt to taste
Fresh ground pepper to taste

Sauce 6:
¼ teaspoon Sambal
2 tablespoons water
1 tablespoons rice vinegar
¼ teaspoon Nam Pla

Let's talk about wine: Raw shellfish is outstanding with a Brut sparkling rose such as **Louis Bouillet Brut Rose,** or **Rondel Rose** or **Moet Rose.** *A Chenin Blanc* such as **Spier** or **Mulderbosch** would add the slightest touch of sweetness to compliment the sauces offered as would a drier Riesling such as the **Dr. Heidemanns Kabinett** or **QBA** *or the* **J. J. Prum Kabinett.**

New Jersey Tomato Tart

1 portion of pizza dough
4 tablespoons extra virgin olive oil
Sea salt to taste

Fresh ground pepper to taste

3 vine ripened summer Jersey or Beefsteak tomatoes, sliced thin

2 tablespoons extra virgin olive oil

2 teaspoons fresh ground black pepper

1 tablespoon fresh oregano, chopped fine

¼ cup asiago cheese, shredded

2 tablespoons grated parmesan cheese

Coat a deep cookie sheet with the olive oil. Spread the dough evenly over the sheet. Season the dough with salt and pepper. Cover the dough with the sliced tomatoes pressing them into the dough. Drizzle the top with additional olive oil and ground black pepper. Sprinkle with asiago and parmesan cheeses and oregano. Bake at 350 degrees until the bottom is golden.

Variation #1: Top with seeded, sliced hot cherry peppers before baking.

Variation #2: Use one of your favorite melting cheeses in addition or instead of the asiago.

Variation #3: top with 6-8 anchovy filets before baking.

Let's talk about wine: Here we offer our first *Pinotage* suggestions: **Spier** or **Graham Beck** from South Africa would add much as lighter reds. A nice *Pinot Noir* such as one of the **Belle Gloss Wines**, or **Angeline RRV** or **Muirwood** would also pair very well. In addition, you might try a bolder red such as a *Brunello f*rom Italy such as the **Vasco Sassetti Brunello 2003.**

Mustard Glazed Cedar-Planked Alaskan Salmon

1 large salmon filet with the skin (3+ pounds and about 18 inches long)

1 teaspoon extra virgin olive oil

¼ teaspoon sea salt

¼ teaspoon fresh ground black pepper

¼ teaspoon fresh ground white pepper

1 untreated cedar plank, large enough for the fish and soaked in water for 2 hours

Glaze:

2 tablespoons fresh lime juice

2 tablespoons seasoned rice wine vinegar

1 teaspoon Dijon mustard

1 tablespoon maple syrup

2 scallions, minced

1 clove garlic, finely minced

½ teaspoon sea salt

½ teaspoon fresh ground black pepper

½ seeded and chopped jalapeño

¼ cup extra virgin olive oil

For the glaze, combine all the ingredients except the oil, in a blender and blend until smooth. Slowly drizzle in the olive oil until well blended. Bake the cedar plank at high heat until the edges begin to smoke. Place the salmon, skin side down, on the plank. Brush with oil and sprinkle with black and white pepper. Pour half the dressing over the salmon and spread evenly. Bake at 425 degrees until slightly pink on the inside-about 15 minutes. Serve with the remaining glaze.

Let's talk about wine: Salmon is one type of fish that cries for a great *Pinot Noir*. Try **Bell Gloss Meiomi** ; **Estancia** or **Montoya.** This dish may call for a real splurge to the top with **Goldeneye** by **Duckhorn** or my favorite **Pahlmeyer** one of the best that is produced.

New Orleans Chicken and Sausage Jambalaya

3 tablespoons unsalted butter

2 tablespoons extra virgin olive oil

3 pounds chicken, cut into 10 pieces

2 large sweet onions, chopped

8 scallions. chopped

4 cloves garlic, chopped

1 sweet red pepper, chopped

3 stalks celery. chopped

1 pound pork stew meat

1teaspoon fresh ground black pepper

½ teaspoon ground white pepper

¾ teaspoon cayenne pepper

½ teaspoon mild chili powder

½ teaspoon herbs de province

1/3 cup fresh flat leaf parsley, chopped

1/8 teaspoon cinnamon
1 pound cooked, sliced Italian sweet sausage
1 cup diced fresh ham
1 cup white rice
1 can diced tomatoes
½ cup tomato sauce
2 cups chicken stock

In a large pot, melt the butter with the oil. Fry the chicken in batches until golden brown and set aside. Turn heat to medium, add the pork, and cook until brown on all sides. Add the onion, scallions, garlic, red pepper and celery. Cook until vegetables are tender. Then, add the salt, peppers, chili powder, bay leaves, herbs de province, parsley and cinnamon, sausage, rice, ham, tomatoes, tomato sauce and chicken stock. Stir pot well, and return the chicken to the pot. Bring pot to a boil, reduce heat, and simmer with pot covered for about 20-30 minutes. Simmer an additional 10-15 minutes uncovered and serve.

Variation #1: Use hot Italian sausage and hot chorizo instead of the sweet sausage.

Variation #2: If you want to kick it up another notch add a chopped jalapeño.

Let's talk about wine: For the sweet version of the dish a *Grenache* would be great as a pairing. **Tres Ojos Old Vine Garnacha** from Spain would be great. **Sawtooth Riesling** from Idaho would be a great white paring. If you are doing very spicy you might want to try a sweet late harvest *Riesling* like **Washington Hills LH** or **B. Lovely**. A good red to pair would be the **Kunde Cabernet** or the **Courtney Benham Zinfandel**.

San Francisco Ciopino

Broth:

2 pounds white fish bones, such as cod or turbo
24 ounces canned San Marzano tomatoes
½ pounds Italian sausage, removed from casing
1 fennel, rough chop
1 yellow onion, Rough Chop
2 carrots, rough chop

½ cup fresh basil, rough chop
½ cup garlic cloves
2 lemons, cut in half
3 cups dry white wine
1 tablespoon red pepper flake
½ gallon water
24 ounce low sodium clam juice
2 tablespoons fennel seed

Seafood:

½ ounce olive oil
1 tablespoon garlic, chopped
12 littleneck clams
24 PEI mussels
½ cup dry white wine
12 ounces cod, or other mild fish, cut into 2 ounce pieces
8 ounces sea scallops

Thoroughly, rinse the fish bones under cold running water. Remove the Italian sausage from the casing and crumble up the meat. In a large stock pot over medium heat, add the Italian sausage meat. Render the sausage until cooked; ¾ of the way. Add the fennel, onion, carrot, and garlic to the pot. Begin to cook the vegetables, tossing occasionally so they start to caramelize, about 15 minutes. Once vegetables are a nice light brown, add the fish bones, and deglaze the pot with the white wine. Cook for 5 minutes more, and then add the water, tomatoes, pepper flake, clam juice, and fennel seed. Bring pot to a boil, then allow to simmer for 1 ½ hours. Strain stock through a fine sieve, and set aside for dish preparation.

In a small sauce pot, over medium high heat, add the olive oil. Once hot, add the garlic and allow the garlic cook to a light golden brown. Add the clams, mussels, and white wine. Cover pot with a lid, and cook until the clams are just beginning to open. Add the scallops and the fish and 1 quart of the fish broth. Return lid to pot, and poach the "Fish Stew" until the fish and scallops are opaque, and the clams and mussels are open.

Serve Ciopinno in a bowl with lots of broth, and some crusty sourdough bread.

Let's talk about wine: A great wine to add to the dish and to pair with it would be a *Pinot Grigio* such as **Kupelwieser, Barone Fini Alto Adige** or **Santa Margarita**. You might also try a nice *chardonnay* such as **River Road Sonoma**, **La Crema**, **Angeline RRV**, **Oak Grove** or **Martin Ray RRV**. This would be a great place to pair a good *white Burgundy* such as **Chateau Tour de l'Ange Macon-Villages** or **Domaine Saint-Martin Saint-Veran.**

Boston Corned Beef and Cabbage

1 five pound corned beef brisket 15 pounds or one five pound?
4 tablespoons pickling spices
3 parsnips cut into 2 inch pieces
4 carrots cut into 2 inch pieces
2 large yellow onions cut into large chunks
6-8 russet potatoes cut into large pieces
1 large head cabbage, cut into wedges.

In a large pot of water, place the corned beef and the pickling spices. Bring to a boil and simmer for 1-3 hours depending on the size of the brisket. The meat should be fork tender when fully cooked. Remove the brisket from the pot and place it in a baking dish; place in a 250 degree preheated oven.

Add the parsnips, carrots, onions and potatoes to the corned beef poaching pot. Simmer for about 10-15 minutes; then add the cabbage to the pot. Simmer until all the vegetables are tender. Remove the beef from the oven; cut across the grain into nice size slices and serve with the boiled vegetables.

Let's talk about wine and beer: When you think of corned beef and cabbage, you think of beer and rightly so. You might want to try an **English Porter** or a **Guinness** or **Murphy's Irish Stout**. A **Pikes IPA** would also go well with the meal as would a rich **Sam Adams Bock**. A rich red such as a *Cabernet* would also pair well and you might want to try one such as **Madrone**

Knoll; Rudy 2008 or **Martin Ray Diamond Mountain 2007**.

New England Clam Chowder

10 pounds small quahogs or large cherrystone clams, rinsed well, (discard open clams)
6 slices bacon, cut crosswise into 1/2-inch strips
4 tablespoons unsalted butter
2 medium leeks, white and light green parts only, halved lengthwise and thinly sliced crosswise (2 1/2 to 3 cups)
1 cup onions, finely chopped
1 cup celery, finely chopped
2 teaspoons garlic, minced
½ cup all purpose flour
6 sprigs fresh thyme
2 bay leaves
2 pounds potatoes, peeled and cut into 1/2-inch cubes (about 5 cups)
2 cups heavy cream
1/2 teaspoon freshly ground black pepper
1 1/4 teaspoons sea salt (or to taste)
1/4 cup fresh parsley, finely chopped
1/4 cup fresh chives or green onions, finely chopped

In a large stockpot, bring 3 cups of water to a boil. Add the clams to the pot, cover, and cook for 5 minutes. Uncover the pot and quickly stir. Replace lid, and cook 5 to 10 minutes longer (this will depend on the type and size of the clams), or until most of the clams are open.

Strain the clams into a large bowl through a fine-mesh sieve, being careful to strain out the sand. (You should have about 8 cups of clam broth. If not, add enough water to bring the volume up to 8 cups.) When the clams are cool enough to handle, remove the meat from the shells and chop into 1/2-inch pieces. Set the clam meat and broth aside.

Cook the bacon in a large heavy pot over medium heat until crisp and the fat is rendered. Pour off all the bacon fat, except 2 tablespoons. Add the 4 tablespoons butter, leeks, onions, and celery.

Cook until softened, about 5 minutes. Add the garlic and continue to cook one minute. Then add the flour and incorporate evenly. Add the clam broth, and bring to a simmer. Add the thyme, bay leaves, and potatoes. Lower the heat, cover, and simmer until the broth thickens slightly, and the potatoes are very tender, about 30 minutes. Be sure to stir chowder to keep ingredients from sticking to the bottom of the pot. Remove from the heat and discard the thyme stems and bay leaves. Stir in the clams and cream and season with the pepper and the salt to taste. Cook for 10 more minutes, and remove from heat.

Set the chowder aside for 1 hour, covered, to allow the flavors to marry. When ready to serve, place the pot over low heat and slowly reheat, stirring frequently, being careful not to boil. Garnish each bowl with some parsley, chives, and some oyster crackers. Serve hot.

Let's talk about wine: The creamy nature of the dish calls for a crisp white such as a *Sauvignon Blanc*. **Kim Crawford**, **Cottesbrook** , **The Crossings** and **Stony Bay** are nice New Zealand style wines with lots of grapefruit in the tastes. For a grassy finish you might want to try the **Courtney Benham Napa**, **Amici** or my favorite **Adler Fels.** A *Pinot Noir* would also go well and you might want to try a light one such as the **Angeline California** or **Kudos.**

Manhattan Clam Chowder

1 stick unsalted butter
2 tablespoon extra virgin olive oil
3 stalks celery with their leaves, chopped
3 carrots, chopped
1 large yellow onion, chopped
1 large green pepper, chopped
4 cloves garlic, minced
2 cups low sodium vegetable or chicken broth
1-6 ounce can tomato paste
1-16 oz can diced tomatoes
2 cups low sodium clam juice
2 baking potatoes cut into 1 inch cubes
1teaspoon dry thyme

1 teaspoon dry basil
½ teaspoon fresh ground black pepper
1/8 teaspoon cayenne pepper
2 bay leaves
1 quart fresh chopped chowder clams with their juices
Sea salt to taste
Ground black pepper to taste
½ cup dry sherry

In a pot, melt the butter in the olive oil. Add the onion, carrots, celery and pepper and cook until tender. Add the garlic and cook an additional minute. Add the clam juice, broth, tomato paste and tomatoes and blend well. Bring to a boil. Add the potatoes, Thyme, basil, black pepper, cayenne pepper and bay leaves. Reduce heat and simmer until the potatoes are tender. Add the clams with their juices and simmer an additional 5-10 minutes until the clams are just done. Remove from the heat, discard the bay leaves; adjust the salt and pepper; stir in the sherry and serve.

Let's talk about wine: Although the soup is tomato based, we feel that you can easily pair the same wines that we suggested for the New England clam chowder. If you want to go red, choose a lighter one such as **G & D Beaujolais** or a Rose such as **Travel**.

Maine Lobster Rolls

1 ½ pounds cooked Maine lobster, cooled, cracked well, meat removed
1 chive, finely chopped
Juice of ½ lemon
½ cup good quality mayonnaise
Salt sea to taste
Ground black pepper to taste
"Lanky" rolls or frankfurter rolls
Unsalted butter, soft

Blend the lobster meat with the other ingredients except the rolls and refrigerate for one hour.

Generously butter each side of the "Lanky" roll and toast until a golden brown. Line the rolls with a piece of red leaf lettuce and fill with the lobster mixture. Garnish with a wedge of lemon and serve.

Let's talk about wine: Nothing goes with lobster like excellent *champagne*. Serve a grand one such as **De Margerie** or **Billecart-Salmon** or a great *Brut* such as **Moet** or **Montaudon.** If you want an extra special wine, serve the **Montaudon Classe M or Veuve Clicquot.**

Baked Virginia Ham

1 shank or butt portion of a fully cooked smoked ham on the bone—about 6-8 pounds
2-3 whole cloves
1 small can pineapple slices (4) in their own juice
1 cup orange juice
½ cup maple syrup
1 teaspoon ground fresh ginger
1 tablespoon Dijon mustard
¼ cup honey

Place the ham on a rack in a baking pan, fat side up. Score the ham in a crisscross pattern. In the scored spaces, stud the ham with the whole cloves.

In a bowl, blend the juice from the can of pineapples, orange juice, maple syrup, ginger and mustard. Pour the mixture over the ham. Bake in a 350 degree pre heated oven about 20 minutes per pound, basting with the pan juices every 20 minutes. For the last 20 minutes, brush the honey over the ham and top with the pineapple slices. Serve with the pan juices as gravy.

Let's talk about wine: Here is the perfect dish for a *dry rose*. Remember, that these wines are dry and they are not the sweet pink wines that you might think. There are a number of great rose wines that you might choose: **Mulderbosch**, **Muga, Bougrier Rose d'Anjou**, **Salmon Sancerre Rose**, **Chateau de Nages Costières-de- Nimes** are all wonderful rose wines that will compliment this dish very well.

Mom's Midwest Meatloaf

2 pound ground beef
2 pound ground pork
2 pound ground veal
2 cups white bread, no crust, ground to crumbs
6 large eggs
Sea salt to taste
Ground black pepper to taste
2 oz Lea & Perrins chicken marinade
½ cup fresh parsley, chopped
¼ cup carrots, minced
¼ cup celery, minced
¼ cup onion, minced
1 tablespoon garlic, chopped
4 ounces evaporated milk
3 ounces ketchup
2 ounces A-1 steak sauce

Combine all ingredients in a large mixing bowl, and mix well. Pre-treat a large bread baking pan with some non-stick spray. Work the meatloaf into the pan. Smack the pan down on a flat surface several times to remove all air pockets in the meatloaf. Bake in 350 degree oven for 25 minutes. Take internal temperature of meatloaf to make sure the meatloaf is fully cooked. (Temperature should be at least 155 degrees.) Allow meatloaf to rest before removing from pan.

Variation #1: Top the loaf with strips of bacon before baking.

Variation #2: Instead of bacon, top the meatloaf with slices of pancetta.

Let's Talk about wine: This is the dish for a hearty red. A nice California *cabernet* would go well such as: **Dominican Oaks Napa, Rudy, Titus, Robert Mondavi Napa**, **Jordan** or if you want to really go for it you might want to try one of the **Caymus 2008** greats. There are also some great Malbec that would go well such as **Norton**, **Mendoza Station** or **Tupungato**

Texas Style Beef Ribs

4-5 pounds beef ribs or baby back pork ribs

Dry Rub:

2 teaspoons sea salt
1 teaspoon fresh ground black pepper
1 teaspoon fresh ground white pepper
1 teaspoon dry thyme
1 teaspoon paprika
1 teaspoon garlic powder
1 teaspoon onion powder
1 teaspoon sugar
½ teaspoon dry mustard
½ teaspoon ground cumin
½ teaspoon ground fennel

Braising Liquid and Sauce:

2 shallots, minced
4 clove garlic, minced
2 tablespoons extra virgin olive oil
12 cups tomato sauce
1 cup dry red wine
2 jalapeño peppers, seeded and minced
1 cup brown sugar
1 tablespoon apple cider vinegar
Sea salt to taste
Ground black pepper to taste

To prepare the dry rub, combine all ingredients and set aside for preparation.

To prepare the sauce, cook the shallots in the oil, in a sauté pan, over medium heat until soft. Add the garlic and cook an additional 30 seconds. Add the remaining ingredients and simmer for 10 minutes.

To prepare the ribs, rub the ribs generously with the dry rub and allow them to stand for 45 minutes. Grill the ribs over high heat, "marking" them well with grill marks. Then, place ribs in a braising pan, rib side down. Pour the prepared sauce over the ribs, cover the pan with foil, and place ribs in a 325 degree oven for 2 hours. (Cook time for ribs may vary.) Once ribs are tender, when the meat is "falling off the bone", carefully remove the ribs from the pan and place on a serving platter.

Pour the braising liquid in a sauce pan and reduce to a thick consistency. Brush the ribs with the sauce and serve. Serve with additional sauce on the side.

Let's talk about beers: Nothing goes better with a rack of ribs that an ice cold beer. Try an *Indian Pale Ale* such as **Dogfish Head** or an *amber lager* such as **Sam Adams**. You might also try the New **Reserve by Sapporo**. The **Monk in a Trunk Organic Ale** would also be great. If you really want to experiment with a great beer you might want to **try Arrogant Bastard**.

Chesapeake Bay Crab Cakes

½ cup Mayonnaise
1 egg
1 tablespoon whole grain mustard
1 teaspoon Old Bay seasoning
Juice of 1 lemon
2 tablespoons chives, chopped
½ teaspoon Tabasco
Pinch ground black pepper
½ teaspoon Worcestershire sauce
2/3 cup Ritz cracker, crushed
½ pound back fin crab meat
1 pound jumbo lump crab meat
Panko bread crumbs
2 tablespoon unsalted butter
1 tablespoon olive oil

In a large mixing bowl, combine the mayonnaise eggs, mustard, Old Bay seasoning, lemon juice, chives, Tabasco, black pepper, and Worcestershire sauce, and mix well. Add crushed Ritz crackers to mayonnaise base, mix well, and let sit, allowing the crackers to absorb some of the moisture. (About 10 minutes.) Add the back fin crabmeat to the bowl and "fold" gently. Then, add jumbo lump crabmeat, and "fold" very gently to mix, try to prevent the lump crab meat from falling apart. Cover and refrigerate the mixture for 2 hours.

Shape the mixture into 4-6 cakes being careful not to press together too firmly. Dust the cakes with some Panko breadcrumb. In a pan, on medium-high heat, place 2 tablespoons unsalted butter and 1 tablespoon olive oil. Brown the cakes quickly on both sides; finish the cakes in a preheated 350°oven until heated through, about 5 minutes.

Let's talk about wine: Let me start by suggesting and *Extra Dry Champagne* such as the **Martell Extra Dry**. The ever so slight sweetness will go well with the richness of the crab. The **Dr. Heidemanns Riesling QBA** would also pair well. Another nice white would be the **Rene Sparr One Alsace**

Key West Shrimp

2 pounds large shrimp, cleaned and deveined, tail off
½ cup extra virgin olive oil
2 tablespoons white wine vinegar
2 tablespoon key lime juice
1 tablespoon fish sauce
½ teaspoon salt
¼ cup shallots, chopped
3 cloves garlic, sliced thinly
½ teaspoon white pepper
½ teaspoon ground black pepper
¼ teaspoon cayenne pepper
½ sweet red pepper, seeded and thinly sliced
½ sweet yellow pepper, seeded and thinly sliced
1 small red onion, thinly sliced
2 stalks celery with leaves, thinly sliced

2 tablespoons nonpareil capers

Cook the shrimp in boiling water, drain and allow cooling. Combine all the ingredients in a nonreactive bowl and blend well. Cover and refrigerate for at least 4 hours. Serve.

Let's talk about wine: A nice *California chardonnay* that is not too oaky would complement the shrimp. Try the **Martin Ray RRV, River Road Sonoma**, **Edna Valley** or the excellent high end **Mer Soleil Silver** or **Lloyd**.

Gulf Shrimp Bisque

¼ pound pancetta, cut into small chunks
¼ cup extra virgin olive oil
1/3 cup flour
1 large yellow onion, chopped coarsely
3 cloves garlic, minced
1 red pepper, coarsely chopped
2 stalks celery with leaves chopped
5 large scallions, chopped
1 quart shrimp stock, low sodium chicken broth or water
3 tablespoon tomato paste
1 teaspoon dry thyme
1 teaspoon dry basil
½ cup chopped fresh flat leaf parsley
1/8 teaspoon ground cloves
1/8 teaspoon allspice
1/3 teaspoon fresh ground black pepper
1/3 teaspoon ground white pepper
2 tablespoon lime juice
2 pounds cleaned and deveined gulf shrimp
Salt and cayenne pepper to taste

In a large pot, sauté the pancetta in the olive oil until the fat is rendered and the pancetta is just crisp. Add the onions, garlic, red pepper, celery and scallions and cook until soft. Add the flour, and stir continuously until a light brown roux develops. Add the stock and stir until well blended; blend in the tomato paste while stirring. Add the thyme, basil, ground cloves, ground all spice, black pepper white pepper and lime juice. Bring pot to a simmer for one hour. Adjust the flavor with salt and cayenne pepper. Add the shrimp and cook until the shrimp are just done, about 2-3 minutes. Serve over cooked rice or pasta.

Let's talk about wine: see the suggestions for #20 Key West Shrimp.

Mississippi River Fried Catfish

1 ½ cups fine cornmeal
½ teaspoon fresh ground black pepper
½ teaspoon ground white pepper
1/3 teaspoon cayenne pepper

6 large catfish filets
1 cup buttermilk
Olive oil for frying
Salt to taste

Combine the cornmeal, black pepper, white pepper and cayenne in a flat dish and blend well. In a large sauté pan over medium high heat, add the oil. Dip the filets in the buttermilk then coat with the cornmeal mixture. Fry the catfish in the hot oil until a deep golden color. Salt to taste as the filets are removed from the frying pan.

Let's talk about wine: Because of the spiciness of the peppers we suggest that you go with a wine that has a bit of sweetness such as the *Vouvray* **Bougrier "V"** or the **Mulderbosch Chenin Blanc** from South Africa. The **Zind Riesling** would also stand up well to the dish.

Great Lakes Roasted Duck

5 pound duck, washed and dried
1 teaspoon salt
1 tablespoon fresh ground black pepper
1 tablespoon ground white pepper
1 teaspoon Spanish paprika
½ teaspoon cayenne pepper
1 teaspoon onion powder
1 teaspoon garlic powder
1 teaspoon dry thyme
1 cup cream sherry

Preheat the oven to 425 degrees. With a very sharp knife, score the duck skin in a crisscross pattern being careful not to cut into the meat.

In a bowl, combine all the spices and blend well. Rub the entire duck inside and out with about ¾ of the spice mixture and refrigerate for 1 hour.

Place the duck on a rack in a baking pan and roast the duck in the preheated oven for about 1 hour. After 1 hour, pour off the excess fat out of the roasting pan and discard. Sprinkle the remaining spice mixture over the duck and return to the oven for an additional 45-60 minutes. Test for doneness (juices should run clear to very slightly pink). Allow the duck to rest for 15 minutes before carving.

While the duck is resting, skim the excess fat from the roasting pan. Deglaze the pan with the sherry and serve the pan gravy with the duck.

Variation #1: The same spice mixture can be used with a whole chicken. The cooking time for a chicken should be about 60 minutes depending on the size.

Variation #2: Use the spice rub on your favorite roast (pork or beef) and cook to the desired doneness.

Let's talk about Wine: a *Rhone blend* such as one of the **President's Domaine** wines is a good match as is the **JV Fleury Rouge**. Also try a rich *Pinot Noir* such as **A to Z** or **Flowers** with the dish, or its variations. A rich full bodied *chardonnay* could be used such as **River Road Mills Vineyard**, or **Dariosh.**

Chapter 6:

Let's Travel To Some Exciting Places

Bulgarian

17. **Cucumber Soup**

GREECE

18. **A Real Greek Salad**

Norway

19. **Coleslaw**

Poland

20. **Herring in Sour Cream**

Finland

21. **Salmon Soup**

Ireland

22. **Irish Stew**

England

23. **Steak and Kidney Pie**

Holland

24. **Stuffed Cabbage**

India

25. **Curried Fried Chicken**

26. **Minced Meat with Potatoes and Peas**

27. **Curried Hard Cooked Eggs**

28. **Curried Meatballs**

29. **India: South Indian Shrimp Curry**

    And 1 variation

Thailand

30. **Shrimp Salad with Champagne Mayonnaise**

31. **Nam Sod**

32. **Mussels with Lemon Grass and Thai Basil**

33. **Beef with Noodles**

34. **Sweet & Sour Shrimp**

Viet Nam

35. **Pork and Shrimp Rolls**

36. **PHO**

Indonesia

37. **Hot and Sour Shrimp**

38. **Chicken in Coconut Milk**

39. **Meatballs with Coconut**

40. **Crisp-fried Beef**

Cambodia

41. **Raw Fish Salad**

42. **Shrimp and Cucumber Curry**

Burma

43. **Noodles with Curried Chicken**

Sir Lanka

44. **Beef Curry**

The Philippines

45. **Fried Noodles**

Lets Travel To Some Exotic Places

If you live in a major cosmopolitan city, you may have come across a restaurant or two that specializes in foods from a country you have only heard about, but have never been. What better way to introduce ourselves to different cultures from around the world, then to learn about the food they eat?

There is nothing more meaningful in a culture than when you are invited to share in the food of the family. Peace offerings are made through the offering of food. Entire cultures are defined by the food they offer.

I can still remember when living at home, the first words out of my own mother's mouth when someone came to visit. "Would you like something to eat?" If someone were to walk in at dinnertime, they were suddenly welcomed to the table.

You were almost required to sit at the table and join the family…. "Let me offer you something;" …. "Please, at least a serving of pasta;"…. "You can't leave without having a cup of coffee;"…. It is like this with every culture. A food offering to a guest in one's home, is the universal symbol of welcome. As a result, the guest is obliged to accept the food offering from the host.

For this reason we have devoted this section of the book to some of the cultural dishes from cultures you may not be familiar with. As you prepare these dishes, remember the sharing of food is the unifying aspect of all human cultures. As you prepare each of these dishes, imagine yourself being welcomed at the table of the people who have created them. Think of sharing the dish with a family. Think of laughing with them, and sharing the food with glass of wine. Think of breaking down the barriers between people. Think of these things so we may begin to better understand others, and bring peace to this volatile planet.

In this chapter, we will present to you a few dishes each from the various parts of Asia. Here, as in other sections, we make no attempt to be all-inclusive. We have chosen our favorite dishes, and ones that can be made at home with much success. There are thousands more dishes that await you in your exploration of the Asian cuisine.

Do you remember when eating Asian food meant: "Choose 1 from column A and 1 from Column B"? Remember when the only soup choices were egg drop or won tong? And weren't we all thrilled by that soggy onion preparation known as chow mein? Those were the days when the only ethnic Asian restaurants in the US were Chinese, and the only part of China represented was Canton. I don't even remember if there was "Take Out".

We have come a very long way since then. Today, in many cities and even in small towns, we have the choice of Chinese from various parts of China, in addition to Thai, Korean, Japanese, Malaysian etc, etc, etc. Just recently, before I moved to Florida, a restaurant specializing in food from Tibet opened down the street from my home.

Where once, no home cooks would attempt to duplicate the Asian dishes eaten at their favorite restaurants, today any serious home cook welcomes the challenges that these foods represent.

One of the greatest challenges is the various complex sauces and ingredients that are necessary to create the dishes we wish to make. Thanks to globalization, in most areas of the country, you should not have any trouble finding the ingredients, and prepared sauces for these recipes.

Once you have located a good Asian market, much of the really difficult parts are done. Unless you are a diehard purest, there is no need to make all the curries and sauces that are called for in these recipes. In a good Asian market, you should be able to find the difficult to make sauces and curry pastes, many imported from Asia. Feel free to use them as I do myself.

You will need a very good quality soy sauce (I like vegetarian soy from Viet Nam) and Nam Pla, a fish sauce from south East Asia. You will also need Asian Five Spice Powder, fresh shallots, garlic, ginger, lemon grass and Sambal or some other Asian garlic/chili sauce. Other than that, always strive to use the freshest ingredients available, and the best quality prepared sauces you can find.

In this chapter, the longest in the book, we will also journey through countries in Africa, the Middle East, Europe and South America. Here too, you may find some ingredients difficult to fine. We have tried to substitute whenever possible. For example we did feel it might be a bit tough to locate a butcher who supplies "assorted bush meats" for the Boerewors so we suggested beef and pork.

Many of the dishes we offer in this chapter go as well with a nice beer as they do with wine. In fact some really cry out for a nice yeasty beer. With that in mind, we will offer you suggestions for both wine and beer pairings, and hope you experiment with all the suggestions we offer.

Recipes from some of these countries will have extended sections in other parts of the book. Because of the sheer magnitude of possibilities, we have not been able to cover every country in total detail. Perhaps in future volumes we will be able to do so. For those countries we have not covered in greater detail, we hope the dishes we have will peak your interest, and will make you seek other sources for additional recipes. We hope you enjoy your journey as much as we have enjoyed bringing these cultural recipes to you.

SOUTH AFRICA

Boerewors

3pounds ground beef
3 pounds ground pork
1pound bacon
¾ cup red wine vinegar
4 cloves garlic, minced

1 large yellow onion, chopped fine
8 tablespoons Worcestershire
2 ½ tablespoons fresh ground black pepper
2 ½ tablespoons curry powder
2 tablespoons ground coriander
½ teaspoon ground thyme
½ teaspoon ground nutmeg
¼ teaspoon ground cloves
4-6 ounces canola oil
2 28 ounce cans crushed tomatoes
1 8 ounce can tomato paste
Sea Salt to taste

To start out, you can use store bought ground beef and pork, or chunk the beef and pork and pass it, along with the bacon, through the medium-course grinding plate of a grinder. Mix the meat with all the other ingredients except for the crushed tomatoes and tomato paste. Refrigerate the mixture for 24 hours.

In a large pot over medium heat, add the canola oil. Add the meat to the pot, and cook the mixture until the meat is grey throughout. Add the crushed tomatoes and tomato paste. Bring the pot to a simmer and cook for 2-3 hours. Stir the pot from time to time to prevent sticking. Adjust the flavor with salt and serve alone or over flatbread.

Variation #1: Mix the same ingredients listed above except for the crushed tomato and tomato paste. Let ingredients stand refrigerated for 24 hours. Place the mixture into natural sausage casing or make into patties or small meatballs. Grill, BBQ or fry. Make an accompanying sauce of one large chopped yellow, and 4 cloves of chopped garlic---sauté in 3 tablespoons of extra virgin olive oil with 2 teaspoons crushed red pepper flakes, and one can of crushed tomatoes. Add a bit of salt and pepper and simmer together for 20 minutes.

Let's Talk about wine: South Africa has become one of the best wine producing nations in the world. For this great rich dish you should definitely stay with a *Pinotage* such as: **Graham Beck Pinotage** or the **Spier Pinotage Special Selection**. The *Mulderbosch Cabinet* **The Faithful Hound** would also compliment the dish well. Also think of a great *Cab Franc* such as **Beaucannon, Titus,** or **Horton Towers**.

ETHIOPIA

Red Lentil Stew

4 tablespoons extra virgin olive oil
4 cups yellow onion, chopped
8 cloves garlic, chopped
2 tablespoons fresh ginger, grated
1-8 ounce can tomato paste
1/8 teaspoon ground cloves
1/8 teaspoon ground cumin
1/8 teaspoon ground cinnamon
1/8 teaspoon ground coriander
1/8 teaspoon ground all spice
1/8 teaspoon chili powder
1/8 teaspoon ground ginger
½ tsp sea salt
½ tsp fresh ground pepper
6 cups low sodium chicken broth
2 cups dry red lentils
½ cup fresh cilantro for garnish
2 cups Basmati rice
4 cup reduced sodium chicken broth

In a pot over medium high heat, cook 2 cups of rice in 4 cups of chicken broth until done. In a large pot over medium high heat, add the olive oil. Add the onion and sauté until tender. Add the garlic and cook an additional minute. Add the ginger and cook an additional minute. Add the tomato paste and all the spices. Blend and cook for 2 minutes. Add the broth and again blend well. Bring pot to a simmer, and then add the lentils. Simmer partially covered for about 35 minutes until the lentils are tender. Adjust the flavor with the salt and pepper.

In a large serving platter, even distribute a bed of the rice. Layer the lentils over the rice; sprinkle with the cilantro and serve.

Let's talk about beers and wines: For this dish we are suggesting pairing it with a beer such as **Bass Ale, Samuel Smiths Nut Brown Ale** or **Brooklyn Local #1.** As for A wine a rich Rhone blend would complement the dish such as **Ch. De S. Casme Gigondas 2007**

MOROCCO

Rib Eye Marinade

4-20 ounce rib eye steaks, about 1 inch thick

Marinade:

4 cloves garlic, minced
2 large shallots, minced
2 tablespoons fresh ginger, grated
½ cup flat leaf parsley, chopped
3 tablespoons fresh basil, chopped
½ cup extra virgin olive oil
Zest of one lemon
Zest of one orange
Zest of one lime
1 teaspoon paprika
½ teaspoon ground cumin
½ teaspoon sea salt
¼ teaspoon fresh ground black pepper
¼ teaspoon fresh ground white pepper
¼ teaspoon allspice

Combine all the ingredients except the steaks in a food processor; blend until smooth. Spread the mixture over the steaks. Allow the steaks to sit for 1-2 hours.

Place the steaks on a preheated grill at a high temperature. Turn the steaks over and continue to grill, turning the steaks every couple of minutes to achieve desired doneness on each side of the steaks. Cook until you reach the desired wellness for the steaks.

Variation #1: This same marinade can be used for other meats that you intend to grill such as lamb or chicken.

Let's talk about wine: This dish cries for a rich *GSM—Rhone Blend*. Try **Clos Saint Michel 2005** or the **Chante Cigale**. The **Rasteau Cote du Rhone** would also work well. Another good choice would be a rich cabernet such as **Chimney Rock 2009** or **Elderton Friends.**

TUNISIA

Grilled Halibut

4-10 ounce halibut filets, about 1 inch thick

Paste:

Juice of one lemon
Juice of one lime
2 tablespoons paprika
1 teaspoon ground cumin
1 teaspoon ground ginger
1 teaspoon onion powder
1 teaspoon garlic powder
1 teaspoon sea salt
¼ teaspoon fresh ground black pepper
¼ teaspoon fresh ground white pepper
2-3 ounces extra virgin olive oil

Blend all the ingredients for the paste in a bowl and mix well. Allow the paste to stand 30 minutes. Spread the paste on both sides of the halibut filets and allow the filets to sit refrigerated for 1-2 hours.

In a sauté pan, over medium-high heat, place the olive oil to heat. Sear the filets until done and flakey. Serve immediately

Variation #1: Use salmon instead of halibut

Variation #2: Use skinless boneless chicken breasts instead of fish.

Variation #3: Use chunks of lamb with the spread. Allow t he lamb to stand overnight. Grill the lamb on a high temperature for best results.

Let's talk about wine: see the Rhone selections in the last two recipes.

ISRAEL

Noodle Kugel

1 pound wide egg noodle
4 tablespoons melted unsalted butter
1 pound cottage cheese
1 pound sour cream
4 eggs, beaten
½ cup granulated sugar
2 tablespoons vanilla extract
1 teaspoon sea salt
½ cup pecans
1 teaspoon ground cinnamon
1 cup golden raisins
¼ cup granulated sugar

Cook the egg noodles in boiling water until soft, but not mushy. Drain and rinse noodle under cold water.

In a large bowl, blend the noodles with melted butter, cheese, sour cream, eggs and sugar. In a separate bowl mix the pecans, cinnamon, raisins, and remaining sugar.

Grease a 9X13 baking dish with cooking spray. Pour the noodle mixture into the baking pan. Spread the noodles evenly. Sprinkle the pecan-raisin mixture over the noodles evenly. Bake in a 350° preheated oven for 60 minutes. Allow the Kugel to cool about 30 minutes before serving.

Let's talk about Wine: This pairs well with one of the *sweet dessert wines* such as **Sobon Orange Muscat, Osborne Tawny Port, Bellini VIN Santo** or **Washington Hills Late Harvest Riesling of try one of the great Tokays from Hungary**.

AUSTRALIA

Meat Pies

Filling:

2 tablespoons canola oil

2 large yellow onions, coarse chop
2 pounds ground chuck
1 8 ounce can tomato paste
4 tablespoons fish sauce
1 ½ cups beef gravy
Sea salt to taste
Ground black pepper to taste

Pastry:

3 packages (2 shells per pack) store bought piecrust
Baking spray

Sauce:

1 tablespoon olive oil
2 shallots, minced
2 16 ounce cans tomato sauce
4 tablespoons red wine vinegar
3 tablespoons granulated sugar
Sea salt to taste
Ground black pepper to taste

In a large sauté pan over medium heat, add the canola oil. Sauté the onions until tender. Add the ground chuck, and continue to sauté until beef is cooked throughout. Add the tomato paste and fish sauce. Add the beef gravy and simmer the mixture for 10 minutes, stirring occasionally. If it appears too dry, add 1-2 Tb water. Set aside to cool.

Spray individual ramekins or a cup cake pan (12 or 24 count) with cooking spray. Cut the piecrust into individual circles that will fit the cups and overlap the top slightly. Fill each cup ¾ of the way with the meat mixture. Cut small circles of the dough to cover the top, and seal the edges. Bake the pies in a preheated 350° oven for about 30 minutes, or until the crust is golden. Turn the pies out of their containers and serve either hot or room temperature with a small amount of the sauce.

To make the sauce: add the oil to a pan and sauté the shallots until tender. Add the sauce, vinegar, and sugar. Simmer for 15 minutes, and adjust flavor with the salt and pepper.

Let's talk about wine: Let's stay in Australia

with one of their many fine shirazes. There are so many, but a few you might consider are **Gumdale Reserve**, **Molly Dooker (The Boxer)**, **Elderton Friends**, **Two Hands, Max's Garden**, **Colonial Estates Explorer**.

NEW ZEALAND

Sweet and Sour Meatballs

Meatballs:

3 pounds ground pork
4 medium yellow onions, minced
8 tablespoons fresh ground ginger, minced
4 large eggs
10 tablespoons Panko Bread Crumbs
Canola oil for deep frying

Sauce:

4 cups good quality low sodium chicken stock
7 tablespoons sugar
3 tablespoons rice wine vinegar
3 tablespoons soy sauce
6 tablespoons Ketchup
10 tablespoons water whisked together with 6 teaspoons of cornstarch

In a large bowl blend together all the ingredients for the meatballs except the oil. Shape the meat into bite size meatballs. Heat the oil to 350° and fry the meatballs in small batches until they are golden and crisp.

For the sauce, place the chicken stock in a pot and heat to just below boiling. Add the sugar, vinegar, soy and ketchup, mix well and bring to a simmer. In a separate bowl, whisk together the water and the cornstarch into smooth slurry. Add the slurry to the simmering mixture slowly; whisking at all time. Cook for 5 minutes, or until the sauce has slightly thickened. Remove from heat. Set aside to cool.

Serve the sauce as a dipping sauce for the meatballs.

Let's talk about wine: Here we stay with the

wonderful *New Zealand Sauvignon Blanc* such as **Kim Crawford**, **Stony Bay**, **Nobilo**, **The Crossings**, and **Cottesbrook.**

CHILE

Chilean Empanadas

½ cup golden raisins
2 tablespoons dark rum
3 tablespoons extra virgin olive oil
1 small yellow onion, chopped fine
¼ teaspoon ground cinnamon
Pinch of red pepper flakes
12 ounces cooked corned beef, shredded
½ cup pitted black olives, chopped
4 hard-cooked eggs, chopped fine
¼ cup flat leaf parsley, chopped
Sea salt to taste
Ground black pepper to taste
1 pound phyllo dough
1 cup clarified butter

Toss the raisins with the rum and let stand 30 minutes. Heat the oil in a pan over low heat. Add onions and cook for about 10 minutes. Stir in cinnamon, pepper flakes, and corned beef. Add the olives and raisins with the rum. Cook for one minute. Remove the pan from the heat, and transfer to a bowl. Allow the corned beef to cool. Once cool, fold the eggs and parsley in the bowl. Season with the salt and pepper. Refrigerate until ready to use.

When working with phyllo dough, it must be kept covered with a very lightly moistened kitchen towel. Lie out one sheet of phyllo dough on a dry surface; brush the entire surface of the sheet with butter, then lay a second sheet on top of the first. Cut into 3-inch wide strips.

Place 1 teaspoon of the filling at the end of the phyllo strip; fold the strip the entire length of the dough into a triangle shape. Brush with butter. Place completed empanadas on a cook sheet and bake in a 350° degrees oven for about 15 minutes or until golden brown.

Let's talk about wine: What can we say about the wonderful wines coming out of Chile? For this dish, we would recommend pairing it with **Anekena Carmenere Single Vineyard** or **Brisandes Cabernet**. A wonderful mid-high end Cabernet that would be an elegant pairing would be the **Concha y Toro Don Melchor 2007** (2 hours to open).

ARGENTINA

Porterhouse Steak with Chimichurri Sauce

1-20 ounce Porterhouse steak, about 2 inches thick
2 tablespoons extra virgin olive oil
1 teaspoon Sea salt
2 tablespoons ground black pepper
Chimichurri Sauce
1 cup extra virgin olive oil
4 tablespoons fresh lemon juice
2/3 cup flat leaf parsley, minced
2 cloves garlic, minced
4 small shallots, minced
1 teaspoons fresh basil, minced
1 teaspoon fresh thyme, minced
2 teaspoon fresh oregano, minced
Sea Salt to taste
Ground black pepper to taste

Brush the steak with the olive oil. Sprinkle both sides with the salt and pepper. Grill steak on a high temperature until desired doneness.

Combine all the ingredients of the Chimichurri sauce, and let stand for at least 2 hours before serving with the grill steak.

Let's talk about wine: Argentina says *Malbec* for reds; **Norton Malbec Reserve**, **Cruz Alta Malbec Chairman's Blend.** A wonderful blend that would really enhance this dining experience would be the **Tupungato,** and a Reserve Malbec that would do the same is the **Alamos Malbec Reserve.** The **Horton Towers Cab Franc** would be a fine pairing for those who might like a less traditional one.

MEXICO

Pork Mole

2 pounds boneless pork shoulder
3 cups water
1 small yellow onion, minced
1 bay leaf
3 dried New Mexican Chilies
Water
1 slice white bread
3 garlic cloves, chopped
¼ teaspoon ground cinnamon
1/8 teaspoon ground cloves
¼ teaspoon ground black pepper
1 tablespoon lard
1 ½ teaspoon sea salt
2 teaspoons red wine vinegar
2 teaspoons granulated sugar

Trim the fat from the pork shoulder, and cut into 1" chunks. Place the pork in a large saucepot with 3 cups water, the onion and bay leaf. Bring the pot to a boil. Skim any foam that may form at the surface. Reduce the heat, and simmer the pork for another 45 minutes to an hour. Drain the pot, reserving the liquid.

Place the chilies in a medium saucepot and cover with some water. Bring the pot to a boil, then immediate turn the heat off, and let the chilies sit in the hot water until soft. Drain the chilies.

Remove stems and the seeds the chilies and discard. Place the chilies in a blender with the white bread, garlic, and ¼ cup of the reserved liquid. Puree the chilies until smooth; add some more of the reserved liquid if needed. Run puree through a fine sieve to eliminate the peel. Stir in the cinnamon, cloves, and pepper and set aside.

In another large saucepot, add the lard. Add the chili puree to the pot and sauté for 1 to 2 minutes, then stir in the pork pieces. Add 2 more cups of the reserved liquid to the pot along with the salt, vinegar and sugar. Bring to a boil; reduce heat, cover and simmer for another 45 minutes. To thicken sauce, uncover pot, and simmer for another 10 to 15 minutes longer. Serve in soup bowls.

Let's talk about beer and wine: There are some fine Mexican Beers that will pair well: **Dos Equis Larger or Dark** and the **Mondello Larger and Dark.** In addition **Red Hook Ale** is a fine compliment. If you want to go with a wine, **Macchia Petite Sirah** would do well as wood the **Kendall Jackson Pinot Noir** or the **Kunde Merlot.**

JAMAICA

Meat Patties

1 ½ pounds ground chicken
3 t extra virgin olive oil
1 red pepper, chopped
1 large yellow onion, chopped
4 cloves garlic, minced
1-2 fresh jalapenos, minced (seeded or not)
2 tablespoons fresh cilantro, minced
2 tablespoons curry powder
1 8 ounce can tomato sauce
Juice of 1 lime
1 package store bought pie crusts (2 in a pack)

Add the olive oil to a pan over medium-high heat, and sauté the pepper and onion until tender. Add the jalapenos, and cook 2 minutes more. Add the garlic and cook 1 minute more.

Add the chicken, and cook until the meat has cooked through. Add the cilantro, curry powder, tomato sauce and limejuice and bring to a simmer for 20 minutes.

Cut the piecrusts in quarters, resulting in 4 pieces each. Place a large dollop of the meat mixture on each piece; fold the crust over, and seal with a fork. Brush both sides of the pie with some of the liquid at the bottom of the pan, and place on a greased cookie sheet. Bake the pies at 350° until the piecrusts are done---about 15 minutes.

Let's talk about beer and wine: The **Red Hook Ale or Kalik Gold** would pair well with the dish, as would a Thai Beer **Chang.** If you are choosing a wine I would stick with a slightly sweet red for this dish like the **Dr. Heidemanns RED** or a **Cardinale Red Blend.**

TURKEY

Spiced Lamb Patties

2-pound ground lamb
1 medium yellow onion, minced
2 cloves garlic, minced
5 tablespoons paprika
1-tablespoon sea salt
1 tablespoon ground black pepper
1 teaspoon ground white pepper
1 tablespoon fresh oregano, minced
1-teaspoon ground cumin
2 tablespoons fresh, chopped fine
2 tablespoons flat leaf parsley, chopped fine
3-4 tablespoons extra virgin olive oil

In a large bowl combine the lamb with all the other ingredients except the olive oil. Blend well. Form the mixture into 10-12 patties, about 3 to 4 ounces each. Cover and refrigerate for 1 hour.

Remove patties from the refrigerator. Brush each patty with some olive oil and grill until cooked to desired temperature

Serve with some plain yogurt, or yogurt blended with some chopped cucumber, some chopped fresh dill, and a squeeze of fresh lemon juice as a garnish.

Let's talk about wine: The richness of the dish and the middle eastern spices need a wine that will hold up well and compliment the complexity of the dish. Try a rich *oaky chardonnay* such as **Barnett's Vineyard**, **Dariosh**, **La Crema** or **Mer Soleil Gold.** A *Pinot Noir* such as **Acacia**, **Castle**

Rock, **ERATH**, and **OFV Willamette** are excellent pairing reds.

RUSSIA

Hot Borscht

2 tablespoons extra virgin olive oil
Sea salt to taste
Ground black pepper to taste
2-3 pound chuck roast
1 large yellow onion, cut in quarters
3 celery stalks with leaves, cut in 4 pieces
2 carrots, cut in four pieces
1 small bunch fresh dill
1 cup dry red wine
3 cups low sodium beef broth
4 cups water
2 pounds fresh red beets
4 tablespoons extra virgin olive oil
Sea salt to taste
3 large russet potatoes, peeled and cut into ½" cubes
1 medium size head green cabbage, sliced thin
½ cup red wine vinegar
1 teaspoon caraway seeds
Chopped fresh dill, chopped flat leaf parsley, and sour cream for garnishes.

Season the chuck roast with salt and pepper. In a large pot over medium high heat, place 2 tablespoons of olive oil. Sear the roast on all sides until Brown. Add the onion, celery, carrot, dill, wine, broth and water, and bring to a boil. Reduce the pot to a simmer, and slowly cook the meat until very tender, about 1-2 hours.

While the meat is cooking, brush the beats with some olive oil and season lightly with salt and pepper. Wrap each beet in aluminum foil and bake in the oven at 350° until tender, about 90 minutes. When the beets are done, remove the skins and chop fine.

Set aside.

When the meat is done, remove it from the pot

and break it into small pieces. Strain the liquid in the pot, and discard the vegetables. Return the stock to the pot, and add the potatoes; cook the potatoes over medium heat for 2-3 minutes. Add the cabbage and cook an additional 4-5 minutes. Reduce the heat; add the meat, beets, vinegar and caraway seed. Adjust the flavor with some salt and pepper. Simmer an additional 4-5 minutes and serve.

Serve with chopped fresh dill and flat leaf parsley and sour cream as garnishes.

In keeping with the Russian tradition, one might pair this hearty soup with vodka. I would recommend **Russian Standard**, and place it in the freezer the day before the meal along with the pony glasses you will use for service. Take the glasses out of the freezer—fill with vodka and serve immediately.

GERMANY

Sauerbraten

1-4 pound beef roast (shoulder or chuck)
2 tablespoon lemon pepper
16 oz dry red wine
16 oz apple cider vinegar
4 small yellow onions, peeled and studded with
  3 whole cloves each
6 cloves garlic, smashed
2 bay leaves
10 juniper berries
1 tablespoon fresh thyme
20 black peppercorns
¼ pound pork belly or bacon, sliced thin
¼ cup flour
Sea salt to taste
Fresh ground pepper to taste
3 carrots, sliced in rounds
3 celery stalks with leaves, sliced thin
1 large yellow onion, sliced thin
1/3 cup+ crushed gingersnaps

Rub the beef with the lemon pepper and set aside. In a large sauce pot over medium high heat, place

the wine, vinegar, studded onions, garlic, bay leaves, juniper berries and peppercorns, and heat the mixture to a boil.

In a large non-reactive bowl or pan, place the beef and pour the hot liquid over it. Cover tightly and allow meat to marinate in the refrigerator 3-6 days.

Remove the beef from the marinade, pat dry, and coat with a dusting of flour. Strain the marinade. In a large baking pot or Dutch oven, render the pork belly. When pork is rendered about ¾ of the way, add the beef to the pot and brown on all sides. Return the strained marinade to the pot along with the carrots, onions and celery. Cover pot and cook at a low simmer for about 1 ½ to 2 hours until the beef is tender.

Remove the beef from the pot and slice. Add the gingersnaps to the pot to thicken the broth to into gravy. If necessary, add a bit of roux to help thicken.

Serve with Potato pancakes or Spaetzle

Let's talk about beer: With this dish I would stick with a cold German beer such as **Hofbrau Muchen Original** or **Hafe Wizen**. Two wines that would hold up well to the high acid nature of the dish might be **Ch de Nages Blanc VV** or the **JV Fleury Cotes du Rhone Blanc**. You could also go with a good Dornfelder such as the **Dr. Heidemanns RED.** Two merlots I think of when I think of this dish are **Duckhorn Estates 2007** and **Courtney Benham 2008**

AUSTRIA

Wiener Schnitzel Holstein

4-8 ounce size pieces of veal cutlet, pounded
  thin
Sea salt to taste
Ground black pepper to taste
1 cup flour
1 cup breadcrumb

2 eggs, scrambled
1 tablespoon extra virgin olive oil
4 tablespoons unsalted butter
4 whole eggs

Pound the veal thin to make it tender using a kitchen mallet. Set aside. In separate bowls place the flour, scrambled eggs and breadcrumbs. Season each cutlet lightly with some salt and fresh ground black pepper. Dredge the pieces of veal in the flour, then the egg and finally the breadcrumbs.

In a large sauté pan over medium high heat, place the olive oil and butter. Cook the veal in the oil about 2 minutes on each side. Remove the veal and drain. In the same pan, crack and fry the eggs sunny side up or over lightly. Serve each cutlet with a fried egg on top.

Let's talk about Wine: The wine of choice would be the **Hugal Veltliner** or the **Winzer Krems Veltliner** or **Achlieten Stockkultia Gruner.**

HUNGARY

Goulash

¼ cup olive oil
½ cup unsalted butter
1 large yellow onion, chopped
1 carrot, diced ½"
1 parsnip, diced ½"
2 stalks celery, diced ½"
2 medium tomatoes, peeled and chopped
2 medium potatoes, sliced
1 teaspoon caraway seeds
1 teaspoon fresh thyme
1 teaspoon flat leaf parsley, minced
2 cloves garlic, minced
Grated zest of one lemon
1 tablespoon Hungarian paprika
1 ½ cups dry white wine
2 pounds pork shoulder, cut into 2 inch pieces
Water as necessary
Sea salt to taste
Ground black pepper to taste

In a large saucepot over medium high heat, place the oil and melt the butter. Add the onion, carrot, parsnip, and celery and cook until tender. Add the caraway seeds, thyme, parsley, garlic, lemon zest and paprika and cook until aromatic. Be careful not to burn. Add the wine, tomatoes, potatoes and the pork. Add just enough water to cover all ingredients, cover and cook at a simmer for about 1 ½ to 2 hours. Adjust flavor with the salt and pepper. Serve with sour cream as a garnish.

Let's talk about wine: To *ADD* , try a *nice full-bodied chardonnay* such as the **Paul Hobbs** or the **Muirwood.** To *PAIR*, we think a rich and fruit forward *merlot* would be nice, such as **Markham, Red Knot, Blackstone, Coastline** or **Cakebread.** To really treat yourself you might try the **Duckhorn Napa** or **Twomey.** You might even try using one of the merlots in the ADD portion to see how it changes the dish. A classic red from Hungary, **Bulls Blood**, would also add much.

BULGARIA

Cucumber Soup

2 cups cucumbers, peeled and seeded, diced ¼"
1 teaspoon sea salt
¼ teaspoon fresh ground black pepper
¼ teaspoon ground white pepper
½ cup chopped fresh unsalted walnuts
3 tablespoons extra virgin olive oil
2 cloves garlic, minced
2 tablespoons fresh dill, chopped
1 cup plain Greek style yogurt
½ cup light chicken stock

In a large bowl, combine all ingredients and blend well. Cover and refrigerate until well chilled. Correct flavor with the salt and pepper and serve.

Let's talk about wine: This dish needs the crispness of a sauvignon Blanc such as the **Amici** or **Courtney Benham Lake Country.** You would also do well with the **Badegas Naia Verdejo**

GREECE

A Real Greek Salad

1 pound Roma tomatoes, diced ½"
1 cucumber, diced ½"
1 large red onion, sliced very thin
12 pitted Calamata Olives, halved
1/3 pound Feta Cheese, crumbled
Anchovies for garnish

Dressing:

1/3 Cup extra virgin olive oil
2 tablespoons red wine vinegar
Juice of a half lemon
Pinch of fresh oregano, minced
Pinch of fresh basil, minced
Sea salt to taste
Ground black pepper to taste

Combine the tomatoes, cucumbers, onion, olives in a large bowl. Add the dressing and fold gently. Adjust the flavor with some salt and pepper. Crumble the feta over the top and serve with the anchovies on the side.

Let's talk about wine: For this salad you could use one of the most well known of the Greek wines, either the **Domestica White** or the **Domestica Red,** depending what your next course might be.

NORWAY

Coleslaw

1 medium head green cabbage, shredded
1 tablespoon sea salt
½ cup granulated sugar
3 tablespoon extra virgin olive oil
1 cup white wine vinegar
2 stalks celery with their leaves, sliced thin
1 yellow onion, sliced thin
1 green bell pepper, chopped ¼"
1 red bell pepper, chopped ¼"
2 carrots, shredded

Place the shredded cabbage in large bowl. Season the cabbage with the sugar and salt.

In a pan over medium heat, add the olive oil. Add the celery, onions, peppers and vinegar to the pan and sauté the vegetables until tender. Add the hot mixture to the cabbage and blend well. Adjust flavor with some salt and pepper. Allow to stand refrigerated for 24 hours before serving:

Let's talk about wine: This dish would probably be served as a side with some other dish, therefore it might be best for you to decide on the wine based on the selection of the main dish.

POLAND

Herring in Sour Cream

1 pound pickled herring, sliced in 2 inch pieces
1 large yellow onion, sliced thin
1 tablespoon fresh dill, minced
1 pound sour cream
5 hard cooked eggs, sliced.

Blend the onions, sour cream and dill in a large bowl. Add the herring and blend. Allow to marinate 3-4 days refrigerated. Serve with the sliced hard cooked eggs as a garnish.

Let's talk about wine: If served alone as an appetizer, this dish can best be paired with a light white such as a **Viho Verde** from Portugal. A light sparkling wine such as the **Rondel Cava** or **Fresxenet** would be nice also. If you wanted to go more high end, we would suggest the **Pommery Brut.**

FINLAND

Salmon Soup

1 one pound salmon filet cut in 2 inch chunks
1 quart water
1 pound russet potatoes, peeled and cut into a ½" dice

2 medium yellow onions, ½" dice
1 cup heavy cream
1 teaspoon sea salt
1 teaspoon ground black pepper
1 teaspoon ground white pepper
2 tablespoons fresh dill, chopped
3 tablespoons unsalted butter
Fresh chopped dill for garnish
Sour cream for garnish

In a large pan heat the water. Add the potatoes and onions and boil for about 10 minutes. Reduce the heat. Add the cream, black pepper, white pepper and dill and simmer for 2 minutes. Add butter and the salmon and cook just until the salmon is firm---about 3-4 minutes. Serve with fresh chopped dill and sour cream as garnishes.

Let's talk about wine: A rich dish that calls for a rich *Pinot Noir*. We recommend **Patz & Hall**, **Barnett's Vineyard**, **Paul Hobbs** or **HK1 Reserve.**

IRELAND

Irish Stew

3 pounds lamb shoulder, cubed into 1 inch chunks
½ cup flour
½ cup canola oil
2 cups sweet onions, 1-inch dice
2 cups celery, ½" dice
2 cups carrots, peeled and sliced ¼ inch thick
3 cloves garlic, chopped
1 pint Guinness stout
2 quarts beef stock, or as needed
3 large russet potatoes, peeled and cubed
1 tablespoon fresh rosemary, chopped
1 tablespoon fresh thyme, chopped
¼ cup fresh parsley, chopped
1 bay leaf
1 cup pearled barley (optional)
Sea salt to taste
Ground black pepper to taste

If you use the barley (which you should do if you want a more authentic Irish stew), cook it for 20 minutes in 3 cups of lamb or beef stock. You'll add it to the stew later.

In a large, heavy braising pot, over medium high heat, add the oil. Season the lamb cubes with salt and pepper. Dust the lamb with flour and add it to the pot, browning it on all sides. Remove lamb from the pot and set aside.

Immediately add the onions, celery, carrots, and garlic to the pot. Mix well to coat the vegetables with the oil and lamb rendering. Add the Guinness and beef stock to the pot. Return the lamb to the pot along with the potatoes and the cooked barley. (You need just enough stock to just cover the ingredients). Drop in the rosemary, thyme, parsley, and bay leaf. Bring the pot to a very low simmer, partially covered for 2-2 ½ hours. Stir the pot every 20-30 minutes during cooking time so that the bottom doesn't stick. Meat should be very tender once done. Most, if not all of the liquid should have been absorbed during the cooking process. Serve.

Let's talk about beer/wine: As with adding wines to a dish, when cooking with beer, it is best to add an excellent beer. Serve the same stout that you add to the stew. For those who may not like a stout, you might try an IPA (India Pale Ale) such as **Pikes** or a darker lager such as **Sam Adams** or **Yuengling.** Of course a pint of stout would always be in order for this great dish. If you would prefer a wine to pair, a nice *cabernet* would go well. Try **Dominican Oaks Napa, Decoy by Duckhorn**, **Edgewood** or **Franciscan**. If you have the time to allow the wine to open, you could use a red *Bordeaux* such as: **Chateau Tours de Charmail Haut Medoc** (3+ hours to open) or **Chateau Haut-Maillet Pomerol** (3+ hours)

ENGLAND

Steak and Kidney Pie

1 ½ pounds of lean beef steak (top round), sliced thin
¾ pounds veal kidney
3 tablespoons extra virgin olive oil
1 cup all purpose flour
Sea salt to taste
Ground black pepper to taste
2 cups low sodium beef broth
1 cup dry red wine
1 sheet piecrust

Dredge the slices of meat in flour seasoned with salt and pepper. In a greased deep-dish baking pan, layer the slices of meat. Add the wine and beef broth. Cover with aluminum foil and bake in a pre heated 350° oven for 2 hours.

In the interim, slice the kidneys in half. In a sauté pan over medium high heat, sauté the kidneys for 30 seconds. Season with salt and pepper and set aside.

After the beef has baked for 90 minutes, remove the foil from baking dish. Layer the kidneys on top of the beef. Return the foil to cover the baking pan again, and bake for another 30 minutes. Remove the pan from the oven and cover the meat with the piecrust. Raise the oven temperature to 400° and bake for 12-15 minutes until the crust is golden. Serve.

Let's talk about beer/wine: This would be a great dish to serve with beer. Try one of the great *Samuel Smiths from England*: **Organic Lager**, **Nut Brown Ale**, **Oatmeal Stout** or any of the others. As for wine, a *pinot noir* like the **Louis Latour** or the **Merry Edwards** would pair well.

HOLLAND

Amsterdam Stuffed Cabbage

Filling:

8 large cabbage leaves
1-pound ground chuck
1 small yellow onion, minced
2 garlic cloves, minced
3 tablespoons flat leaf parsley, chopped
½ teaspoon sea salt
1 teaspoon ground black pepper
¼ teaspoon ground white pepper
1 teaspoon herbs de province
Pinch of cayenne pepper
2 tablespoons red wine vinegar
3 tablespoons brown sugar
2 tablespoons capers, chopped
4 ounces unsalted butter

Braising Sauce:

1 tablespoon olive oil
1 garlic clove, minced
16 ounces tomato sauce
2 teaspoons paprika
½ cup sour cream

Blanch the cabbage leaves in boiling water until soft. Remove and reserve. Place the remaining ingredients in a bowl and blend well. Divide the meat mixture among the cabbage leaves and roll into tight rolls. Place in a greased baking dish and dot the cabbage rolls with the butter.

For the braising sauce, in a separate pot, over medium high heat, add the oil. Add the garlic, cook to a golden color, then add the tomato sauce and bring to a simmer. Add the paprika and the sour cream and blend well. Pour sauce over the cabbage rolls in the baking dish. Cover with aluminum foil and bake the cabbage rolls in a preheated 350° oven for about 45 minutes, or until the cabbage is very tender. Serve.

Let's talk about beer: Here is another dish crying out for a good beer. Try one that is richer in flavor such as the **Hofbrau Muchen Hafe**

Wizen, **Murphy's Stout, Rogue Stout** or the **Sierra Nevada Bock.** Each will compliment the dish.

A Journey through Asia

Let's talk about Wine and Beer right away:

We felt that in a cookbook highlighting dishes from around the world, we simply could not leave out Asia. However, there are indeed some problems. Because of the intensity of the spices both in "heat" and in complexity (curries), it is very difficult to pair wines with dishes from many Asian countries.

So much depends on the intensity of the hot chilies used in the preparation and in the depth of the curry. When made properly, there is no wine in the world that could stand up to a Vindaloo Curry from India or to some of the super intense dishes from Thailand.

Therefore, in this section of the chapter, there will be very little discussion of wines. Consequently, we will strongly recommend the pairing of beer with the spiciest dishes from Asia. Beers that have a rich hoppiness go very well such as **Chang** or **Singha** from Thailand. You could also try the **Tsingtao** from China, or **Kirin** or **Sapporo** from Japan. The rich *stouts* also stand up well such as **Guinness** or **Murphy's**. I particularly like amber and brown ales such as **Bass Ale, Pike's Double Brown**, and **Red Hook Ale** as well as **Arrogant Bastard**. In addition you might choose some of the rich IPAs such as **Pikes IPA** or Pikes **Double IPA.**

If you choose to make the dishes milder, then you may venture try some of the more fruit forward wines such as Zinfandels like **Sobon Rocky top**; **7 Deadly Zins**; or one of **the Oak Ridge**.

However, even here, it will be very difficult to "compliment" the intense curries with a wine. For these, I would recommend medium sweet to sweet *Sherries* and *ports* such as **Harvey's,**

Osborn, Quinta, Offley, and **Taylor**. Medium to sweet sparklers may also work well such as **Rondel Semi Seco, Botter sweet Prosecco**, and **San Orsola Muscotto d'Asti.** There are also some wonderful Rieslings that will pair well such as **Columbia Valley; Ch. Saint Michelle; Washington Hills** or one of the great German Rieslings such as **JJ Prum or Dr. Heidemanns.**

Remember the "more heat—more sweet" we spoke about in previous sections. As you increase the spice of the dish try to offset it with slightly sweeter wines. Even those of you who say "I don't like sweet wines." will recognize the way they compliment very spicy dishes.

This is a section of adventure in the dishes we offer and in your selection of beers and wines to pair. Remember to choose hoppy beers and as for wines, "The More Heat—The More Sweet. For some of the dishes we will make additional specific suggestions, denoted by ***, but you can't go too wrong if you follow the general suggestions in this introduction to this section of the book.

INDIA

Curried Fried Chicken

3 pounds chicken, cut into 10 pieces
1-8 ounce can coconut milk
2 cloves garlic, minced
1 large shallot, minced
1 teaspoon fresh ground ginger
1 tablespoon curry paste (choose your style and heat)
1 cup all purpose flour
1 tablespoon garlic powder
1 tablespoon onion powder
1 teaspoon sea salt
1 teaspoon ground black pepper
2 tablespoon curry powder
Vegetable oil for frying

Blend the coconut milk, garlic, shallot, ginger and curry paste in a large bowl. Add the chicken pieces, and allow the chicken to marinate for 6 to 8 hours, or overnight.

Remove the chicken from the coconut milk. Blend the flour, garlic powder, onion powder, salt, pepper and curry powder in a large plastic bag. Dredge the chicken in the seasoned flour and fry in the vegetable oil until done.

***<u>Montaudon Brut Rose</u>

Minced Meat with Potatoes and Peas

4 tablespoons unsalted butter or vegetable oil
1 large yellow onion, minced
2 cloves garlic, minced
1 teaspoon fresh ground ginger
1 teaspoon ground cumin
1 pound ground chuck
2 cups frozen peas
2 cups potatoes cut in ¼" pieces
1 teaspoon ground cloves
1 teaspoon garam masala
2 cups Basmati Rice
4 cups chicken broth
1 teaspoon garam masala

In a large pan over medium heat, add the butter. Sauté the onion until tender; then add the garlic, ginger and cumin. Sauté for an additional minute. Add the meat to the pan, and continue to cook, stirring all the time. Add the ground cloves, potatoes and peas. Add the chicken broth and the rice and stir. Add the garam masala and stir. Bring to a slow simmer; cover and cook until the rice is done—about 15 minutes.

***<u>Mano a Mano Tempranillio</u> from Spain or <u>Cataldi Montepulciano</u> from Italy.

Curried Hard Cooked Eggs

6 eggs, hard boiled and peeled

2 tablespoons unsalted butter or vegetable oil
1 large yellow onion, sliced thin

4 cloves garlic, sliced thin
2 teaspoons fresh ground ginger
2 teaspoons ground coriander
2 teaspoons ground cumin
½ teaspoon ground turmeric
½ teaspoon curry powder
1 tablespoon fresh cilantro, minced
Juice of 1 lemon
4 plum tomatoes, seeded and diced
½ teaspoon garam masala

Heat the butter in a sauté pan over medium high heat. Sauté the onions, garlic and ginger until soft. Add the coriander, cumin, turmeric, curry powder and cook an additional minute. Add the cilantro and lemon juice. Simmer until the gravy is thick. Cut the hard boiled eggs in half and add them to the pan. Cook until heated through and serve.

***<u>Ch Chiagle CH. N de Pape Blanc</u>

Curried Meatballs (Kofta)

2 pounds ground lamb
1 ½ teaspoon fresh ground ginger
2 tablespoon Sambal chili sauce
1 ½ teaspoon ground coriander
1 teaspoon curry powder
2teaspoon garam masala
1 teaspoon sea salt
¾ cup plain yogurt
1 teaspoon ground black pepper
1 teaspoon white pepper
1 teaspoon cayenne pepper
1 teaspoon granulated sugar
1 teaspoon powdered milk or flour
¼ teaspoon cinnamon
¼ teaspoon ground cardamom
Oil for frying

In a large bowl, combine all the ingredients except the oil and blend well. Shape into patties or meatballs. Fry in the oil until done and serve with rice.

***<u>Edna Valley Chardonnay or Chalk Hill Chardonnay</u>

South Indian Shrimp Curry

1 tablespoon dry unsweetened coconut

1 tablespoon cornstarch

2 cups coconut milk

2 tablespoon melted unsalted butter

2 small sweet onions, chopped

6 cloves garlic, chopped

3 teaspoons ground fresh ginger

2 tablespoons Madras Curry Paste

1 teaspoon Sambal chili sauce

2 tablespoons fresh limejuice

1ounce vegetable oil

2 pounds large shrimp, peeled and deveined, tail off

Sea salt to taste

Place the dry coconut, cornstarch and ½ cup coconut milk in a blender and blend well. In a medium sauce pan over medium-high heat, add the butter. Allow the butter to melt, then add the onion and garlic and cook until translucent and soft. Add the ginger and cook an additional minute. Add the curry paste and Sambal and cook for another minute. Add the blended coconut milk mixture, the remaining coconut milk to the pan and incorporate the ingredients. Cook for another five minutes.

In a separate sauté pan over medium-high heat, add the oil. When oil is hot, carefully add shrimp and sear for 1-2 minutes on each side. Immediately, reduce heat to medium-low and add the curry sauce. Cook until shrimp are opaque throughout. Add the lime juice and serve.

Variation #1: use chunks of skinless boneless chicken breasts instead of shrimp. Be sure to cook them until done.

***Sparr One Pinot Blanc**

THAILAND

Shrimp Salad with Champagne Mayonnaise Dressing

1 ½ cups basmati rice

3 cups low sodium low fat chicken broth

¼ cup extra virgin olive oil

2pounds medium shrimp, cooked & cut into thirds

1 large or 2 small Asian pear, large chop

1 small yellow onion, chop fine

3 stalks celery, chopped fine

1 cup high quality or homemade mayonnaise

1 tablespoon nam pla

1 tablespoon Sambal

Juice of one lime

½ cup high quality brut champagne

4-5 grinds of fresh black pepper

¼ teaspoon white pepper

Belgium endive leaves for service

1-2 teaspoons fresh squeezed lemon juice

In a small sauce pan over medium high heat, place the olive oil. Add the rice and sauté for 30 seconds. Add the chicken broth, cover pan tightly, and cook the rice until all the water is absorbed. Cool the rice completely.

Combine the shrimp, pears, celery and onion in a large bowl. In a separate bowl, combine the mayonnaise, black pepper, cayenne, lime juice, nam pla, Sambal and champagne and mix thoroughly. Adjust the flavor with some salt and pepper.

Once the rice has chilled completely, add the dressing and the shrimp mixtures to the rice, and mix thoroughly. Chill the mixture overnight. Remove the leaves from the Belgium endive. Place a dollop of the salad on each leaf and serve as an appetizer.

***Dr. Heidemanns Spatlese**

Nam Sod

2 pounds ground chicken or pork

1 tablespoon of ginger, minced

3 cloves of garlic, minced

½ small yellow onion, minced

2 tablespoons extra virgin olive oil

3-4 tablespoons soy sauce

3-4 tablespoons Thai fish sauce

1 or more teaspoons Asian garlic/chili paste or
  Sambal
Juice of 3 limes
½ cup cilantro leaves, torn
4-5 large shallots, sliced thin
1 head Iceberg lettuce, sliced thin
Sea salt to taste
Ground black pepper to taste

In a large wok or frying pan over high heat, add
the extra virgin olive oil and then add the ginger,
garlic and onion. Sauté quickly until they are
tender and aromatic, stirring all the time. Add
the meat and continue cooking and stirring until
almost done. Add the soy, fish sauce, lime juice
and chili paste. Cook until done and adjust the
flavor with salt and pepper. Add "heat" to taste.

Remove from the heat and allow cooling. Add the
shallots and cilantro. Serve at room temperature
over the lettuce.

***Jean Albrecht Gewürztraminer

*NOTE: be sure to review the wine/beer/Asian
discussion at the beginning of this section.*

*NOTE Be sure to read the entire wine/beer/
Asian food discussion at the start of this
section.*

Mussels with Lemon Grass and Thai Basil

2 pounds mussels, cleaned
2 cups water
1 cup dry white wine
2 stalks lemon grass (hard outer leaves discarded),
  crushed and cut into 3-4 inch pieces
Zest from one lime (green part only)
6 cloves garlic, crushed
3 large slices of fresh ginger
¼ teaspoon white pepper
5 Thai chilies, crushed
1 cup Thai basil leaves

Examine the mussels. Discard any mussels that
are open and don't close when handled. Add the

water, wine, lime zest, garlic, ginger and pepper.
Bring to a boil and simmer for 5 minutes.

Bring pot back to a rolling boil. Add the mussels
and cook covered for 4-5 minutes until the
mussels open. Discard any that do not open.
Transfer the mussels to a large bowl. Add the
crushed chilies and ¾ cup of basil to the water
and simmer 2 minutes. Strain the broth through
a fine strainer into the bowl with the mussels.
Sprinkle the remaining basil over the mussels
and serve. Provide soup bowls so that people can
take broth along with the mussels. Additional hot
sauce, such as Sambal can be served for those who
would like it.

***Adler Fels Sauvignon Blanc

Beef with Noodles

1 flank steak (1-2 pounds), cut in half and then
  sliced thin across the grain
2- 4 tablespoons peanut oil
1 tablespoon shallot, minced
1 tablespoon garlic, minced
1 tablespoon fresh ginger, minced
1 large yellow onion, sliced thin
1 tablespoon soy sauce
1 teaspoon nam pla
1 tablespoon Sambal
1 cup packed Thai basil or other basil leaves
1 cup low sodium chicken broth
1 pound lo mien noodles

Cook the lo mien noodles in salted water until
al dente. In a wok, heat the oil and sear the beef
slices until just done. Remove and reserve.

Add the shallot, garlic and ginger to the wok,
and cook one minute. Add the onion and cook
until tender.

Add the soy, nam pla and Sambal to the wok.
Add the basil and cook until just wilted. Add
the chicken broth and bring to a boil. Return
the beef to the wok and heat through. In a large

bowl, combine the beef mixture with the lo mien noodles and serve. Offer additional Sambal as a condiment.

Dom Baisson Cotes de Rhone 2009

Sweet and Sour Shrimp

16-20 medium shrimp, shelled and deveined, tail on
2 tablespoon peanut oil
1 large yellow onion, minced
10 cloves garlic, minced
3 teaspoon ginger, minced
1 tablespoon soy sauce
2 tablespoons nam pla
3 tablespoons granulated sugar
2 tablespoons seasoned rice vinegar
1 teaspoon Sambal or other hot paste

Once the shrimp have been cleaned, deveined and shelled (leave the tails on), butterfly them. In a very hot wok, add the oil, onion, ginger and garlic. Stir for 1-2 minutes being careful not to burn. Add the shrimp, and stir fry about 45 seconds until just done. Add the sugar, soy sauce, nam pla and vinegar and then stir fry an additional 20 seconds. Serve.

Osborne Medium Dry Sherry

VIET NAM

Pork and Shrimp Rolls

1 tablespoon peanut oil
1 shallot, minced
1clove garlic, minced
½ teaspoon fresh ginger, minced
½ pound ground pork
7 ounces shelled, deveined shrimp, chopped
1 tablespoon good quality soy sauce
1 teaspoon nam pla
¼ teaspoon white pepper
¾ cup bean sprouts
6 scallions, sliced thin on the bias

Chinese spring roll wrappers
Oil for frying
Iceberg lettuce leaves
Fresh coriander leaves
Fresh mint leaves

Dipping sauce
2 chilies chopped finely
1 clove garlic, mashed and finely chopped
1 teaspoon sugar
1 tablespoon seasoned rice vinegar
1 lemon, skin and internal membranes removed
1 tablespoon water
1 tablespoon good quality soy sauce
4 tablespoon nam pla

Heat the oil in a wok. Add the shallot, garlic and ginger and stir 20 seconds. Add the pork and cook while constantly stirring. Add the shrimp, soy, pepper and nam pla and cook an additional minute. Remove the pork mixture from the heat and allow cooling to room temperature.

Once the pork mixture has cooled, blend in the scallions and bean sprouts. Place 1-2 teaspoons of the mixture on a spring roll wrapper and roll into a tight, completely closed roll. Use a small amount or water to seal the edges.

Fry the completed rolls in the oil until golden. Place one roll in a piece lettuce leaf, along with 1-2 mint and/or coriander leaves and a few drops of the dipping sauce.

To prepare the dipping sauce place all the ingredients in a blender and blend until smooth.

Amici Sauvignon Blanc

Pho

2 quarts good quality low sodium beef broth
1 large yellow onion, sliced
1 cinnamon stick
3 large slices fresh ginger
1 tablespoon whole black peppercorns
1 teaspoon whole white peppercorns
½ pound rice noodles, cooked
1 pound bean sprouts

6 plum tomatoes, cut in quarters

6 hard boiled eggs, cut in half

2 onions, sliced

1 pound beef roast, sliced very thin

Fish sauce as garnish

Soy sauce as garnish

Lime wedges as garnish

Fresh chilies, chopped as garnish

Sambal as garnish

Fresh coriander leaves as garnish

Fresh mint leaves as garnish

In a large pot, place the beef broth, onion, cinnamon stick, ginger and peppercorns. Bring to a boil and simmer 30 minutes. Strain the broth and keep heated.

In 4-6 large bowls divide the rice noodles, tomatoes, bean sprouts, eggs, and sliced beef. Fill with the hot broth and serve. The heat of the broth will cook the beef.

Serve with the remaining ingredients as condiments and garnishes as desired.

***<u>Kirin Ichiban Beer</u>

***<u>Mer sole Gold Chardonnay</u>

INDONESIA

Hot and Sour Shrimp

1 pound 21/25 shrimp, peeled and cleaned, tail off

2 tablespoons peanut oil

1 yellow onion, chopped fine

2 cloves garlic, minced

1 teaspoon fresh ginger, grated

1 teaspoon Sambal

1 teaspoon anchovy paste

1 teaspoon ground cumin

1 teaspoon ground coriander

1 teaspoon curry powder

3 tablespoon tamarind juice

Sea salt to taste

In a wok over medium high heat, place the oil.

Add the onion, garlic and ginger. Cook until the onion is soft. Add the Sambal, anchovy paste, cumin, coriander and curry powder and cook an additional minute. Add the shrimp and cook 1 minute. Add the tamarind juice and cook until the liquid is almost dry. Serve with rice.

***<u>Pikes Double IPA</u>

<u>*NOTE: Be sure to read the entire wine/beer/ Asian food discussion at the start of this section.*</u>

Chicken in Coconut Milk

1-3 pound chicken, cut into 10 pieces

5 cloves garlic, crushed

½ teaspoon fresh ground black pepper

2 teaspoon fresh ginger, grated

2 tablespoons chopped peanuts

3 teaspoons ground coriander

1½ teaspoons ground cumin

½ teaspoon ground fennel

4 tablespoons peanut oil

3 yellow onions, sliced thin

2 cups coconut milk

1 cup chicken broth

1 teaspoon curry paste

3-2 inch pieces of lemon peel

1 cinnamon stick

2 tablespoons lemon juice

Sea salt to taste

Sambal

In a bowl, make a paste of the garlic, pepper, ginger, peanuts, coriander, cumin, fennel and 1 tablespoon oil. Rub the paste all over the chicken pieces and let stand 1-3 hours.

Place 1 tablespoon oil in a pan and sauté the onions until tender. Remove the onions and set aside. Add the remaining oil to the pan, and over high heat, sauté the chicken pieces just until they get a little color. Add the coconut milk, chicken broth, curry paste, lemon peel and cinnamon stick. Reduce heat and cook at a simmer until the chicken is done—about 20 minutes. Remove the cinnamon stick and lemon peel. Adjust the flavor with salt and serve with rice. Offer Sambal as a condiment.

Meatballs with Coconut

8 ounces dried, unsweetened, shredded coconut
5 tablespoons hot water
1 pound ground beef
1 teaspoon anchovy paste
3 cloves garlic minced
1 teaspoon salt
1 teaspoon Sambal
½ teaspoon ground black pepper
½ teaspoon ground white pepper
1 teaspoon ground coriander
1 teaspoon ground cumin
1 teaspoon grated, fresh ginger
2 eggs
Oil for deep frying

Combine the dried coconut and hot water in a bowl and allow sitting until the water is absorbed. Add the garlic, salt, Sambal and the rest of the spices and mix well. Add the beaten eggs and mix again. Combine with the beef and mix well. Shape the mixture into small balls and deep fry until golden brown. Serve as a snack or with rice.

***Banfi Rose**

Crispy-Fried Beef

1 ½ pounds beef tenderloin
2 teaspoons sea salt
5 cloves garlic, minced
5 anchovies, minced
2 tablespoons lemon juice
½ teaspoon ground black pepper
½ teaspoon white pepper
1 teaspoon chili powder
2 teaspoons ground coriander
½ cup peanut oil
4 dried Thai chilies, seeds removed
4 tablespoons onion powder
2 teaspoons garlic powder

2 green onions, diced ¼ inch bias

Trim any fat away from the meat and then cut into very thin slices. Cut each slice into strips; 1 inch long and ½ inch wide.

In a bowl, blend the meat, salt, garlic, anchovy, lemon juice, black and white pepper, onion powder, garlic powder, and coriander. In a large wok, over medium-high heat, add the oil and fresh chilies. Cook until just crisp. Add the meat. Blend and toss frequently until done. Remove and serve over white rice or in iceberg lettuce cups. Garnish with green onion.

***Poppy Pinot Noir 2009**

NOTE: *Be sure to read the entire wine/beer/ Asian food discussion at the start of this section.*

CAMBODIA

Raw Fish Salad

1 pound very fresh white fish filets
½ cup fresh lemon juice
5-6 fresh green chilies, seeded and thinly sliced
8 scallions, thinly sliced on the bias
2 cloves garlic, finely minced
¼ teaspoon Sambal
½ teaspoon soy sauce
1 tablespoon nam pla
For serving:
Lettuce leaves
Mint leaves for garnish
Coriander leaves for garnish

Chop the fish into small chunks. Add the lemon juice and mix well. Combine with the other ingredients and blend. Allow to sit refrigerated overnight.

Place a small amount of the mixture in a lettuce leaf along with a few mint and/or coriander leaves and serve. Offer additional Sambal as a condiment.

***Frank Bonville Grand Cru Rose**

Shrimp and Cucumber Curry

1 pound medium shrimp, shelled and cleaned
2 cucumbers, peeled, seeded and sliced thin
5 cloves garlic, minced
2 shallots, chopped
2 teaspoons fresh ginger, chopped
½ teaspoon curry powder
½ teaspoon ground fennel
½ teaspoon ground cumin
1 tablespoon ground coriander
½ tsp ground white pepper
4 tablespoons peanut oil
2 cups coconut milk
3 tablespoons lemon juice
1 tablespoon nam pla

In a bowl, place the garlic, shallots, ginger, and all the ground spices. Heat the oil in a wok over medium high heat. Add the spice mixture and cook until very aromatic. Add the shrimp and cook; stirring for about 2 minutes. Add the coconut milk and bring to a very slow simmer. Add the cucumber and remaining seasoning and cook until the cucumber is just tender but not soft. Serve with rice.

***Beringer White Zinfandel**

BURMA

Noodles with Curried Chicken

1-3 pound chicken, cut into 10 pieces
3 tablespoons peanut oil
6 cloves garlic, minced
1 large yellow onion, minced
2 tablespoons fresh ground ginger
2 tablespoons fish sauce
2 tablespoons sesame oil
1-2 Thai chilies, minced
4 cups coconut milk
3 tablespoons corn starch
1 pound thin egg noodles
Sea salt to taste
Ground black pepper to taste

Season the chicken pieces with some salt and pepper. In a large pot over medium high heat, sauté the chicken pieces in the oil until brown on all sides. Remove and reserve.

Reduce the heat; add to the pan, the garlic, onion, ginger, fish sauce, sesame oil and chilies. Cook for 30 seconds until aromatic. Add the coconut milk and bring to a boil. Return the chicken to the pot and continue to simmer until the chicken is done (about 30 minutes).

Mix ¼ cup of the cooking liquid with the cornstarch and return it to the pot to thicken the broth. Serve on top of the cooked noodles.

***Martini and Rossi Asti**

SIR LANKA

Beef Curry

3 tablespoons olive oil
1 yellow onion, sliced very thin
6 cloves garlic, minced
5 green chilies, sliced very thin
1 teaspoon fresh ginger, peeled and minced
3 cardamom pods
1 ½ cinnamon sticks
1 teaspoon cumin, ground
1 teaspoon coriander, ground
1 teaspoon turmeric, ground
1 teaspoon garlic powder
1 teaspoon cayenne pepper
1 cup water
2 pound boneless beef chuck, cut into 1 inch cubes
Sea salt to taste

Heat the oil in a pan over medium heat. Add the onions and cook until soft and translucent; about 5 minutes. Reduce heat to medium low and continue to cook onions until very tender and dark brown; about 15-20 minutes. Stir in the garlic, green chilies, ginger, cardamom pods, and cinnamon. Combine and cook for 3 to 5 minutes, or until the garlic begins to turn a light golden brown. Stir in the cumin, coriander, turmeric, garlic powder, cayenne, and water. Simmer until most of the water has evaporated and the mixture has thickened.

Add the beef chuck and stir well, coating the meat with the mixture. Cook the meat over a medium low heat, stirring occasionally, until the meat is cooked through and tender, 1 ½ to 2 hours. Serve over rice.

***Adler Fiels Sauvignon Blanc**

THE PHILIPPINES

Fried Noodles

1 pound thin egg noodles, cooked al dente
2 tablespoons extra virgin olive oil
1 pound medium shrimp, cleaned and cut in half
1 chicken breast, boiled and shredded
¼ pound pork belly or pancetta, chunked
¼ pound ground chuck
¼ pound ground pork
4 cloves garlic, minced
1 large yellow onion, minced
1 cup Napa cabbage, shredded
2 tablespoons soy sauce
1 teaspoon rice vinegar
½ teaspoon white pepper
Sea salt to taste
Fresh ground black pepper to taste

Cook the noodles in salted water until very al dente. Strain noodles and reserve liquid.

In the same water, cook the shrimp until just done. Remove and cut in half.

In a frying pan, cook the pork belly or pancetta until just short of crisp. Add the ground chuck and cook about 3 minutes. Then, add the ground pork and cook an additional 3 minutes, or until brown throughout. Add the onion and garlic and continue cooking, stirring all the time. Add the soy, vinegar and white pepper. Adjust the flavor with salt and pepper. Add the cabbage and stir until just wilted. Serve over the cooked noodles.

***Graham Beck Brut Rose**

SINGAPORE

Singapore Noodles

1 pound medium size shrimp
1 tablespoon extra virgin olive oil
6 cups low sodium, low fat chicken or beef stock
½ pound ground pork
1 tablespoon soy sauce
1 tablespoon sesame oil
1 tablespoon oyster sauce
1 shallot, minced
4 cloves garlic, minced
½ teaspoon fresh ground ginger
½ pound vermicelli, cooked al dente
¼ teaspoon Chinese 5 spice powder
4 scallions, thinly sliced on the bias
½ cup bean sprouts
2 tablespoons fresh cilantro, chopped

In a frying pan or Wok over high heat, add the oil. Cook the shrimp quickly in the oil and remove. Add the ground pork and cook until done. Add the soy, sesame oil, shallot, garlic, five spice powder and ginger. Incorporate and cook for one minute. Return the shrimp to the pan. Add the cooked vermicelli and mix to combine. Transfer to a large bowl and top with the scallions, bean sprouts and cilantro and serve.

***Kirin Ichiban Beer**

JAPAN

Udon

6 cups low sodium, low fat chicken or beef broth
½ cup soy sauce
½ cup dry sherry
¼ teaspoon rice wine vinegar
½ pound Crimini mushrooms, diced
½ pound shrimp, cooked and diced
1 skinless boneless chicken breast, cut into thin, bite size pieces.

1 pound Udon noodles

2 scallions, chopped

1 tablespoon cilantro, chopped

Cook the noodles in a large pot of salted water until tender. In a separate pot, bring the stock to a boil, and add the soy, sherry, vinegar and mushrooms. Add the chicken breast, and return to a boil. Cook for 2 minutes. Add the shrimp, and cook an additional 30 seconds. Serve in large bowls with the Udon and broth. Garnish with the scallions and cilantro.

***Sapporo Reserve Beer**

KOREA

Stir-fried Cucumbers with Beef

8 ounces flank steak, cut into paper thin slices

2 teaspoons sesame oil

1 tablespoon soy sauce

½ teaspoon sea salt

½ teaspoon granulated sugar

¼ teaspoon cayenne pepper

2 large English cucumbers peeled, seeded and sliced thin

1 tablespoon vegetable oil

2 tablespoons sesame seeds

Slice the beef into strips; 1 inch long by ½ inch wide. Place the sliced beef in a bowl with the sesame oil, soy, salt, sugar and cayenne pepper. Mix well and allow standing for 5-10 minutes.

Add the oil to a very hot wok. Add the beef and allow cooking for about 30 seconds. Add the cucumber and cook an additional 30-45 seconds. Serve the beef over white rice and garnish with sesame seeds

***Robert Mondavi Cabernet Napa**

CHINA

Crispy Beef in Oyster Sauce

1-2 pound flank steak

2 eggs, beaten

4 tablespoon cornstarch

2 tablespoon soy sauce

2 tablespoon sesame oil

1 tablespoon oyster sauce

1 teaspoon ground white pepper

Oil for deep frying

1 tablespoon peanut oil

1 large shallot, minced

2 cloves garlic, minced

2 tablespoons fresh ginger, minced

1 large yellow onion, sliced thin

3 tablespoon soy sauce

4 tablespoons oyster sauce

4 green onions, chopped

Cut the flank steak thinly, across the grain, into 3 inch pieces. In a large bowl, blend together the eggs, corn starch, soy, sesame oil, oyster sauce and white pepper. Add the beef and coat well with the mixture. Deep fry the beef in small batches until crispy. Set aside.

In a wok, over medium-high heat, add the peanut oil. Sauté the shallot, garlic, and ginger for one minute. Add the onion and sauté until it is just tender. Add the soy and oyster sauce and cook 20 seconds. Add the reserved beef and cook, coating the beef with the sauce. Sprinkle with the scallions; drizzle with additional sesame oil and serve.

Variation #1: Add 2 crumbled hot Asian peppers to the mixture just before serving.

Variation #2: Use pork instead of beef and Hoisin sauce instead of Oyster sauce.

Variation #3: Try using chunks of chicken breast.

***Columbia Crest H3 Merlot**

NOTE: Be sure to review the discussion of wine/Asian pairings at the beginning of the Asian section of this chapter.

Chapter 7:

Classic And Not So Classic Italian Section I

CLASSIC AND NOT SO CLASSIC ITALIAN

There are more Italian restaurants in the United States than any other type of ethnic restaurants. From you local pizza joint to elegant dining establishments, Americans eat more Italian food than any other type. Similarly, when it comes to wine, Italy is the largest producer of some of the finest wine in the world. There's nothing better than great Italian food paired with a great Italian wine.

All Italians think their food is the best. I am no different. I am convinced that no other person can prepare good Italian foods as well as I can. Nevertheless, I still enjoy finding new and better Italian restaurants that offer not only the classics, but also new innovations on those classis Italian dishes. You might ask how I judge the quality of the food in an Italian restaurant. Besides the quality of their Ragu (sauce), I judge a restaurant on their preparation of two key dishes, Pasta Putanesca (see page); and a veal or chicken, and in particular, a Sole Francese. The first is a bold pasta dish that should have multiple layers of flavor that combine into a wonderful whole. The second is a delicate dish with nuances of flavor that should melt in your mouth.

As you review the recipes in this section, you will notice that we have drawn recipes from various parts of Italy. Many of them are classic dishes, so we hope you enjoy making them. We have also drawn some recipes from some of the lesser known sections of Italy such as Puglia, in the hope and expectation that you will enjoy them and seek out additional recipes from the many other regions of the country.

The biggest controversy in Italian cooking is over the preparation of the Ragu. No, that is not a brand name. Some families will call it ragu, others call it sauce, and still others call it gravy. Basically, it is the stuff mama makes on Sundays for when the entire family sits down to dinner at about 1:30-2:00 in the afternoon.

In these pages, we have offered recipes from the North and from the South. But remember, that ragu---sauce---gravy made for Sunday dinner is the single most personal dish created in the Italian household and not two recipes are exactly the same. For example, if Nona (grandma) is still with us and she had five children each of who have 4 married children, you can bet that there are at least 20 variations on that most sacred of Sunday preparations.

We have offered a number of recipes here, but we have in no way scratched the surface on Italian food preparation. Considering the fact that we are only scratching the surface on the magnitude of Italian recipes, if you are looking for particular suggestions or recipes not contained here, remember to visit our question and answer website. **www.wineanddine123.com** Just send your questions and we will be sure to get back to you ASAP.

As for Italian wines, every town and village, if not every household in Italy produces its own variation of wine. While Sangiovese is the omnipresent grape varietal, local growing conditions will change the characteristics of the wine produced. As in the other sections, we will be suggesting not only Italian wine, but wines from other countries as well.

Let's Do Cutlets

When most people speak about Italian food and they talk about <u>cutlets</u>, they most often refer to veal <u>cutlets</u> or *veal scaloppini*. The following recipes are for all types of <u>cutlets</u> and fish filets. They can be used for veal, chicken, turkey or pork. Many can be used for filets of fish such as flounder, sole, tilapia, or fish local in your area. The general ideas will hold true for any of these food items. You need only adjust the cooking time to accommodate the protein you are using. Let's begin...

Variation #1: Milanese

Using the protein of your choice, lightly dust each piece in seasoned flour. Dredge each a piece in an egg wash, and then in breadcrumbs; with a ratio of half seasoned bread crumbs and half pecorino or parmesan cheese. Sauté each piece in a canola-olive blended oil over medium heat (some prefer not to fry in extra virgin olive oil because the flavor of extra virgin can overpower the flavor of the protein). Top each portion with a blend of chopped plum tomato, a clove of chopped garlic, some fresh, chopped basil and some extra virgin olive oil. Adjust flavor with some salt and pepper. You can also use some baby arugula with shaved red onion, or some shaved fennel tossed in lemon vinaigrette.

Lemon Vinaigrette:

Fresh lemon juice
Extra virgin olive oil
Sea salt to taste
Ground black pepper to taste
Fresh basil, chiffonade (cut into strips)
Sugar, granulated

Variation #2: Piccata

Dredge portions of the protein of your choice, in seasoned flour. In a large sauté pan, over medium heat, add a mixture of ½ olive oil and ½ unsalted butter. Add the protein and cook on one side until done; turn protein over. Immediately, add the juice of one lemon and a tablespoon or so of capers "around the rim" of the pan. Remove the protein from the sauté pan. Add one minced clove of garlic, and sauté until golden, and ¾ cup white wine. Reduce by a third. Add a ½ cup clear broth related to the protein to the pan. (Chicken broth would be used if preparing chicken, for example).

Place the protein back in the pan; add a tablespoon or so of whole unsalted butter and cook an additional minute until butter is incorporated. Adjust flavor with some sea salt and fresh ground pepper. Serve on a large platter. Garnish with some lemon wheels, some grated cheese, and some chopped parsley.

Variation #3: Francese

Dredge 4 serving size portions of the protein of your choice in seasoned flour and then into an egg wash. In a large sauté pan, over medium heat, add a mixture of ½ olive oil and ½ unsalted butter. Add the protein and cook on both sides until done. Remove the protein when cooked.

Add one clove garlic and one shallot minced. Sauté for one minute. Add ¾ cup dry white wine and the juice of ½ a lemon. Reduce by a third. Add a ½ cup of chicken stock and a tablespoon of whole butter. Return the protein to the pan and cook for 1 minute. Adjust the flavor with salt and pepper and serve.

Variation #4: Marsala Wine & Mushrooms

Dust 4 serving size portions of the protein of your choice in seasoned flour. In a large sauté pan, over medium heat, add a mixture of ½ olive oil and ½ unsalted butter. Add the protein and cook on both sides until done. Remove from pan and set aside.

Add 2 minced cloves of garlic and one minced shallot. Cook until a light golden color, then add a ½ pound sliced mushrooms and stir. Cook for one minute. Add ¾ cup Marsala wine to the pan and continue to cook until the mushrooms are tender and the liquid has reduced by half. Return the protein and cook an additional minute. Add 1 cup (more or less) of veal demi-glace, and a tablespoon of whole butter. Cook until slightly thickened. Adjust flavor with salt and pepper.

Variation #5: Sorentino

Place a very thin slice of prosciutto on one side of a cutlet and set aside. In a sauté pan with some olive oil over medium heat, sauté a thin slice of pre-breaded eggplant on both sides. Set aside. In same pan, sauté the prosciutto layered protein, prosciutto side first. Cook until prosciutto is crisp. Turn protein over and place the reserved sliced eggplant on top. Cook for one additional minute; remove and reserve.

Add ½ cup dry white wine to the pan; reduce by ½, and then a ½ cup marinara sauce to the pan. Return the <u>cutlets</u> to the pan, eggplant side up. Place a slice of fresh mozzarella on each <u>cutlet</u>, and cover the pan. Adjust flavor with salt and pepper. When the cheese has melted, serve.

Variation #6: Saltimbocca

Lay the <u>cutlets</u> on a flat service. Sprinkle a bit of fresh sage overreach piece, then press a thin slice of prosciutto on top of the <u>cutlets</u>. In a sauté pan with olive oil over medium heat, sauté the <u>cutlets</u>, prosciutto side down until prosciutto is crisp. Turn <u>cutlets</u> over and cook until done. Remove from pan and reserve. Drain off excess oil.

Place a bit of olive oil and unsalted butter in the pan. Place 3 cloves of garlic, sliced thin, in the pan. Sauté one minute. Add ½ lb of fresh spinach and ½ lb of sliced mushrooms to the pan and cook another minute, or until the spinach starts to wilt. Add ¾ cup Marsala to the pan and continue to cook until the mushrooms are tender and the liquid has reduce by half. Return the protein and cook an additional minute. Add 1 cup (more or less) of veal demi- glace, and a tablespoon of whole butter. Cook until slightly thickened. Adjust flavor with salt and pepper.

Suggestion: When returning the protein to the pan to reheat, layer each piece with some shredded provolone, asiago, or fresh mozzarella cheese.

Let's talk about wine: Once again we have chosen to group recipes and speak in some general as well as specific terms about wines. When using a lighter protein such as fish or chicken you can stay with a white such as **Santa Margarita Pinot Grigio** or **Barone Fini Alto Adige.** As you move up in the richness of the protein you can change to a light red such as the **Montresor Valpolicella**

or a light *Pinot Noir* such as **Angeline California** or **Mark West.** A *rose* such as **Bougrier Rose d'Anjou** or **Salmon Sancerre Rose** would pair with the light and the more heavy proteins. Then, when you move into variations 4, 5 and 6 you could look to a little heaver red such as **Trecciano Chianti** or for a really high end enjoyment the **San Guido Guadalberto** (decant 3-5 hours before drinking).

Ragu alla Toscana /Tuscan Meat Sauce

8 tablespoons unsalted butter
½ cup extra virgin olive oil
8 ounces prosciutto, chopped
10 anchovy filets, chopped
2 large yellow onions, fine chop
2 celery stalks, fine chop
1 large carrot, fine chop
2-3 pounds boneless chuck roast, cut into ½" pieces
1 pound sweet Italian sausage removed from the skin (use hot if desired)
2 28 ounce cans crushed tomatoes
4 cups low sodium beef or chicken broth
1 ½ cups Italian red wine
1 tablespoon lemon zest
4 tablespoons lemon juice
½ teaspoons ground cinnamon
½ teaspoon fresh ground nutmeg
½ teaspoon ground Rosemary
1 teaspoon crushed dry Basil
1 teaspoon crushed dry oregano
½ cup Pecorino Romano

In a large pot, over medium heat, add the extra virgin olive oil and butter. Once butter has melted, add the prosciutto and anchovies and cook 2 minutes. Add the sausage and chuck, and continue to cook until brown throughout.

Add the onion, celery, and carrot, and sweat for 10 minutes or until the vegetables are soft and translucent. Add the wine, scraping the bottom of the pot to pull the 'fond" off the bottom. Reduce the wine by half. Add the tomatoes, broth, lemon zest and juice, cinnamon, rosemary, basil, oregano, and nutmeg. Cook over medium heat for about 2 hours. Be sure to stir the sauce occasionally so the ingredients don't stick to the bottom of the pot.

Serve with pasta such as penne or rotini. Top with pecorino Romano cheese.

Let's talk about wine: Here is where the big bold Italian reds come into play. The **Vasco Sassetti Brunello** (decant 3-5 hours before drinking) and **San Lorenzo** (decant 3-5 hours before drinking). You could use a rich bold *Chianti* such as **San Andrea Reserva** or **Devolve Reserva.** A great high end red would be the **Antinori Tignanello** (decant 3-5 hours before drinking). But don't forget the very nice Italian Table Wines like the **Montepulciano d'Abruzzo** or the Southern Italian **Nero d'Avola.**

Italian Herbed Pork Roast

5+ pound Pork Roast
10 cloves garlic, finely minced
2 shallots, minced
6 tablespoons Italian parsley, fine chop
6 tablespoons fresh rosemary, fine chop
2 teaspoons fresh thyme, fine chop
2 teaspoons fresh basil, fine chop
½ cup extra virgin olive oil
¼ cup grated cheese
Sea salt to taste
Ground black pepper to taste
2 cups dry wine
1 cup low sodium chicken broth

Finely chop the garlic, shallots, and the fresh herbs, and combine. Slowly add the extra virgin olive oil to the blend, to form a paste. Adjust flavor with salt and pepper.

Using a knife, "score the outside of the roast about 2 inches apart, about a ½" deep. Use about ¾ of the paste to fill the slits. Spread the remaining paste over the roast and rub in to coat completely. Let stand at room temperature for 30 minutes. Place the pork roast in a roasting pan with a

rack, fat side up. Place the roast in a 350° oven for about 1 ¾ hours, or until the internal temperature is 150 degrees. Remove the roast from the oven and let stand.

Place the roasting pan on the stove top over medium heat. Add with the wine, scraping the bottom of the pan, and simmer for about 3 minutes. Add a bit of whole butter. Whisk until well incorporated. Slice the roast thin and serve with pan juices.

Variation #1: Use a leg of lamb instead of a pork roast.

Variation #2: Use a fresh ham as an alternative.

Let's talk about wine: The pork dishes would go very well paired with a *dry Rose* such as **Dom Fantanyl** from France or **Mendoza Station** from Argentina. One of the **Travel Roses** from France would also be very nice with this dish. It also pairs well with a *Pinot Noir* from Burgundy such as the **Chateau Tour de l'Ange**. The **Plunger head** or **Rudy** *Zins* would also support the flavors of the dish as would the **Bridgeman Merlot.** If you wanted to treat yourself to a more upscale wine, a good choice would be **Pinot Noir Goldeneye** by Duckhorn.

Prosciutto Appetizer

2 pounds of Prosciutto, sliced "paper thin"
2 red onions, sliced thin
1 cup baby arugula, washed well and dried
2 tablespoons extra virgin olive oil for cooking
2-3 tablespoons high quality extra virgin olive oil for dressing
2-3 tablespoons Balsamic Vinegar
½ pound good quality blue cheese like gorgonzola or Maytag blue cheese

Slice the red onions very thin. In a large pan, over medium low heat, add 2-3 tablespoons extra virgin olive oil. Add the onions, season with salt and pepper and sauté until tender and transparent. Add the balsamic vinegar and continue cooking until the onions are well glazed, and are a deep, dark purple color. Remove onions from the heat and allow cooling. In a large bowl, dress the arugula with a high quality extra virgin olive oil, and salt and pepper. Crumble the blue cheese in a separate bowl.

Assembly: Lay out one slice of prosciutto. Place 1-2 leaves of the dressed arugula, 1-2 small pieces of the glazed onions and some crumbled blue cheese. Roll into a package and serve as an appetizer.

Let's talk about wine: OK—your turn. You didn't think we were going to hand it all to you on a silver platter. Which wine(s) do you think would pair well with the rich/salty/sweet/peppery appetizer? Experiment and let us know what you have chosen---if it worked and why it did or didn't.

Citrus Shrimp with Shaved Fennel

3 pounds large shrimp, peeled, cleaned and deveined
1 medium yellow onion, shaved very thin
1 yellow pepper, julienned
1 orange pepper, julienned
¾ cup extra virgin olive oil
4 tablespoon orange juice
3 tablespoons lemon juice
2 tablespoons orange zest
3 teaspoons lemon zest
2 Fennel Bulbs, top fronds removed, cut in quarters and shaved very thin
1 tablespoon fresh basil, chopped
Sea salt to taste
½ teaspoon white pepper
½ teaspoons ground black pepper
¼ teaspoons crushed red pepper flakes

Quickly poach the cleaned shrimp in rapidly boiling water and cook until opaque. Immediately remove shrimp from the pot when cooked and place in an ice bath. Cool completely. Drain well.

In a large bowl, combine the extra virgin olive oil, citrus juice, citrus zest, fennel, basil, onion,

and peppers and blend well. Add the shrimp to the bowl, and toss to blend well. Adjust flavor with the salt and the white and black peppers. Refrigerate 8 hours, or overnight to allow the shrimp macerate. Serve room temperature on toasted Italian bread or rounds.

Let's talk about wine: **This** is a great summer dish and would pair well with whites such as: **Salneval Albarino**, **Veramonte Sauvignon Blanc**, **Banfi Rose**. I guess you would also expect us to suggest a sparkler since we are trying to convince people that they are wonderful food wines so you might try: **Nino Franco Prosecco**, **Montaudon Brut Rose** or one of our favorites **De Margerie Grand Cru**.

Mushroom and Pork Ragu

8 ounces button mushrooms, sliced
8 ounces Crimini mushrooms, sliced
8 ounces assorted wild mushrooms, sliced
5-6 cloves garlic, minced
2 pounds boneless pork with some fat, cut into ½ inch pieces
8 ounces Guanchali or pancetta, chopped
5 links sweet Italian Sausage with fennel, casings removed (mild or hot sausage may be substituted)
1 bottle dry white wine; such as Sauvignon Blanc ("grassy style")
2 large sweet onions, fine chop
2 carrots, fine chop
2 stalks celery, fine chop
1-28 ounce can whole tomatoes, hand crushed
8 ounce tomato paste
2-3 cups low sodium pork or veal stock (chicken stock can be substituted)
2 tablespoons fresh basil, chopped
¾ cup grated pecorino Romano
1 teaspoon dry oregano, crushed
Extra virgin olive oil
Sea salt to taste
Freshly ground black pepper
Ground black pepper to taste
Grated pecorino Romano cheese for garnish

Crushed Red Pepper Flakes for garnish

Heat 2-3 tablespoons of extra virgin olive oil in a large frying pan over medium-high heat. Add the garlic, half the onions and mushrooms. Cook just until the mushrooms begin to soften. Add 3-4 grinds of pepper to the pan. Add about 1/3 bottle of wine and cook an additional 2-3 minutes and set aside.

In a large pot, heat 2-3 tablespoons extra virgin olive oil. Season the pork with some salt and pepper and cook over high heat until browned throughout. Remove pork from the pot, set aside, and lower heat to medium. Add the Guanchali. Stir 1 minute. Add the sausage and cook for 3 minutes to render out some of the fat. Add the remaining onions, carrots, and celery. Cook until soft. Add remaining wine and cook until it is almost absorbed. Add tomatoes, tomato paste, 1 ½ cup stock, reserved pork, basil, oregano, cheese, and additional pepper if needed. Cook on high to bring to a boil; then reduce heat to a simmer. Simmer the ragu until pork is tender; (about 1 hour). Add additional stock along the way if "ragu" starts to get too dry. Add the mushroom mixture after the hour and warm throughout. Adjust flavor with some additional salt and pepper if needed and serve.

Let's talk about wine: For the wine addition to the recipe, you might try a nice southern Italian white like **Kaila Grillo Inzolia Sicilia** or its red alternative **Kaila Nero d'Avola Sicilia .** These wines are also a good choice to pair with this dish. You could also ADD/PAIR a nice unoaked or low oaked *Chardonnay* like **Sonoma Lobe** or **Mer Soleil Silver**. If you wanted to treat yourself to a more upscale wine, a good choice would be the **Du MOL**. Although you might want to experiment with light reds and we encourage you to do so, we recommend you stay with rich whites.

Mozzarella in Carrozza

1 pound fresh mozzarella, sliced into ¼ inch slices
Slices of ciabatta Bread, ½" thick
3 eggs, beaten
¼ teaspoon salt
¼ teaspoon fresh ground black pepper
4 tablespoons canola oil
2 tablespoons unsalted butter
2 anchovy filets, chopped
1 clove garlic, minced
1 shallot, minced
2 tablespoons lemon juice
½ cup dry white wine
Sea salt to taste
Ground black pepper to taste

Heat a large sauté pan over medium heat, add the canola oil and one tablespoon of butter to the pan. Make sandwiches of the fresh mozzarella and the bread. In a dish beat the eggs with the salt and pepper. Dredge the sandwiches in the egg and fry in the oil until a light golden brown. Remove and set aside.

To the pan, add the butter, shallot, garlic and anchovies. Cook until tender and the anchovies have melted. Add the lemon juice and wine and cook until the liquid has reduced by half. Adjust the flavor with some salt and pepper. Pour over the Carrozza and serve.

Variation #1: Using sliced Italian bread, place some fresh mozzarella and bacon in the center of two slices of bread, dip into the egg and cook like French toast. Drizzle some maple syrup over the top and serve for breakfast.

Let's talk about wine: A nice light Italian white like the **Bolla Orvieto**, or the **Bellini Orvieto** or a *Pinot Grigio* like the **Conti Priola** or **Luna de Luna** or **Bella Sera** would all compliment this great appetizer. You could also go with a great Prosecco such as **Nino Franco Rustico**.

Chicken Cacciatore

1-3 pound chicken, cut into 10 pieces
Sea Salt to taste
Ground black pepper to taste
3 tablespoons extra virgin olive oil
1 large yellow onion, sliced
3 carrots, split in half and sliced thin
2 stalks of celery with leaves, sliced thin
5 cloves garlic, sliced thin
8 ounces tomato paste
2 cups dry white wine
1 28 ounce can Italian tomatoes, hand crushed
1 cup low sodium chicken broth
2 tablespoons flat leaf parsley, chopped
1 tablespoon fresh basil, chopped
Sea salt to taste
Ground black pepper to taste

In a deep sauce pot, over medium high heat, add the oil. Season the chicken with some salt and pepper, and fry the chicken in small batches until golden. Remove and reserve.

Reduce the heat to medium, then add the onion, celery, carrots and garlic to the pot, and cook 5 minutes, stirring regularly. Add the tomato paste and cook an additional minute. Add the wine and cook until reduced by half. Add the tomatoes and chicken broth and parsley. Return the chicken to the pan. Add additional chicken stock if necessary to just cover the chicken. Cook at a low simmer for about 40 minutes until the chicken is done. Serve with Orzo or rice tossed with a bit of olive oil.

Variation #1: Try adding 3 pickled hot cherry peppers that have been seeded and cut in half.

Variation #2: Instead of using a dry white wine, try using a light dry red wine such as Valpolicella.

Variation #3: Instead of chicken use a 2-3 lb chuck roast. Cook until tender (it will take longer to cook) and serve.

Variation # 4 Instead of chicken use rabbit

Let's talk about wine: Here, as in other dishes, we encourage you to choose a wine to ADD that is one you would choose to PAIR. Once again we say don't cook with a wine you wouldn't drink. Some ADD/PAIR wines for this great Italian dish would be: **Barone Fini Pinot Grigio, Santa Margarita Pinot Grigio, Vasco Sassetti il Ginepro Sangiovese, Santi Nello Prosecco, Armani Pinot Grigio Friuli, Montresor Valpolicella**.

Chicken Scarpariello

4 sweet Italian sausages
2 tablespoons extra virgin olive oil
2 skinless boneless chicken breasts, cut in 2 inch cubes
2 shallots, minced
4 cloves garlic, minced
¾ cup dry white wine
2 tablespoons balsamic vinegar
¾ cup chicken stock
½ teaspoon fresh oregano, fine chop
Sea salt to taste
Ground black pepper to taste
1-2 tablespoons unsalted butter

In a large pan over medium heat, sauté the sausage until they are almost done. Remove sausage and slice into bite size pieces and reserve. Add the chicken pieces to the pan and sauté them until almost done. Remove and reserve with the sausage.

Add the shallot and garlic to the pan and cook 30 seconds. Add the wine and continue cooking for 1-2 minutes, reducing the wine by half. Add the vinegar and chicken stock. Return the sausage and chicken to the pan and cook 1 minute. Adjust flavor with the salt and pepper. Once heated through, place chicken and sausage on serving platter. Add the whole butter to the sauce; bring to a boil, reduce slightly to thicken. Pour over chicken and serve.

Variation #1: Use chicken thighs instead of the breast or a whole chicken.

Variation #2: Add 5 hot pickled cherry peppers that have been seeded and sliced in 4's to the pan before returning the chicken and sausage. You may also have to add some chicken stock to augment the gravy.

Variation #3: Add some crispy roasted potatoes to the pan at the same time you add the chicken and sausage. Toss well and serve.

Let's talk about Wine: This dish would go well with a light Italian red such as **Bellini Chianti**, or a **Montepulciano D'Abruzzo.** You could also use a nice *Pinot Noir* such as **Acacia**, **Estancia** or **Bell Gloss, Clark & Telephone.** A rich *merlot* would also compliment the dish. You might choose **Cupcake, Dynamite** or **Duckhorn.**

A Classic Muffaletta

1 loaf of round Tuscan bread, most of the center dough removed
¼ cup red wine vinegar
½ cup extra virgin olive oil
1 clove garlic, minced
1 shallot, minced
½ cup oil cured black olives, pitted and chopped
½ cup Italian green olives, pitted and chopped
1 hot cherry pepper, seeded and chopped
¼ cup pimento peppers, chopped
¼ cup marinated artichokes, chopped
Fresh ground pepper to taste
¼ pound thin sliced mortadella
¼ pound thin sliced hard salami
¼ pound thin sliced pepperoni
¼ pound sliced provolone
¼ cup grated Romano cheese
¼ pound thin sliced prosciutto
1 large sweet onion, sliced thin
2 cups arugula
1 tablespoon red wine vinegar
2 tablespoon extra virgin olive oil
Sea salt to taste

Ground black pepper to taste

In a bowl, combine the red vinegar, garlic, shallot, olives, cherry peppers, pimentos and artichokes. Season with a bit of pepper.

Split the bread loaf down the middle diagonally; remove most of the dough center. Spread ¼ of the olive mixture on the bottom of the bread bowl. Layer the meats and cheeses pressing each layer into the bowl. From time to time, spread a little of the olive mixture over one of the layers. Toss the arugula with some, olive oil, salt and pepper. Make this the top layer of the bowl. Spread the last of the olive mixture on the top of the bread. Press the top down and wrap the entire loaf tightly in plastic wrap. Allow the sandwich to sit 4 hours to overnight. Slice into wedges and serve.

Let's talk about beer: Although wine would always be a good choice, this dish would be great with an ice cold beer instead. You could choose a nice Italian lager such as **Birra Moretti** or a more substantial bear such as **Samuel Smith's Nut Brown Ale** , **Yuengling lager** or **Monk in a Trunk**.

Pizza Rustica

I package (2crusts) store bought pie crust or make your own
1 pound frozen baby spinach, thawed and squeezed dry
3 tablespoon extra virgin olive oil
1 medium yellow onion, sliced thin
3 cloves garlic, minced
Sea salt to taste
Ground black pepper to taste
1 pound ricotta
½ cup grated Romano cheese
3 extra large egg yolks
2 tablespoons flat leaf parsley, chopped
1 cup mozzarella, shredded
¼ pound prosciutto, cut into thin strips
¼ pound sweet Soppressata, sliced thin
¼ pound hot Soppressata, sliced thin
1 small roasted red pepper, seeds removed and peeled
1 small roasted yellow pepper, seeds removed
2 small jars marinated artichokes, drained and quartered
1 egg (for egg wash)

Heat the oil in a pan over medium heat. Add the onion and cook until tender. Add the garlic and cook an additional minute. Add the spinach and sauté until heated through. Adjust flavor with salt and pepper. Remove from the pan and reserve to cool.

Blend the ricotta with the Romano, egg yolks and parsley until smooth. Set aside. Evenly distribute each of the ingredients onto one of the pie crusts. Begin with the spinach, then the mozzarella, ricotta mix, prosciutto, sweet Soppressata, hot Soppressata, roasted peppers, artichokes, onions, and peppers. Cover the filling with the second pie crust. Tightly roll and seal the edges. Brush the top lightly with an egg wash and bake in a pre heated 375° oven for about 1 hour until the crust is a deep golden color. (You may have to cover the pie crust with aluminum foil to prevent burning. Allow the pizza to cool for about 2 hours before serving.

Let's talk about beer: Here again is another recipe where beer pairs very nicely. The beers mentioned in previous recipes in this chapter would go very well. Additionally, consider beers such as: **Bass Ale**, **Red Hook Ale** and **Pikes double Ale.**

salt, pepper and oregano. Place the mixture in the center of the baking pan with the sausage surrounding it. Blend the wine and water and pour into the pan. Bake in a 350° preheated oven for one hour, turning the sausage and mixing the potato mixture after about 30 minutes of cooking. Serve immediately.

Variation # 1: Try using hot Italian sausage instead of sweet.

Variation #2: Instead of oil cured olives, try using sun-dried tomatoes packed in olive oil, sliced into thin strips.

Variation #3: Try adding 1/3 cup grated Romano cheese into the potato mixture.

Let's talk about wine: This dish would pair well with a light *Chianti* such as **Bolla** or **Reffino**. A rich *merlot* such as **Edgewood** or **Blackstone** would also go well, The **Norton Malbec** or the **Phebus MMC** would also pair well. A great wine not often used in this country would be the Italian **Rocca Felice Barbaresco 2004**. You could also go with a Rhone valley blend such as **Tardieu-Laurent Vacqueyras 2007**

Sausage with Potatoes, Olives and Onions

6 pieces sweet Italian sausage with fennel
3 large baking potatoes, cut into 2 inch chunks
1 large yellow onion, sliced thin
6 cloves garlic, sliced thin
¼ cup Calamata or Gaeta black olives, pitted and cut in half
1/3 cup extra virgin olive oil
1 teaspoon sea salt
1 teaspoon fresh ground black pepper
1teaspoon fresh oregano
¼ cup dry white wine
¼ cup water

Arrange the sausage around the edge of a large deep baking pan. In a large bowl, mix together the potatoes, onion, garlic, olives, olive oil,

Eggplant Parmigiana

1 large eggplant, peeled and sliced into ¼" rounds
4 tablespoons sea salt
2 cups dry seasoned bread crumbs
¾ cup grated Romano cheese
1 tablespoon onion powder
1 tablespoon garlic powder
1 teaspoon fresh ground black pepper
1 tablespoon fresh basil, chopped
1teaspoon fresh oregano, chopped
1 cup flour seasoned with salt and pepper
3 eggs beaten
4-6 tablespoon canola oil for frying
1 pound fresh mozzarella, sliced
1 cup grated Romano cheese
3 cups marinara sauce

Peel the eggplant, and slice it into ¼ inch slices.

Layer it in a colander, sprinkling each layer with some sea salt. Cover with plastic wrap and weigh down the eggplant slices with a pot filled with water. Allow the pot to sit on top of the eggplant for 2 hours. After 2 hours, remove the weight and wash the slices with fresh water, then pat dry.

In a large dish, combine the breadcrumbs, Romano cheese, garlic and onion powders, pepper, basil, and oregano. In a second dish, beat the eggs. In a third dish, place the seasoned flour. Dredge the slices of eggplant in the flour, then the egg, and then the seasoned breadcrumbs. Heat the oil in a large pan over medium high heat. Fry each piece golden brown and allow the eggplant to drain on a rack or paper towels.

In a baking dish, place a coating of sauce on the bottom, and then place a layer of the cooked eggplant slices. On top of the eggplant, place slices of the mozzarella cheese. Sprinkle with some Romano cheese and coat with additional sauce. Repeat until all the eggplant is used. The final layer should be mozzarella, grated cheese and sauce. Bake in a preheated 350° oven until bubbly.

Let's talk about wine: This is really a peasant dish but one with great richness and structure when made properly. For that reason we recommend a rich red to pair with it. Let your heart experience great Italian reds such as: **San Guido Guadalberto** (decant 3-5 hours before drinking), or the greatest of the great Italian reds, **Sassicaia**

Panzanilla Salad

(Bread and Tomato salad)

2 cups hard, stale, thick-crusted Italian bread
6 very ripe plum tomato, cut into chunks
1 pound fresh mozzarella, cut into ½" cubes
1 red onion, sliced thin
2 cloves garlic, minced
½ cup plus extra virgin olive oil
1 tablespoon small capers

¼ cup red wine vinegar
2 tablespoon fresh basil, chopped
Sea salt to taste
Ground black pepper to taste
1 head romaine lettuce, sliced thin
1 head frisee lettuce, pulled apart and washed
1 cup (packed) baby arugula
1 head radicchio, sliced thin
Grated Romano cheese
Anchovies as garnish

In a large bowl, mix the cubed bread, tomatoes, mozzarella, red onion, garlic, capers, and basil. Add the olive oil, vinegar, and salt and pepper to taste. Toss well and allow to stand refrigerated for 15 minutes, or until the bread starts to soften.

On a platter, combine the romaine, frisee and arugula. Add the tomato salad over the top of the lettuce blend. Drizzle with additional extra virgin olive oil and serve with the Romano cheese and anchovies as garnish.

Let's talk about wine: Ok here is another for you, our audience, to choose. Could it take a rich white? What about a Rose? Could I choose a light red? What do you think? Remember you have the acidity of the tomatoes, the aroma of the Basil and garlic. Since it is a salad might you choose a sparkler? Choose a great wine and be surprised.

Mom's Pork Chops with Hot Peppers

4-1 inch thick, center cut pork loin chops
Sea salt to taste
Ground black pepper to taste
3 tablespoons extra virgin olive oil
5-6 pickled hot cherry peppers, seeded, cut in half
3 tablespoons extra virgin olive oil
½ cup red wine vinegar
1 tablespoon small capers
¼ cup Italian parsley, chopped

Season both sides of the pork chops with the salt and pepper. In a large frying pan over medium high heat, add the olive oil. Sear the chops until just done---about 5 minutes per side. Remove to a large serving platter. Drain the frying oil from the pan and add the extra virgin olive oil. Add the cherry peppers and toss quickly to heat through. Then, add the capers and deglazed the pan with the red wine vinegar. Add the chopped parsley. Pour the mixture over the pork chop. Serve with some crusty Italian bread.

Let's talk about wine: Remember, when we eat spicy foods, "the more heat—the more sweet." As you shift from mild peppers to very hot peppers, you could move up the ladder of sweetness and try a sparkling wine like **Nino Franco Dry Prosecco, Botter Medium Sweet Prosecco, Soria Asti** or **Cardinale Lanata Muscotto d'Asti**

Yellowtail Snapper Scampi

4 serving size pieces of yellowtail snapper filets, skin and pin bones removed
Seasoned flour
2 tablespoons olive oil
1 tablespoon unsalted butter
2 shallots, minced
5 cloves garlic, minced
¾ cup dry white wine
Juice of ½ lemon
4 ounces unsalted butter
½ tablespoon fresh basil, chiffonade
Sea salt to taste
Ground black pepper to taste
Flat leaf parsley for garnish

Dredge the snapper lightly in the seasoned flour. Preheat a large sauté pan over medium high heat. Add the olive oil and melt the butter in the pan. Carefully place the snapper in the oil, skin side up, and sauté the snapper for about 2-3 minutes. Carefully turn the snapper over with a spatula, being careful not the break the filets. Continue to cook the snapper for another 2-3 minutes, or until the fish is cooked through. Place the snapper on a serving tray and reserve.

Drain some of the oil from the pan and reduce the heat to medium. Add the shallots and garlic to the pan and cook 10-15 seconds. Add the

wine and reduce by a third. Add the lemon juice. Reduce the heat to low and add pieces of the cold, unsalted butter to the pan, incorporating the butter into the sauce until completely melted. Adjust the flavor with salt and pepper. Add the fresh basil. Pour the sauce over the snapper in the serving dish. Sprinkle with fresh flat leaf parsley and serve.

Variation#1: Try the same recipe using flounder or sole filets or your other favorite white fish filet. It can also be used for small whole fish such as whiting.

Let's Talk about wine: Let's try some non-Italian non-traditional whites that will really pair well with this dish. Remember, use the wine suggested in the preparation and then drink it with the finished dish. *From France*: **Rothschild Blanc** ; *From Germany*: **Thanisch Badstube Kabinett Riesling**; *From Austria*: **Winzer Krems Gruner Veltliner**; and *from Napa*: **Caymus Conundrum**.

Italian Bread Soup

¼ cup flat leaf parsley, coarsely chopped
¼ cup fresh basil leaves, coarsely chopped
¼ cup fresh oregano, coarsely chopped
¼ cup baby arugula, coarsely chopped
¼ cup radicchio, coarsely chopped
¼ cup chicory coarsely chopped
8 cups good quality low sodium chicken stock
1 large red onion, minced
3 cloves garlic, minced
3 large potatoes, cut into ½ inch cubes
2 thick (2-3 inches) slices of dense Italian bread, crust removed
Sea salt to taste
Ground black pepper to taste
Extra virgin olive oil for drizzle
Grated cheese for garnish
Chopped, pickled cherry peppers for garnish

Chop all the fresh herbs and place in a bowl for later use. Place the chicken stock in a large pot. Add about 1 cup of the herb mixture, the potatoes, onion and garlic. Bring the pot to a simmer and cook until the potatoes are just tender; about 15-20 minutes. Break the Italian bread into small pieces and add them to the pot. Continue simmering until the bread is broken down and the soup has thickened. Just before serving add the last ½ cup of the herbs. Adjust the flavor with salt and pepper. Serve the soup with grated cheese, a drizzle of olive oil, and chopped pickled cherry peppers as a garnish.

Let's talk about wine: This would be a very nice place for an *oaky chardonnay* to compliment the cooked and fresh herbs in the soup. Try **River Road Mills Vineyard**, or **Muirwood Single Vineyard**, or **La Crema, Sonoma.** If you want to go all out with a great wine paired with a simple dish try **Newton Unfiltered.**

Antoinette's Cannelloni

This dish calls for the use a crepe shell instead of a pasta shell. It makes it much more delicate and light.

Crepes:

1 cup whole milk
1 cup all purpose flour
4 extra large eggs
Pinch of salt
Pinch of white pepper
1 stick unsalted butter, melted and clarified to remove solids.

For the crepe batter, place the cold milk in a large mixing bowl. Using a whisk, add the eggs, and whip into a froth. Add the flour, a little at a time to form a batter. Season the batter with salt and pepper.

To make the crepes, use an 8 inch nonstick frying pan, over medium low heat. Brush the pan with a scant amount of butter; pour a ¼ cup of the batter mixture into the pan. Gently turn the pan to coat the bottom. Return to the heat and cook about 30 seconds until the crepe is "set". Flip quickly with a rubber spatula, cook

for another 30 seconds and then remove from the pan and set aside. Repeat the same process, using the remainder of the egg mixture, stacking the crepe shells as they are done. The mixture should generate about 16 crepes. (It may take some practice the first time you make the crepes, so you may break a few.)

Filling:

1 pound fresh ricotta cheese, low moisture
½ pound mozzarella, shredded
½ cup grated Romano cheese
2 eggs, beaten
½ teaspoon white pepper
¼ cup fresh flat leaf parsley, chopped
4 cups of marinara sauce

For the crepe filling, blend the ricotta, mozzarella, grated cheese, eggs, white pepper and parsley in a bowl. To fill the crepes, place each shell on a clean, dry surface. Add 2 to 3 tablespoons of the cheese mixture across the crepe shells starting at the 9:00 position, and filling the crepe across to the 3:00 position. Roll each crepe into a tube. Heat the marinara and use it to assemble the dish. Place a thin layer of the sauce on the bottom of a baking dish. As you roll the cannellini, place them in the baking dish. Once finished, coat the top with additional sauce and bake in a preheated 350° oven for 30 minutes.

Variation # 1: Add one pound of frozen spinach that has been defrosted and squeezed dry with the ricotta mixture for the filling. Instead of using a tomato sauce use a béchamel sauce or a butter sauce.

Variation # 2: Use a Bolognese sauce. Cover the cannellini with the sauce and sprinkle the top with grated cheese or shredded mozzarella before baking.

Let's talk about wine: Here you have a dish that can be made with a rich buttery white sauce or a red sauce. You can use just about any meat ragu and also make the dish a bit spicy if you wish. It is a dish limited only by your imagination and because of that you will have to choose a wine depending on the type of sauce and fillings you choose. For that reason we leave it up to you. Experiment!

Maria's Meatballs and Potatoes

For the meatballs:

1 ½ pounds ground sirloin
¾ pounds ground pork
1 cup seasoned breadcrumbs
½ cup Romano cheese grated
2 eggs
1 tablespoon fresh basil, fine chop
1 teaspoon fresh oregano, fine chop
1 teaspoon fresh ground black pepper
1 yellow onion, minced
2 cloves garlic, minced
1 tablespoon flat leaf parsley, minced
Olive oil for frying

To prepare the dish:

4 tablespoons extra virgin olive oil
2 large potatoes, cubed
2 yellow onions, sliced thin
½ cup dry white wine

In a large bowl, combine all the ingredients for the meatballs and mix well; be careful not to over working the meat. Form the meatballs about 2-3 inches in diameter each.

In a large frying pan, fry the meatballs until a deep golden color. Remove meatballs from the oil and reserve.

Drain the frying oil from the pan. Add the extra virgin olive oil to the pan over medium heat. Add the potatoes and the onions to the pan and sauté 4-5 minutes. Add the wine and continue cooking until the potatoes are almost done. Return the meatballs to the pan and cook together until the potatoes are done. Serve with lots of crusty Italian Bread.

Variation #1: Try using ground chicken or turkey instead of the beef when making the meatballs.

Variation #2: When you start cooking the potatoes and onions, add 2-3 anchovy filets to the pan.

Variation #3 Instead of meatballs, use 1 ½ pounds of Italian Sausage cut into bite size pieces.

Variation #4: use hot sausage and kick it up a notch.

Let's talk about wine: If using beef you can choose a nice deep red such as **Montresor Amarone Brevettata**. Chicken meatballs would still pair well with a red but lighter such as **Villa Maffei Valpolicella** or **Valpolicella Rio Albo, Ca' Rugate**. Also consider **Vecchia Cantina Vino Nobile** or Chianti such as **Da Vince** or **Trecciano Chianti Senesi**

Arborio Rice (Risotto)

1 tablespoon extra virgin olive oil
4 ounces unsalted butter
1 small yellow onion, chopped
1 tablespoon garlic, chopped
16 ounces Arborio rice
6 ounces white wine
24 ounces or more of low sodium chicken stock
Sea salt to taste
Ground black pepper to taste
1 tablespoon fresh basil, chopped

In a large sauce pot over medium heat, add the oil and unsalted butter. As soon as the butter has melted, add the onions and sweat until translucent. Add the garlic and cook until aromatic. Add the Arborio rice and sauté for one minute to coat the rice. Add the wine to the pot. Stir the rice until wine has absorbed.

Begin to add the chicken stock to the rice, a bit at a time, stirring constantly. Continue to add the stock until the risotto begins to take on a creamy consistency. Once most of the stock has evaporated and the risotto is tender, but not mushy, add some Romano cheese, and adjust flavor with the salt and pepper. Add some fresh chopped basil, and some more Romano cheese on the side.

Variation #1: Just before serving, add ½ pound cooked medium shrimp and 2 tablespoons chopped scallions.

Variation #2: Halfway through the cooking, add 1 pound par cooked asparagus.

Variation #3: Just before serving, add 1 pound of sliced mushrooms that have been sautéed until soft in 1 tablespoon of extra virgin olive oil and 1 tablespoon of unsalted butter.

Variation #4: Just before serving, add the meat from 2 Italian sausages (sweet, hot, or parsley cheese) that have been removed from their casings and fried in 2 tablespoons of extra virgin olive oil.

Variation #5: For red risotto, use a dry red wine instead of a white at the beginning of the cooking.

Variation #6: Half way through the cooking, add one head of par cooked broccoli to the pan and continue cooking.

Variation #7: Half way through the cooking, add the florets from one small head of cauliflower to the pan and continue cooking.

Variation #8: Just before serving, crumble ¼ cup gorgonzola cheese or feta cheese into the rice and serve.

Variation #9: About half way through the cooking, add the kernels and milk from one ear of fresh corn to the mixture and continue cooking.

Variation#10: Just before serving, add the zest from one lemon.

Variation #11: In a separate pan, fry ¼pound pancetta cut into small chunks until just slightly crisp. Add the pancetta and the rendered fat to the risotto.

The variations for flavor additions to the basic risotto recipe are almost limitless. Use your imagination but remember that you just want to add a condiment to compliment the rice, not overpower it. You may make some mistakes in the beginning, but we are sure this will become one of your favorite dishes or sides.

Let's talk about wine: As you can see from the 11 variations of risotto offered here and the discussion that the additional are almost limitless, it would be imposable to offer specific wine suggestions for so many dishes. Keep in mind as you choose a wine for your risotto; match the intensity of the wine with the intensity of the dish. Light buttery risottos will call for lighter wines like **Pinot Grigio** or **Orvieto.** Rich risottos can handle rich wines like **Brunello** or **Nero de Avola**. Those in between, will take to wines in between.

Chapter 8:

Classic And Not So Classic Italian Section II

1. **Let's Talk About Pasta!**

2. **Penne with 3 Cheeses**

3. **Bucatini Putanesca**

4. **Angel Hair with Cauliflower**

   And 1 variation

5. **Linguini with Marinara Sauce**

   And 2 variations

6. **Gemelli with Fresh Cherry Tomato Sauce**

7. **Thin Spaghetti (#8) with Garlic and Oil**

   And 7 variations

8. **Fettuccine alla Carbonara**

   And 1 variation

9. **Gnocchi in Butter Sauce**

10. **Penne with Sausage and Cream**

    And 2 variations

11. **Ditalini with Peas**

    And 1 variation

12. **Tagliatelle with Mushrooms**

13. **Cavatelli with Sausage and Broccoli Rabe**

    And 5 variations

14. **Tortellini in Brodo**

15. **Linguine with Shrimp and Radicchio**

16. **Fusilli all'amatriciana**

17. **Spaghetti with Five Onions**

    And 3 variations

18. **Cavatelli with Pesto Genovese**

19. **Orecchiette with Prosciutto and Mushrooms**

    And 2 variations

20. **Goat Cheese Sacchetti with Herbs, Chicken & Garlic Broth**

21. **Spicy Capellini**

    And 1 variation

22. **Pappardelli with Chicken & Mushrooms**

23. **Vermicelli with Clams**

    And 2 variations

24. **Broken Thin Spaghetti with Cannellini Beans**

    And 2 variations

25. **Orzo with Lemon Butter Shrimp**

26. **Flaked Sole Over Spaghetti**

27. **Fusilli ala Limone**

28. **Bucatini BLT**

29. **Taglitelle Bolognese for Four**

Part II: Let's Talk about Pasta

No meal in Italy, with the exception of perhaps breakfast would be complete without some sort of pasta dish as one of the courses.

As most of us have noticed, there are so many sizes and shapes of pasta. Why all the different shapes? Believe it or not, the shape of pasta has a purpose. Each shape enhances the taste of the sauce used, and therefore the whole eating experience. We have suggested as many shapes of pasta as we could and offer them with the knowledge that they can be purchased dried, fresh, or frozen in most communities.

For this section on pasta, we have chosen recipes in which the sauces can be prepared in the time it takes to boil the water to cook the pasta. Also, remember to salt your pasta water, and always cook the pasta al dente (slightly firm to the tooth).

The recipes in this section are designed to make enough sauce to accommodate one pound of pasta. Remember the sauce is a condiment and not intended to drown the pasta. If you would like to make more or less than what the recipe calls for, you can adjust the recipes accordingly.

Also remember, you should reserve 1 cup of the cooking water for use should you feel that the sauce is too thick once mixed with the pasta. You can add a little water at a time until you have the desired consistency. Since the cooking water has salt in it, be careful with the amount of salt you add to the sauces.

In addition, pay careful attention to the sauces that include grated cheese in them, or are served with grated cheese. These recipes will have the additional saltiness from the cheese. As for the grated cheese itself, the types used will depend on the region of Italy that inspires the dish. In the north, the king is Parmesan, and in the south, Romano. Feel free to use these, or one of the other great grating cheeses from Italy, depending on your taste.

As for the dishes that contain seafood, you will notice that we have not included cheeses in the preparation or as a garnish. No, we did not forget. As general rule of thumb, cheese is not served in or with a seafood sauce in Italy. However, I do, on occasion, add grated cheese to seafood. Feel free to do what you like regarding the grated cheese. But if you are in Italy please don't ask for cheese with seafood

One last comment about eating pasta NEVER---NEVER use a fork and spoon when eating any type of long pasta. Rolling the pasta into a ball in a spoon is strictly American. You scoop a few strands of the pasta holding you fork on its side. Move down the strands and scoop a second time. This should be enough. A little slurping is ok.

Enjoy your journey through pasta.

Penne with 3 Cheeses

1 pound Penne pasta, cooked al dente
1 pound ricotta
½ pound mozzarella, cut into small cubes
¾ cup ground Romano or Parmesan
Sea salt to taste
Fresh ground black pepper to taste

After cooking the pasta, add the three cheeses to the pasta in a large bowl and mix well. Add the black pepper to taste. Add pasta water as necessary and adjust the flavor with salt.

Let's talk about wine: Because of the richness and creaminess of the sauce, wines with a crisp clean taste are best. Try wines such as **Kaila Grillo Inzolia Sicilia**, **Kings Estate Pinot Gris**, **Barone Fini Pinot Grigio**, **Robert Mondavi Fume Blanc**, **Adler Fels Sauvignon Blanc** or **Veramonte Sauvignon Blanc.**

Bucatini Putanesca

1 pound Bucatini pasta, cooked al dente
4 tablespoons extra virgin olive oil
8 cloves garlic, sliced thin
8 anchovy filets, chopped
2-28ounce cans San Marzano plum tomatoes, hand crushed
1 cup Gaeta or Calamata olives cut in half
4 tablespoons capers
½ cup hearty red wine
Sea salt to taste
Ground black pepper to taste
Crushed red pepper for garnish

In a large sauté pan, over medium high heat, add the olive oil. Add the garlic and sauté until a light golden color. Add the anchovies and allow them to dissolve in the oil. Add the tomatoes, olives, capers and wine. Bring to a simmer.

Toss the sauce with the al dente pasta. Adjust flavor with fresh black pepper and possibly a pinch of salt (check the flavor before adding salt). Serve with cracked red pepper as garnish.

Let's talk about wine: Use the wine you choose to drink with the dish as the wine you add during preparation. This is a rich tomato sauce that deserves a rich wine. **Duckhorn Merlot Napa, Earthquake Zin, Napa Wine Company Zin, Montresor Valpolicella Repassa, Zenato Amarone** . ½ cup is a small amount and you may not want to use one of these expensive wines to add. Please remember to add a wine that you would enjoy drinking with the dish. Never add a cheap or inferior wine because that will give you an inferior dish.

Angel Hair with Cauliflower

This is one of my favorite—my son and I could eat the entire portion described below with crusty Italian Bread.

1 pound Angel Hair pasta, cooked al dente
1 head cauliflower, cut into small florets
1 large sweet onion, coarsely chop

6 cloves garlic, sliced thin
4 tablespoons extra virgin olive oil
1 cup dry white wine
½ cup chicken stock
10-15 grinds of fresh black pepper
1 teaspoon sea salt
Extra virgin olive oil to finish
Crushed red pepper as garnish
or
Pickled hot cherry peppers, sliced thin as garnish

In a large pot, over medium high heat, add the olive oil and sauté the onions until wilted. Add the garlic and sauté an additional minute or until garlic is a light golden color. Add the cauliflower florets and toss well. Add the wine, reduce by half and then add the chicken stock. Cook covered until the cauliflower is broken down and well cooked. Adjust the flavor with salt and pepper. Cook pasta al dente. Combine the pasta and cauliflower in a large bowl, and drizzle with a good quality extra virgin olive oil. Toss well and serve with the garnishes.

Variation #1: Use broccoli instead of cauliflower.

Let's talk about wine: This dish has some intense flavors because of the cauliflower and tons of garlic and onions and can pair easily with a white burgundy such as a **Macon Villages,** a *rose* such as **Saladire Rose** or a light red such as the **Bolla or Montresor Valpolicella.**

Linguini with Marinara Sauce

This was a great meatless Friday (remember those days) pasta at home and I never got it right until I watched my mother cook it. I couldn't believe that everything went directly into the tomatoes.

1 pound Linguini
½ cup extra virgin olive oil
10 cloves garlic, coarsely chopped
1 cup southern Italian white wine
3-28 ounce cans San Marzano plum tomatoes, hand crushed

8 ounces tomato paste
¾ cup flat leaf parsley, coarsely chopped
1 teaspoon sea salt
Ground black pepper to taste
Cracked red pepper for garnish

In a large saucepot, over medium high heat, add the oil. Add the garlic, and cook until light golden in color. Add the wine, reduce by half, and then add the plum tomatoes, tomato paste, parsley, basil, salt and pepper. Bring sauce to a boil, and then simmer for about 15 minutes. Cook pasta al dente. Toss pasta with a generous amount of sauce. Serve with cracked red pepper as a garnish.

Variation #1: Cracked red pepper is used as a garnish and adds a speck of heat here and there as you eat. For a more aggressive "heat", add 1 teaspoon of cracked red pepper at the beginning of the sauce cooking preparation.

Variation #2: Add 3-4 anchovy filets to the sauce.

Let's talk about wine: Of course we would just bring up a gallon of wine from the cellar but you can use one of the suggested wines that include: **Citra Montepulciano d'Abruzzo**; **San Andrea Chianti Reserva**; **Palazzo Red Blend**; **Sobon Rocky Top Zin**; **St. Francis Red Blend**.

Gemelli with Fresh Cherry Tomato Sauce

1pound Gemelli pasta
1+ pounds cherry or pear tomatoes
1 small sweet onion, finely chopped
2 cloves garlic, minced
2-3 teaspoons fresh basil or 1 tablespoon dried
Fresh ground pepper to taste
½ teaspoon sea salt or more to taste
½ cup extra virgin olive oil
½ cu shaved ricotta salata cheese

Combine in a non-reactive bowl, the tomatoes, onions, garlic, basil, salt, pepper, olive oil, and ricotta salata. Allow the tomatoes to macerate at room temperature for 1-2 hours. Cook the pasta in salted water until it is al dente. Reserve one cup of the pasta cooking water. Strain the pasta, and add to the tomato mixture. If it seems too dry, add some additional olive oil and/or some of the reserved cooking water from the pasta.

Serve immediately with a sprinkle of Pecorino Romano cheese, or chill in the refrigerator and serve as a cold pasta salad.

Let's talk about wine: Although this dish has tomatoes in it, really calls for a light wine such as **Botter Dry Prosecco**, **Villa Lanata Moscato d'Asti**; **Nobilus Vinho Verde.** If you wanted to go a little richer try a full bodied chardonnay such as **Lloyd** or **Newton Unfiltered**

Thin Spaghetti with Garlic and Oil

It doesn't get much better than this---

1 pound thin Spaghetti
¾ cup extra virgin olive oil
10 cloves garlic, cut in slivers
6 anchovy filets, coarsely chopped
¼ cup flat leaf parsley
Sea salt to taste
Fresh ground black pepper to taste

In a pan over low heat, add the oil. Add the garlic to the oil, and simmer gently until the garlic is a light golden color (careful not to overcook the garlic). Cook pasta to al dente. Reserve some pasta water for the dish. Strain pasta and pour spaghetti into the olive oil mix and toss well. Sprinkle on the parsley. Add pasta water if necessary. Serve with cracked red pepper and grated cheese as a garnish.

Variation #1: After blending in the garlic, mix in one 28 ounce can hand crushed Italian tomatoes, (uncooked) blend again and serve as above.

Variation #2: Along with the garlic, sauté 1 thinly sliced yellow onion. Then, serve as above.

Variation #3: Along with the garlic, add one coarsely chopped can of anchovies in olive oil. Blend and serve as above without the cheese.

Variation #4: After blending in the garlic and oil, sprinkle the top with plain toasted bread crumbs. Serve.

Variation #5: A combination of variations 2 & 3 and serve.

Variation #6: To the sautéed garlic, add one can chopped anchovies, ½ cup dry plain breadcrumbs and ½ cup Romano cheese. Sauté until golden and serve over the pasta.

Variation #7: After preparing any of the above variations, add some blanched, fresh French cut string beans and blend again and serve.

Let's talk about wine: Rather than repeat, we suggest you look back at the suggestions for recipe #3 this section. But also remember that at home the wine on the table would have been the one from the barrel in the basement so feel free to go with an Italian red such as lo **Zaccalaro Barbara d' Alba** or the **Macchia Barbara** from California.

Fettuccine alla Carbonara

1 pound Fettuccine pasta
4 ounces pancetta, sliced very thin and julienne
4 tablespoons extra virgin olive oil
4 ounces unsalted butter at room temperature
1 shallot, minced
1 clove garlic, minced
3 egg yolks
¼ cup heavy cream
½ cup (or more) grated cheese

Cook pasta al dente. In a small pan, over medium heat, add the olive oil. Add the pancetta and simmer until crisp. Add the garlic and onion and simmer slowly until translucent. Remove from heat.

In a large bowl, place the hot cooked pasta. Add the pancetta, garlic, and onion mixture and toss well. Fold the butter into the pasta in small batches. Make a "nest" in the center of the pasta. Add the egg yolks. Toss the pasta, coating it with the yolks. Add the heavy cream. Add the cheese

and toss again. Add pasta water as necessary. Serve with ground pepper as garnish.

Let's talk about wine: With the richness of this dish you will want to choose a rich wine such as **Albrecht Gewürztraminer** or **Sparr Pinot Blanc**. Also try **Amici Sauvignon Blanc; Alder Fels Sauvignon Blanc** or one of the white burgundies of **Javillier Bourgogne.**

Gnocchi in a Brown Butter Sauce

1 pound Gnocchi
2 tablespoons extra virgin oil
¼ pound unsalted butter
2 cloves garlic, whole
1/8 teaspoon nutmeg
¼ cup flat leaf parsley

To a pot with boiling water, add the gnocchi. When the gnocchi floats to the top of the pasta water, that means the gnocchi are most likely done. Drain and reserve.

In a sauté pan, over medium heat, melt the butter in the olive oil. Add the cloves of garlic to the oil mixture and simmer until a light golden color. Add the cooked gnocchi to the olive oil blend; toss and continue to cook the gnocchi until they start to brown, and you notice a "nutty" aroma start to emerge. Add the nutmeg and parsley. Toss the gnocchi one final time and serve with grated cheese.

Let talk about wine: For Christmas Day dinner 2010, I (Nick) paired this dish with the **Montaudon Classe M** and it was beyond wonderful. So, I guess I will stop here.

Penne with Sausage and Cream

½ pound Penne pasta
12 ounces of sweet Italian sausage, removed from the casing and crumbled
2 tablespoons extra virgin olive oil
1 small yellow onion, minced
2 cloves garlic, minced

¼ cup dry white wine
½ cup half-and-half
½ cup grated cheese
Ground black pepper to taste
Grated cheese for garnish

In a pan, heat the olive oil and render the sausage until done. Add the onion and garlic and cook an additional minute or two, or until the onion becomes translucent. Add the wine and reduced by half. Add the heavy cream and grated cheese. Stirring constantly, allow the cream to simmer until it starts to slightly thicken.

Cook the pasta to al dente. Add the pasta and some fresh ground black pepper and blend well. Serve with additional grated cheese.

Variation #1: To the sautéed sausage, garlic and onion, add one bunch of torn Swiss chard, leafy part only; cook until tender and proceed with the rest of the recipe.

Variation #2: Use small shells as the pasta and delete the half and half.

Let's talk about wine: For this dish, we offer you three great wines to consider: **Baron De Brane Margaux** (decant 3-5 hours before drinking); **Pahlmeyer Red** (decant 3-5 hours before drinking); or **Caymus Special Select** (decant 3-5 hours before drinking). Yes, I realize that these are all "high end" expensive wines, but once in awhile, we should really treat ourselves. And they would pair with this like no other wines.

Rotini with Peas

1 pound Rotini pasta
4 tablespoons extra virgin olive oil
4 ounces pancetta, sliced thin and julienne
1 small yellow onion, minced
6 cloves garlic, minced
½ cup dry white wine
2 cups frozen peas
Sea salt to taste
Ground black pepper to taste
Grated cheese to taste

In a pan, over medium high heat, add the olive oil. Add the pancetta and cook until crispy. Add the onion and cook until tender. Add the garlic and cook an additional minute. Add the wine, reduce by half, then, add the peas and cook until the peas are tender.

Cook rotini pasta until al dente, reserving some of the water. Add the rotini to the pan, season with salt and pepper. Add reserved pasta water as necessary. Mix with some grated cheese and serve.

Variation#1: Once the pasta is cooked and mixed with the peas, place some of the reserved pasta water in a separate saucepot. Bring the pasta water to a simmer and crack 6 eggs into the simmering water. Cook the eggs until the eggs are just done and the yolks are still soft. Remove with a slotted spoon and serve over the pasta.

Let's talk about wine: The ADD and PAIR suggestions for this dish include: **River Road Chardonnay Sonoma**, **Edna Valley Chardonnay**, **Courtney Benham Napa Valley Sauvignon Blanc**, **Conte Fini Pinot Grigio.**

Tagliatelle with Mushrooms

½ pound Tagliatelle pasta
3 tablespoons extra virgin olive oil
½ pound Crimini mushrooms, sliced thin
½ pound button mushrooms, sliced thin
1 small yellow onion, sliced thin
3 cloves garlic, sliced thin
1teaspoon fresh oregano, chopped
1 tablespoon fresh basil, chopped fine
¼ cup dry white wine
¼ cup heavy cream
Sea salt to taste
Ground black pepper to taste
Grated cheese for garnish

Cook pasta al dente, reserving some of the water. Drain and reserve.

In a sauté pan, over medium high heat, add the olive oil. Add the onion and garlic and sauté until translucent. Increase the heat and add the mushrooms. Sear the mushrooms until tender, and the water from them has evaporated. Add the white wine and reduce by half. Reduce heat to medium. Add the heavy cream and grated cheese, stirring continuously until the sauce starts to thicken. Add the oregano, basil and the pasta to the pan. Season the pasta with salt and pepper. Add pasta water as necessary. Toss until well incorporated. Serve with grated cheese on the side.

Let's talk about wine: Once again, with this dish wine to ADD is also wine to PAIR. A *California merlot* would go well with this dish. Try **Blackstone**, **Coastline**, **Columbia Crest Two Vines** or **Angeline.** Don't hesitate to use a full bodied *Pinot Noir* such as **Argyle** or **Etude** or **Muirwood Reserve**. A very nice high end wine to pair with this dish might be **Goldeneye by Duckhorn.**

Cavatelli with Sausage and Broccoli Rabe

1pound Cavatelli
2 tablespoons extra virgin olive oil
12 ounces sweet Italian sausage (hot is ok too),
  removed from the casing and crumbled
4 cloves garlic, sliced thin
1 small yellow onion, sliced thin
¼ cup dry white wine
1 pound broccoli Rabe
1 pound Cavatelli
Sea salt to taste
Ground black pepper to taste
Crushed red pepper for garnish
Grated cheese as garnish

Wash the broccoli Rabe and discard the bottom ends (about 1 inch). Cut into bite size pieces. Bring a saucepot filled with water to a boil. Add a bit of salt to the water. Place the broccoli Rabe in the water, and "blanch" for 2-3 minutes, or until tender. Immediately, remove the broccoli Rabe from the boiling water, and plunge into an ice

bath. Remove the broccoli from the water when cool and drain well.

Cook pasta al dente, reserving some of the water. In a pan, over medium high heat, add the olive oil. Add the sausage and cook until brown throughout. Add the onion and garlic and continue to cook until tender. Add the broccoli Rabe and the wine and cook until heated through. Add the pasta to the pan, season with salt and pepper. Toss until well incorporated. Serve crushed red pepper and grated cheese as garnish.

Variation #1: Use one large head of radicchio (leaves separated and torn into large pieces) instead of the broccoli Rabe.

Variation #2: Use one large bunch of arugula (leaves separated) instead of the broccoli Rabe.

Variation # 3: Use one large bunch of dandelions instead of the broccoli Rabe.

Variation #4: Use a combination of the above bitter greens in the preparation.

Variation #5: In any of the above variations, add a few of chopped anchovies when you cook the onions and garlic.

Let's talk about wine: Here we are talking about bitter greens and the more you add the more bitter the dish is. A wine with a very slight sweetness would go well to offset the bitterness: **Mulderbosch Chenin Blanc** or **Beringer Chenin Blanc** would go well. The **Sparr Pinot Blanc** from Alsace is great as is the **Hans Schuler Riesling**.

Tortellini in Brodo

Cook the tortellini directly in about 6 cups of good quality chicken stock. I like to use the stock from my chicken soup recipe.

Serve in a soup bowl along with the cooking liquid. Provide fresh ground black pepper, grated cheese, flat leaf parsley and chopped scallions as garnishes.

Let's talk about wine: For this dish lighter is better the **Bolla or Bellini Sauvé** are two that would fill the bill, as would the **Nobilus Vinho Verde.**

Linguine with Shrimp and Radicchio

1 pound Linguini
4 tablespoons extra virgin olive oil
2 shallots, minced
4 cloves garlic, minced
1 cup dry white wine
½ pound large shrimp, 16/20 size, peeled and deveined, tail removed
2 tablespoons unsalted butter
1 head radicchio, sliced thin
Sea salt to taste
Ground black pepper to taste
Crushed red pepper for garnish

In a pan, over medium high heat, add the olive oil. Add the shrimp and sauté one minute; turn the shrimp over and add the shallots and garlic and sauté until tender and the shrimp are opaque. Add the wine to the pan and reduce by half. Add the butter and the radicchio and cook until the radicchio is just wilted.

Cook the pasta and drain, reserving a little of the pasta water if needed. Add the pasta to the pan. Season with salt and pepper and toss well. Serve with crushed red pepper on the side.

Let's talk about wine: While we suggest adding a dry white such as the **Barone Fini Pinot Grigio** to the dish during preparation, you might consider serving a red as a pairing wine. You can certainly serve the ADD wine but you also might consider a nice *Valpolicella* such as the **Masi** or **Montresor.**

Fusilli all'amatriciana

1 pound Fusilli pasta
3 tablespoons extra virgin olive oil
4 ounces pancetta, cut into small cubes
1 medium yellow onion, minced
3 cloves garlic, sliced thin
1/3 cup red wine
1-28ounce can San Marzano tomatoes, hand crushed
4 ounces tomato paste
Sea salt to taste
½ teaspoon fresh ground black pepper
1teaspoon crushed red pepper
Grated cheese as garnish

In a pan, over medium high heat, render the pancetta in the olive oil until crisp. Add the onion and cook until tender. Add the garlic and cook an additional minute (careful not to overcook the garlic). Add the wine, tomatoes, tomato paste and blend well. Add the black pepper and red pepper flakes, and allow the sauce to simmer a few minutes.

Cook pasta al dente, reserving some of the water. Mix the sauce with the cooked pasta. Toss until well incorporated. Add pasta water if necessary. Serve with grated cheese.

Let's talk about wine: Depending on the amount of hot pepper you use and when you add it, you can choose a wine to compliment the spiciness of the dish. You can choose a hearty red to ADD or PAIR with this dish: **Vasco Sassetti IL Ginepro Sangiovese; Arcordini Valpolicella.** Another excellent Italian red for this dish would be the **Masi Amarone** or the **Nipozzano Chianti Rufina Reserva.**

Spaghetti with Five Onions

1 pound Spaghetti
4 tablespoons extra virgin olive oil
1 Vidalia onion, sliced thin
1 red onion, sliced thin
1 yellow onion, sliced thin
1 white onion, sliced thin

8 scallions, sliced thin on the bias
1 cup dry white wine
Sea salt to taste
Ground black pepper to taste
Grated cheese for garnish

Cook pasta al dente, reserving some of the water. Cook the all the onions except the scallions in the olive oil over medium heat. Cook until tender. Add the scallions and the wine and cook until almost all the wine has evaporated. Blend with the cooked pasta. Add pasta water as necessary. Adjust the flavor with the salt and pepper and serve.

Variation #1: Add ½ cup of assorted sliced green and black olives to the dish.

Variation #2: Add 3-4 chopped anchovy filets to the dish.

Variation #3: Combine variations 1 and 2.

Let's talk about wine: A rich white burgundy such as the **Louis Latour Chablis or Macon Villages** would pair well with this dish. If you serve the dish with some hot cracked red pepper, you could move to the **Dr. Heidemanns Kabinett or Spatlese.** You might also celebrate with the **Nino Franco Brut Prosecco.**

Capellini with Pesto Genovese

1 pound Capellini pasta
2 cups packed fresh basil leaves
1/3 cup pine nuts
2 cloves garlic, minced
1 ½ cups grated cheese
½ cup extra virgin olive oil
Sea salt to taste
Ground black pepper to taste

In a blender or food processor, place the basil, pine nuts, and garlic and blend until coarsely chopped. Add the cheese and blend 10 seconds more. Drizzle in the olive oil as your continue to blend the mixture. Adjust flavor with the salt and pepper.

Cook the pasta until al dente, reserving some of the pasta water. Toss pesto with the cooked pasta until well incorporated. Add pasta water as necessary.

Let's talk about wine: The great floral nature of the basil in the pesto would pair well with a *Viognier* such as the **Bridgeman**, or **Gasser.** Also, a nice crisp *Sauvignon Blanc* from New Zealand would add much to the character of the dish. Try: **Kim Crawford, Nobilo, Cottesbrook,** *The Crossings.*

Orecchiette with Prosciutto and Mushrooms

1 pound Orecchiette
4 ounces of prosciutto, cut into julienne slices
3 tablespoons extra virgin olive oil
1 small onion, minced
1 clove garlic, minced
8 ounces crimini mushroom, sliced thin
¼ teaspoon fresh oregano, chopped
1 tablespoon fresh basil, chopped
¼ teaspoon fresh thyme, chopped
½ cup dry white wine
Sea salt to taste
Ground black pepper to taste
Grated cheese as a garnish

Cook the pasta until al dente, reserving some of the water. Render the prosciutto in the olive oil until cooked about half way, but not crispy. Remove the prosciutto and set aside.

Add the onion and cook until translucent. Add the garlic and cook an additional 30 seconds. Add the mushrooms and cook for another 3-4 minutes. Deglaze the pan with the wine and return the prosciutto to the pan; cook until the mushrooms are tender. Add the fresh herbs and adjust the flavor with salt and pepper. Add the pasta to the pan and toss well to incorporate. Add pasta water as necessary. Serve.

Variation #1: Use one of your favorite Italian cured meats, (sweet or hot) instead of the prosciutto.

Variation #2: When frying the onions, add 3-4 chopped anchovy filets.

Let's talk about wine: For the ADD/PAIR selections, we offer the same suggestions as with pasta dish #11 in this section.

Goat Cheese Sacchetti* with Herbed Chicken and Garlic Broth

Chicken:

2 pounds whole roasting chicken
2 tablespoons olive oil
2tablespoons garlic, chopped
1 tablespoon fresh rosemary, chopped
1 teaspoon fresh basil, chopped
1 teaspoon flat leaf parsley, chopped
Sea salt to taste
Ground black pepper to taste

Recipe ingredients:

1 pound Sacchetti (Pasta Purses)
2 tablespoons extra virgin olive oil
3 tablespoons unsalted butter
1 large shallot, minced
2 cloves garlic, minced
1 ½ cups dry white wine
1 cup low sodium chicken broth
1 cup fresh baby spinach
2-3 tablespoons whole unsalted butter
Sea salt to taste
Ground black pepper to taste

Chicken Preparation:

Wash and pat dry the whole chicken with paper towel. Place chicken in a large mixing bowl. Season with garlic, rosemary, basil, parsley, salt and pepper, and massage the bird. Let bird sit for 30 minutes. Preheat oven to 350°. Place chicken in a baking pan with a drip rack. Place chicken in the oven and cook for one hour. Once chicken is done, remove from oven and allow to cool. Once cool, "pull" the chicken meat away from the bones of the bird and set aside for dish preparation.

Recipe Preparation:

Cook pasta until al dente and set aside. In a pan, over medium high heat, add the olive oil and melt the butter. Add the shallot and garlic and cook for one minute (careful not to overcook the garlic). Add the wine and the chicken stock and reduce by 1/3. Add the pulled chicken, whole butter, spinach and the pasta. Toss until well incorporated, and the spinach is slightly wilted. Serve with grated cheese.

*****Sacchetti:** Also known as a pasta "purse" or "Pouch".

Let's talk about wine: This is the perfect place for a unoaked or very slightly oaked *chardonnay* from California for both the ADD and PAIR wine. Try **Edna Valley**, **Wishing Tree**; **Dominican Oaks**, **River Road Sonoma**, **Mer Soleil Silver**, **Newton Unfiltered**.

Spicy Capellini

½ cup extra virgin olive oil
4 ounces pancetta, sliced thin and julienne
1 large yellow onion, chopped
2 cloves garlic, sliced thin
6 hot pickled cherry peppers, chopped
1-28 oz can San Marzano tomatoes, hand crushed
Sea salt to taste
Ground black pepper to taste
1 pound Capellini
Grated cheese for garnish

In a pan, over medium heat, add the olive oil. Add the onion and garlic and sauté until translucent. Add the cherry peppers and cook an additional minute. Add the hand crushed tomatoes and cook until hot. Adjust flavor with the salt and pepper.

Cook pasta al dente. Add the Capellini and toss. Add pasta water as needed, toss well and serve. Serve with grated cheese as a garnish.

Variation #1: Add 3-4 anchovy filets to the sauce.

Let's talk about beer and wine: The hot peppers will add real heat to this particular dish and for that reason we suggest going with an Italian Beer such as **Birra Moretti** or the **Thai beer: Singha.** If you wanted to go with wine choose a red with a slight sweetness such as **Dr. Heidemanns RED** or **Jam Jar Shiraz**

Pappardelle with Chicken and Mushrooms

1 pound Pappardelle, cooked al dente
3 tablespoons extra virgin olive oil
4 tablespoons unsalted butter
½ pound Crimini mushrooms sliced thin
1 large shallot, sliced thin
3 cloves garlic, sliced thin
1 pound boneless, skinless chicken breast, cut
  into 1 inch chunks
Sea salt to taste
Ground black pepper to taste
1 cup dry masala wine
2 cup veal demi glace or a good brown gravy
1 cup green peas
¼ teaspoon fresh thyme
2 cups fresh baby spinach
2 tablespoons unsalted butter
Grated cheese

In a pan, over medium heat, add the olive oil and the butter. Add the chicken and sauté, browning all sides. Remove chicken from the pan and set aside. In the same pan, with the reserved oil still remaining, add the mushrooms and sauté until tender. Add the shallots and garlic and continue to sauté until the garlic starts to become golden in color. Immediately, return chicken to the pan, and add the masala to "deglaze" the pan. Reduce the masala by half, then add the veal demi glace. Reduce heat to low; bring pan to a simmer.

Cook pasta al dente, reserving some of the water. Add the unsalted butter, peas, and spinach. Incorporate quickly, and then add the pasta

and heat through. Season the pan with salt and pepper. Add a bit of pasta water if needed. Serve with the grated cheese.

Variation #1: Add 2 seeded and sliced sweet or hot cherry peppers to the sauce.

Let's talk about wine: For your ADD wine we suggest a *Pinot Grigio* such as **Bella Sera** or **Conti Priola** which can also be served as the PAIR wine for the dish. If you choose a different PAIR wine you might want to move up to a higher end *Pinot Grigio* such as **Kupelwieser, Santa Margarita** or **Barone Fini.**

Vermicelli with Clams

1 pound Vermicelli, cooked al dente
3 dozen small little neck clams
1 cup extra virgin olive oil
1 small yellow onion, chopped
2 cloves garlic, chopped
1 teaspoon sea salt
1 tablespoon fresh ground black pepper
1 tablespoon crushed red pepper flakes
1 cup dry white wine
½ cup fresh flat leaf parsley chopped

In a large covered pot, add the olive oil and heat. Add the onions and garlic and cook until tender. Add the salt, pepper, red pepper, parsley and wine. Bring to a boil. Add the clams and cover. Cook for 3-5 minutes until the clams open. Cook pasta al dente. Discard any clams that do not open. Toss with the pasta and serve.

Variation #1: After adding the wine, add one 28 ounce can of Italian tomatoes; hand crushed and cook 2-3 minutes before adding the clams.

Variation #2: Use mussels instead of clams in either of the above.

Let's talk about wine: If serving the clam sauce "white" then you can stay with the white wines suggested in the last recipe such as **Barone Fini Pinot Grigio** or **Alder Fels Sauvignon Blanc**. If you are adding tomatoes and serving it "red" then a light *Valpolicella* such as the **Arcordini** or **Montresor** would be great to pair with the dish.

Broken Thin Spaghetti with Cannellini Beans

OK, this is one of the few times I will allow you to break the spaghetti, only because this is the way my mother prepared the dish. The only other time spaghetti was broken in our home was for the "noodles" in homemade chicken soup and when making peas and macaroni.

1 pound thin Spaghetti, broken in thirds and cooked al dente
1 small yellow onion, minced
2 cloves garlic, minced
3 tablespoons extra virgin olive oil
2-28 oz cans Italian tomato puree
1-28 ounce can water
16 ounces cannellini beans
Sea salt to taste
Ground black pepper to taste
Cracked red pepper as garnish
Grated cheese as garnish

Cook pasta until al dente and set aside. In a pan, combine the onion and garlic and sauté 1-2 minutes (careful not to overcook the garlic). Add the tomato puree and water. Bring to a simmer and cook for 10 minutes. (The sauce should be thin like a soup). Add the beans and heat through. Add the cooked pasta and serve in soup bowls with cracked red pepper and grated cheese as garnishes.

Variation #1: Instead of cannellini beans, use garbanzo beans.

Variation #2: Instead of cannellini beans, use French string beans.

Let's talk about wine: This really is a lighter dish and served almost as a soup (Pasta Fagole) Pair this dish with a wine such as: **Tenuta di Trecciano Chianti**, **Vasco Sassetti Il Ginepro**, **Citra Montepulciano**, or one of the many great **Nero d'Avola** wines from Sicily.

Orzo with Lemon/Butter Shrimp

1 pound Orzo, cooked al dente
1 tablespoon extra virgin olive oil
3 tablespoons unsalted butter
1 small yellow onion, minced
3 cloves garlic, minced
1 pound large shrimp, 13/15 size, cleaned and deveined
½ cup dry white wine
Pasta water as necessary
Sea salt to taste
Ground black pepper to taste
2 tablespoons fresh flat leaf parsley, chopped

Cook pasta until al dente and set aside. In a pan, melt the butter in the olive oil. Add the onions and sauté until soft. Add the garlic and sauté an additional minute (careful not to burn it). Add the shrimp and cook for 1 minute on each side, then immediately deglaze the pan with the white wine. Cook until the shrimp are opaque. Adjust the flavor with salt and pepper. Place the shrimp over the orzo pasta, sprinkle with the parsley and serve.

Let's talk about wine: See below after recipe #26.

Flaked Sole over Spaghetti

1 pound thin Spaghetti, cooked al dente
2 tablespoons extra virgin olive oil
2 tablespoons unsalted butter
Seasoned flour for dusting
2 pounds filet of sole or flounder, pin bones removed
1 clove garlic, minced
½ cup dry white wine
Juice of one lemon
Pasta water as necessary
Sea salt to taste
Ground black pepper to taste

Cook pasta al dente, reserving some of the water. In a pan over medium high heat, melt the butter in the olive oil. Dust the filets lightly in the flour and sauté in the oil/butter. Cook for about 2 minutes on each side. When just about done, add the garlic, cook for 30 seconds, then add the white wine and lemon juice and cook an additional 30 seconds. Flake the filets in the pan, and add the cooked pasta; toss gently. Add pasta water as necessary, adjust the flavor with salt and pepper and serve.

Let's talk about wine: see below after #26

Fusilli alla Limone

1 pound Fusilli, cooked al dente
6 tablespoons extra virgin olive oil
4 cloves garlic, chopped
½ cup dry white wine
½ cup low sodium chicken broth
Grated zest of 2 lemons
Juice of 2 lemons
Sea salt to taste
Ground black pepper to taste

In a pan over medium heat, add the olive oil. Add the garlic and sauté gently for 1 minute. Add the white wine, broth, lemon zest and lemon juice. Add the cooked pasta to the pan and toss well. Cook an additional minute. Add pasta water as necessary. Adjust the flavor with salt and pepper and serve.

Let's Talk about wine: The last three pasta dishes call for a similar selection of wines. All three are light with a hint of lemon in the sauce. We suggest either French or a California style *Sauvignon Blanc* such as: **Chateau Coucheroy Blanc**, **Rothschild Blanc; Ch Montet; Amici Sauvignon Blanc, Courtney Benham Napa, Alder Fels.** All of these wines would compliment any the three dishes as both ADD and PAIR wines and would bring out the full flavors of the dishes.

Bucatini BLT

1 pound Bucatini
3 tablespoons extra virgin olive oil
¼ pound pancetta, cut into ¼ inch chunks
1 small red onion, sliced thin
2 cloves garlic, sliced thin
1 small head radicchio, sliced thin
1-28 ounce can San Marzano tomatoes, hand crushed
3 tablespoons tomato paste
Sea salt to taste
Ground black pepper to taste
Red pepper flakes as garnish
Grated Romano cheese as garnish

In a pan, over medium high heat, add the oil. Add the pancetta and render out the fat until the pancetta is almost crispy. Remove the pancetta and reserve.

Add the onion the pan and sauté until tender. Add the garlic and sauté an additional minute or until the garlic becomes a light golden color. Add the radicchio, and sauté an additional minute. Add the tomatoes, tomato paste and reserved pancetta and blend well. Bring the sauce to a boil, then reduce the heat and simmer the sauce for 10-15 minutes.

Cook the pasta. Once pasta has become al dente, immediately add to the sauce. Toss well to incorporate. Serve with the red pepper flakes and Romano cheese as garnishes.

Let's talk about wine: The lightness of this dish along with the tomato flavors call for a lighter red such as: **Montresor Valpolicella** or a **Werner Krems Red Gruner.** You could even go with a full bodied white such as the **Lloyd Chardonnay** or the **Jason's Chardonnay**.

Tagliatelle with Bolognese Ragu for 4

1½ pounds Tagliatelle
6 tablespoons extra virgin olive oil
½ cup onions, minced
½ cup carrots, minced
½ cup celery, minced
3 garlic cloves, minced
½ pound ground beef
½ pound ground pork
½ pound ground veal
3 tablespoons dry porcini mushrooms, soak in warm water and chop, reserve soaking liquid*
¼ cup porcini juice*
1 cup red wine
1 cup beef stock
2 cups marinara sauce
1 teaspoon fresh rosemary, chopped
1 teaspoon fresh thyme, chopped
2 tablespoons fresh basil, chopped
1 tablespoon fresh Italian parsley, chopped
Sea salt to taste
Ground black pepper to taste
Grated Parmesan for garnish

In a large saucepot, over medium heat, add the olive oil. Add the onions, carrots, and celery and gently sweat the vegetables for about 2 minutes. Do not let the vegetables caramelize. Add the garlic and cook an additional minute.

Add the beef, pork, and veal and begin to brown, smashing the meat with a spoon to keep it from clumping together. Cook until brown throughout. Add the hydrated porcini mushroom, and continue to cook for a few more minutes, evaporating any liquid. Add the red wine and reduce by half. Then, add the porcini juice and beef stock. Simmer for 2 minutes. Add the marinara sauce, rosemary, basil, thyme, and parsley. Adjust the flavor with salt and pepper. Reduce heat and simmer for 30 minutes.

Cook pasta al dente, reserving some of the water. Once pasta is cook to al dente, toss it with a generous amount of the Bolognese along with some Parmesan cheese. Add some reserved pasta water if the dish seems too dry. Serve with grated Parmesan cheese on the side.

Let's talk about wine: Let's bring out the richness and full flavors of the dish with wines such as; **Vasco Sassetti Brunello 2004** (4+ hours to open)**; Paulo Scavino Borolo 2005** (3+ hours to open); **Silver Oak Alexander Valley 2004** (4+ hours to open); **Martin Ray Diamond Mountain 2007**(2+ hours to open)

Chapter 9:

A BRIEF VISIT TO FRANCE

A Brief Visit to France

In a previous chapter, we presented you with many classic and not so classic recipes from the world of Italian cuisine. We would now like to offer you a number of classic and not so classic recipes from another culinary Mecca…France. We hope you enjoy them as much as the Italian recipes.

As you may or may not of figured out, we have devoted an extensive amount of time devoted to Italian, French, and of course, American cuisines for a number of reasons. First and foremost, these countries are some of the largest producers of wine in the world. They offer a vast selection of whites and reds that can be used in both the preparation of food, and with the consumption of food.

Some of the recipes that follow can be considered the foundation to all things culinary. In fact, a French chef and restaurateur, Auguste Escoffier, is credited with creating the modern methods of food preparation as we do today. Therefore, in this chapter, we have included the best of the classic French recipes. Most have been adapted for the modern cook and simplified without sacrificing the nature of the dish or the classic tastes.

Many of the dishes offered are ones you will probably be familiar with, or at least heard of. It may even be a dish you remember seeing Julia Child or some other celebrity chef prepare. Be that as it may, with many classic cuisines, we may know of the dishes, but have never experienced them--- cooked them----or even tasted them.

As for the wines we have suggested to ADD or PAIR, many will be French, but many will be from vineyards around the world. So, let's begin our adventure through France and its classical dishes.

Filet of Sole in Wine with Mushrooms

1 pound small button mushroom, quartered
2 tablespoons unsalted butter
1 tablespoon extra virgin olive oil
2 tablespoons unsalted butter
6 sole filets, 7-8 ounces each, (may substitute flounder or fluke)
Seasoned flour to dredge
¾ cup heavy cream
½ cup dry white wine
1 tablespoon lemon juice
¼ cup grated aged Swiss cheese
2 tablespoons unsalted cold butter
Sea salt to taste
Ground black pepper to taste

In a sauté pan over medium high heat, place the butter and extra virgin olive oil. Sauté the fish filets in the oil until done, about 2 minutes on each side. Remove and reserve the filets on a serving plate.

Place the additional butter in the same pan. Add the mushrooms, season with salt and pepper, and sauté for 5 minutes or until the mushrooms are soft and most of any water has evaporated.

Reduce the heat low and add the wine, reduce by half, then add the cream and the lemon juice. Add the Swiss cheese and allow to melt into the cream. Add the cold butter and adjust the flavor with salt and pepper. Swirl the butter until completely incorporated. Pour the sauce over the fish and serve.

Let's talk about wine: The richness of this dish calls for a crisp white such as the **Salmon Sancerre** or a California *Sauvignon Blanc* such as **Alder Fields**. You could also pair it with an elegant *pinot blanc* from Alsace such as the **Trimbach** . A light red such as the **Georges Dubuef Gamay** would also go well but be careful with any deeper reds as they might overpower the dish.

Coquilles St. Jacques

1 pound medium sea scallops, cleaned of any
  membrane
2 tablespoons unsalted butter
1 shallot, minced
1 tablespoon unsalted butter
1 tablespoon flour
1 cup dry white wine
2 egg yolks, whisked smooth
½ cup heavy cream
1 teaspoon lemon juice
½ cup Swiss cheese
3 tablespoons unsalted butter
Sea salt to taste
Ground black pepper to taste

In a sauté pan over medium high heat, melt
the 2 tablespoons of butter. Season the scallops
with salt and pepper. Wait until pan is good and
hot, and sear the scallops for 1 minute per side.
Remove and reserve.

In the same pan over medium heat, add the
shallot and additional butter and sauté for 30
seconds. Add the flour and cook an additional
minute stirring all the time to make a roux. Add
the wine and continue stirring. Reduce the heat
to low. While whisking, slowly add the cream
and the lemon juice. Add the egg yolks, a bit at a
time and completely incorporate. Cook until the
sauce slightly thickens.

Divide the scallops into 4-6 oven proof small
plates, egg shires, or small casserole dishes. Pour
on the cream mixture, top with Swiss cheese
and dot with butter. Place under a broiler for
1-2 minutes until the cheese melts and begins to
brown. Serve.

Let's talk about Wine: The suggestions for the
previous dish would pair well with this dish also.
In addition, we would suggest wines such as
Conundrum from California. There is a great
Austrian wine that would go very well— **Krems
Gruner Veltliner**. In addition, a little known
wine a **White Cotes du Rhone JV Fleury** would
bring out the richness of the dish.

Tuna Steaks with Herbs de Province

4 Ahi tuna steaks, 8-9 ounces each, cut into ¾
  inch steaks
2 tablespoons extra virgin olive oil
2 tablespoons unsalted butter
1 medium yellow onion, minced
½ cup dry white wine
2 plum tomatoes, split, seeded and coarse chop
1 tablespoon Herbs de Province
2 tablespoons unsalted butter
¼ cup Italian parsley, chopped
Sea salt to taste
Ground black pepper to taste

Season the steaks with salt and pepper. In a pan
over high heat, place the olive oil and butter. Sear
the tuna steaks to a medium rare doneness—
about 3 minutes per side. Remove and reserve to
a serving platter.

To the same pan, over medium heat, add the
onion and sauté until tender. Add the white wine
and reduce by half. Add the tomatoes and herbs
and sauté 2 minutes. Adjust the flavor with salt
and pepper. Reduce the heat and add the last of
the butter. Pour the sauce over the steaks; sprinkle
with the parsley and serve.

Let's talk about wine: The richness and firm
texture of the tuna, calls for a full bodied white
such as *chardonnay* like Lloyd, or the **Newton
Unfiltered.** This dish is so rich that it could also
pair well with a red such as the **Vasco Sassetti
Rosso** or even an elegant Margaux such as the
Chateau Druzac (decant 3-5 hours before
drinking).

Lobster Thermidor

2 lobsters, 1½-2 pounds, steamed or boiled,
  cooled, meat removed and cut into chunks
2 tablespoons extra virgin olive oil
2 tablespoons unsalted butter
1 large yellow onion, minced
1 celery stalk, minced
2 tablespoons Italian parsley, minced
1teaspoon fresh ground black pepper

¼ teaspoon sea salt
1 tablespoon lemon juice
½ cup dry white wine
¼ teaspoon Herbs de Province
2 egg yolks
½ cup heavy cream
1/3 cup cognac
Garnish with chopped chives

Place the lobster meat in individual crock dishes or bowls. In a pan, place the olive oil and butter. Add the onion and celery and cook until tender and translucent, but not brown. Add the parsley, salt and pepper and lemon juice. Add the wine and the herbs. Reduce the heat to low. Reduce the wine by half, and then begin to add the cream to the pan. Whip the eggs and slowly add them to the cream while whisking all the time. Add the cognac. Allow the sauce to thicken a bit. Pour the sauce over the lobster meat and serve. Garnish with some chopped chives.

Let's talk about wine: When looking for a cognac to add, I would use **Hennessey VSOP**. The wonderful and rich lobster dish calls for a sparkler that will compliment the richness and the taste. Try one such as the **Martell Prestige; Thorn Clark Brut; Montaudon Brut Rose** or **Veuve Clicquot** or as the ultimate treat yourself to **Krug Grand Cru**.

Beef Bourguignon

¼ pound lard or bacon fat
1-3 pound chuck roast, cut into 2 inch pieces
3 tablespoons all purpose flour
Sea salt to taste
Ground black pepper to taste
1 teaspoon Herbs de Province
2 cups + dry red wine
½ pound pearl onions, peeled
12 medium size mushroom caps
1/3 cup Italian parsley, chopped
¼ cup French brandy

In a large pot over medium heat, render down the bacon. Once the fat has been rendered, increase the heat to high, place the beef cubes in the pot

and sear on all sides. Sprinkle with the flour, salt and pepper and continue cooking until brown. Add the herbs de provice. Add enough wine to cover the beef. Bring the pot to a simmer and cook covered for about 1 hour.

After one hour of cooking, add the onions and mushroom caps. Cook for another ½ hour to an hour.

Just before serving, flambé the dish with about ¼ cup French brandy (be careful). Sprinkle with parsley and serve.

Let's talk about wine: For this dish, you could use the same wine to add and pair, but use a younger vintage for the add wine. It will be less expensive but still add the full complexity of flavors to the dish. This dish cries for a **Ch. Larsen Haut-Medoc** (5 hours to open) but be careful when choosing one. They will vary in the blend from year to year and you should choose one with a higher percentage of *Cabernet* to bring out the bold flavors of the beef. Think of the **Chateau Tour Saint Joseph 2005** (decant 3-5 hours before drinking), or the **Wine Maker's Collection 2003; 2005** (decant 5-6 hours before drinking). These wonderful wines are produced in the Medoc region. Each year one of the most outstanding winemakers in the world is asked to come and produce/blend the wine. You can't go wrong with any of these wines produced by the greatest.

Bouillabaisse

1 large yellow onion, minced
4 leeks, white part only, cleaned and sliced thin
16 ounces whole plum tomatoes, hand crushed
6 cloves garlic, minced
½ teaspoon saffron
1teaspoon grated lemon zest
1 teaspoon grated orange zest
8 ounces tomato paste
1 stalk celery with leaves, chopped
4 tablespoon Italian parsley, chopped
1 teaspoon fresh ground black pepper

½ teaspoon ground white pepper

½ cup extra virgin olive oil

1 pound fresh fish such as halibut, snapper or cod

½ pound 13/15 size shrimp, cleaned and deveined

4 lobster tails, 4-5 ounces each, split down the center and cleaned

12 littleneck clams, rinsed

12 oysters, rinsed

24 mussels, rinsed

¾ cup dry white wine

¼ cup Pernod*

Water to cover

Sea Salt to taste

In a large pot, over medium heat, add the olive oil. Add the onion and leeks and sauté until tender, but not brown. Add the garlic and sauté an additional minute. Add the saffron, lemon zest, orange zest, tomatoes, tomato paste, celery, parsley, black pepper, white pepper. Stir all together then add the white wine and the Pernod.

Cut the fish into 3 inch pieces, and add to the pot. (Reserve the shrimp, lobster and/or shellfish to add later). Just cover with water and bring to a simmer.

Poach the fish for 5 minutes. Add the shrimp, lobster and the shellfish and poach until the clams and mussels open; another 5-6 minutes. When the shellfish open, adjust the flavor with salt and pepper and serve. Serve with lots of toasted, buttered French bread.

***Note:** Pernod is a French made Anise flavored liqueur.

Let's talk about wine: A "real" *Dornfelder* from Germany like Dr**. Heidemanns Red**, would play with the richness and the fish of this dish. Be very careful about the cheap German "sweet" reds even if they are called *Dornfelder*. These would not pair well. The **Georges Duboeuf Gamay** would also be a nice red to pair with this dish. Because the sauce is so light, a white would be a good choice. Try the **Jean Albrecht Gewürztraminer** or the **Trimbach Pinot Blanc**. If you choose to

increase the spiciness of the dish you might want to go with a wonderful *Chenin Blanc* from South Africa, **Mulderbosch Chenin Blanc** .

Cream of Onion Soup

4 tablespoons unsalted butter

2 large yellow onions, sliced very thin

1 clove garlic, minced

1 ½ tablespoons all purpose flour

2 cups whole milk

2 cups heavy cream

4 egg yolks, beaten

Dash of paprika

½ teaspoon ground white pepper

½ teaspoon Worcestershire Sauce

Chopped Italian parsley for garnish

To a pot over medium heat, add the unsalted butter and the onions and sauté until tender. Add the garlic and sauté an additional minute. Be careful not to brown either the onions or the garlic. Stir in the flour and cook the flour one minute, being careful not to brown. Lower the heat a bit. While stirring slowly, add the milk and then the cream. Simmer at a low heat until the onions are very tender.

Beat the egg yolks in a bowl. Before adding the egg yolks to the soup mixture, add one tablespoon of the soup mixture to the egg yolks to temper the eggs. Continue to add the soup mixture a little at a time to the egg yolks to temper the eggs completely. Then, slowly add the tempered yolks to the soup stirring continuously. Reheat, but do not allow the soup to return to a boil. Add a pinch of paprika, the Worcestershire, and adjust the flavor with salt and pepper. Serve with the flat leaf parsley as garnish.

Let's talk about wine: This is a difficult dish to pair a wine with, but we think a nice *tawny port* such as the **Illaparra 10 year old** or a dry sherry like the **Osborne Fino** would pair well. In addition the **Rondel Brut Cava** would complement the richness of this classic soup.

Vichyssoise

3 medium size leeks, white part only, cleaned and minced
1 large yellow onion, minced
3 tablespoons unsalted butter
3 large potatoes, peeled and sliced thin
1 quart low sodium low fat chicken stock or broth
1 ½ cups heavy cream
1/8 teaspoon ground nutmeg
Sea salt to taste
White pepper to taste

In a pot, over low to medium heat, melt the butter and sauté the leeks and onions until very tender and translucent. Be very careful not to brown them. Add the potatoes and chicken stock and simmer covered for 15 minutes.

Using a hand blender, or working in small batches, puree the contents of the pot in a blender until smooth. Return to another pot on low heat. While stirring, slowly add the cream. Add the nutmeg and adjust the flavor with the salt and white pepper.

May be served hot immediately or refrigerated and served cold. Chopped chives can be used as a garnish.

Let's talk about wine: Another difficult dish to pair, the richness of this dish, as well as the fact that it is served cold, we feel this soup would be complimented by a light wine like a *pinot grigio* such as **Barone Fine Alta** or the **Nobilus Vinho Verde**.

Mussels Mariniere

4 tablespoons unsalted butter
2 tablespoons extra virgin olive oil
1 yellow onion, chopped
2 clove garlic minced
36+ black mussels,* cleaned
2 cups dry red wine**
1 sprig of fresh thyme
1 bay leaf

Fresh Italian flat leaf parsley for garnish

In a large pot over medium heat, melt the butter with the olive oil and sauté the onion until tender and translucent. Add the garlic and sauté an additional 1-2 minutes. Add the mussels, wine, thyme and bay leaf. Stir together. Cover and cook the mussels for 5-10 minutes.

Transfer to a serving dish and discard any unopened mussels. Sprinkle with parsley and serve with plenty of good French bread.

*Note: Mussels from Prince Edward Island are preferred.

**Note: We are calling for a red wine for a dish that most would think would take a white wine. We believe this adds a new dynamic to a classic dish and hope you will try it.

Let's talk about wine: A great wine to add or pair would be the **Chateau Tour de l' Ange**. You could also add/pair other light *pinot noirs* such as **Ropiteau** or **D'Autrefois**.

Stuffed Tomatoes

4 large ripe tomatoes
3 cups bread crumbs from day old French bread
¼ cup whole milk
¼ cup heavy cream
2 large eggs, beaten
1 tablespoon fresh basil, chopped
2 scallions, chopped
1 tablespoon fresh oregano, chopped
1 tablespoons flat leaf parsley, chopped
1 clove garlic, minced
2 shallots, minced
4 tablespoons Swiss cheese
2 tablespoons dry, unseasoned breadcrumbs
Extra virgin olive oil
Sea salt to taste
Ground black pepper to taste

Cut a thin slice off the top end of the tomatoes and scoop out the seeds and the pulp. Season the interior of each with a small amount of salt and pepper. Set aside.

In a bowl, blend together the day old breadcrumbs, the milk and the cream. Add the eggs, basil, scallions, oregano, parsley, garlic and shallots. Season with a little salt and pepper and fold together. Fill each tomato with the bread mixture. Top each with the Swiss cheese and the dry breadcrumbs. Place the stuffed tomatoes in a greased baking dish. Drizzle each tomato with some olive oil and bake in a 350° oven for 30-35 minutes. Serve immediately.

Let's talk about wine: When we discussed this dish, we all thought a full progression of great Rhone blends. Choose one or more of the following: **Cave de Tain Hermitage 2003 or 2005**; **Clos St. Michel Chat-du-Pape 2008**; **Domaine Cigale Chat -du-Pape 2005 or 2007**; **Amadieu Vacqueyras 2007** or the **Amadieu Romane Machotte Gigondas 2006 or 2007**. All of these wines would certainly add to this wonderful appetizer or side dish.

French Meatballs

3 pounds ground chuck
1 pound ground pork
3 large shallots, minced
4 cloves garlic, minced
3 tablespoon flat leaf parsley, minced
1 ½ teaspoon fresh rosemary, minced
2 tablespoon Herbs de Provence
1 tablespoon ground French 4 Spice*
1cup plain dry breadcrumbs
4 eggs, lightly scrambled
1 cup grated Gruyere cheese
1teaspoon fresh ground black pepper
1teaspoon ground white pepper
½ teaspoon salt
Olive oil for frying
Gravy:
4 large shallots, minced
2 cloves garlic, minced
3 tablespoons extra virgin olive oil
1 tablespoon anchovy, chopped
1 bottle red Bordeaux
1 quart beef gravy

1 or more cups low sodium, low fat chicken broth
2 teaspoons Herbs de Provence
½ teaspoon ground French 4 Spice*
1½pound frozen pearl onions
2 pounds button mushrooms, quartered

Combine all the ingredients for the meatballs in a large bowl and mix well. Moisten your hands and begin to roll the mixture into 1-1 ½ inch meatballs. In a pan over medium high heat, cook the meatballs in olive oil until deep brown in color. Set aside.

In a separate pot over medium high heat, make the gravy. Add the olive oil to the pot and sauté the shallots and garlic for one minute. Add the anchovies and sauté until melted. Add the mushrooms; cook until most of the water has evaporated from the mushrooms. Add the wine to the pot, reduce by half, then add the gravy and mix well. Add the Herbs de Provence and French 4 Spice and stir.

Add the cooked meatballs to the gravy. Add additional chicken stock to just cover the meatballs. Bring to a low simmer and cook for one hour, but 2 hours would be better. At thirty minutes, add the pearl onions and continue to simmer. Serve with cooked egg noodles.

*Note: French four spice is a blend of white pepper, clove, ginger and nutmeg.

Let's talk about wine: This is another case where you could choose red Bordeaux to add and pair. If you choose a younger vintage to add to the dish, you will add the necessary flavors and not pay a premium for an older wine. You could then choose an older more "drinkable" vintage (2003, 2005) to pair with the dish. When you serve it remember to decant for 3-5 hours. A San Julian such as **Chateau Gloria** (decant 8-10 hours) might be one to choose. Other Bordeaux you might consider would be **Ch Druzac Margaux 2005** (6+ hours to open) or a great cab from **Napa Balducci Stage Leap 2006** (3-5 hours to open). Also a must try is the **Ch Pipeau St. Emilion 2005 or 2006** (((6 hours to open)

French Beef Stew with Winter Vegetables

2-3 pound boneless chuck roasts, cut into 1 inch pieces
2 cups flour seasoned with salt, ground pepper and 2 teaspoons ground French 4 spice
4 tablespoons extra virgin olive oil
6 large shallots, minced
6 cloves garlic, minced
2 tablespoons anchovies
1 bottle red Bordeaux wine
Beef broth to cover
4 carrots, 1 inch dice
2 large potatoes, 1 inch dice
2 medium turnips, 1 inch dice
1 large rutabaga, 1 inch dice
4 ribs of celery with leaves, sliced thin
2 pounds pearl onions, peeled (or frozen)
2 tablespoons Herbs de Provence
2 tablespoon of a good quality bouquet garni wrapped in cheese cloth
2 pounds frozen peas

Dredge the beef chunks in the seasoned flour. In a large pot over medium high heat, sear the beef in small batches until deep brown in color. Remove and reserve.

In the same pot, reduce the heat to medium and add the shallots and garlic to the pan. Sauté the shallot and garlic for one minute. Deglaze the pot with the wine; make sure to scrape up the brown bits on the bottom of the pan. Bring to a simmer and reduce by 1/3. Return the meat to the pot along with all the other ingredients except the onions and peas. Add enough beef broth to just cover the ingredients. Bring to a simmer and cook for one hour until the meat is cooked and the vegetables are tender.

At 30 minutes into the simmer, add the onions. During the last 5 minutes add the peas. Remove the bouquet garni adjust the flavor with salt and pepper. Serve with cooked egg noodles.

Let's talk about wine: See the discussion after the previous recipe.

Duck with Apricot Glaze

1 duck (4-5 pounds)
1 tablespoon French 4 Spice Powder
2 sprigs Italian parsley
2 sprigs fresh thyme
2 sprigs fresh rosemary
An orange cut into wedges
A lemon cut into wedges
12 ounces apricot preserves
12 ounces of tawny port wine (**Illaparra 10 Year Old**)
12 ounces orange juice
1 tablespoon Dijon mustard
Zest of one lemon
Zest of one orange
Sea salt to taste
Ground black pepper to taste

Wash the duck thoroughly and pat dry with paper towel. Remove the wing at the elbow and discard. Sprinkle the inside and outside of the duck with salt, pepper and the French 4 spice powder. In the cavity of the duck, place the fresh herbs, lemon and orange wedges. Place the duck on a baking pan with a rack and cook for 30-35 minutes at 350°, then for another 25-30 minutes at 400°. While the duck is baking, make the glaze.

In a sauce pan over medium heat, combine the apricot preserve with the wine, orange juice, mustard, lemon zest and orange zest. Bring to a boil and simmer until reduced by at least half. During the last half hour of baking, brush the duck with some of the glaze several times. Serve with the remaining glaze on the side.

Let's talk about wine: A *sauvignon blanc* from New Zealand without a huge grapefruit punch would go well such as the **Hawke's Bay Framingham;** another great white such as the **Nora Albarino** from Spain would pair well with the apricot glaze and richness of the duck.

Tenderloin of Beef Burgundy

4 -5 ounce cuts of beef tenderloin
Cracked black peppercorns, coarsely ground
2 tablespoons canola oil
2 tablespoons unsalted butter
1 large shallot, minced
1 clove garlic, minced
1 ½ cups button mushrooms, sliced
1 teaspoon Herbs de Provence
1 cup merlot
½ cup veal demi glace*
2 tablespoons unsalted butter
Sea salt to taste
Ground black pepper to taste

Lightly salt the tenderloin. Generously coat the tenderloin with the coarsely ground black peppercorns. In a pan over medium high heat, add the oil and melt the butter in it. Add the beef and sear the tenderloin to desired doneness. Remove and let rest while keeping them warm.

To the same pan, reducing the heat to medium, add the mushrooms and sauté for 2-3 minutes. Add the shallots and garlic and cook for an additional minute. Be careful not to burn the garlic. Add the herbs and then the wine, cook until the wine is reduced by half. Add the demi glace to the pan and bring to a simmer. Remove the pan from the heat and add the additional cubes of cold butter, allowing it to melt and become incorporated with the sauce. Adjust the flavor with some salt and pepper and pour the sauce over meat.

*Note: Demi glace is a rich, concentrated stock made from beef and veal bones, vegetables, and tomato paste. Thicken with flour.

Variation #1: Instead of tenderloin, try using a flank steak. Remember, when you slice the meat for serving, you should slice it across the grain of the meat.

Variation #2: When adding the wine to the pan, add 1 tablespoon Dijon mustard.

Let's talk about wine: We all agreed that the best pairing for this dish would be an excellent *merlot*.

Some excellent add/pair *merlots* are **Bridgman**; **Courtney Benham**, **Blackstone**. You might also consider using one of the very good lower end *merlots* as the add wine and then use an upper end *merlot* as the pair wine when serving the dish. Some upper end merlots you might try are: **Duckhorn Estates**; **Twomey**; **Pahlmeyer.**

Herb Crusted Chicken

8 skinless, boneless chicken thighs
2 tablespoons Italian parsley, chopped fine
2 tablespoons fresh tarragon, chopped fine
1teaspoon fresh thyme, chopped fine
1 teaspoon fresh rosemary, chopped fine
2 tablespoon canola oil
2 tablespoon unsalted butter
1 shallot, minced
¾ cup of a dry red wine
1 tablespoon unsalted butter
Sea salt to taste
Ground black pepper to taste

Lightly salt and pepper the chicken thighs. In a bowl, combine the fresh herbs and blend well. Coat the chicken with a thin layer of the herbs, pressing them firmly into the meat.

In a pan over medium high heat, add the oil and melt the butter. Add the chicken and cook until done. Remove and reserve.

To the same pan over medium heat, add the shallot and sauté 30 seconds. Add the wine and cook until reduced by half. Return the chicken to the pan and heat through. Place the chicken on a warm serving platter. Into the pan, swirl the tablespoon of cold butter; adjust the flavor with salt and pepper and serve.

Variation #1: Use boneless, center cut pork chops instead of chicken thighs.

Variation #2: Before adding the wine, add 1 cup of sliced mushrooms; sauté them 2-3 minutes and then proceed with the rest of the recipe.

Let's talk about wine: Here again, we feel a nice

merlot would be an excellent add or pair wine. You might choose from the ones suggested in the last recipe. In addition, we feel that a full bodied *chardonnay* could be used and the dish would have a completely different taste. If you choose to go with this type of wine you should try: **Muirwood Single Vineyard**; **Lloyd**; **Mer Soleil Gold**; or **Chalk hill.**

Coq Au Vin

4 chicken legs and 4 thighs, skin on**
2 tablespoon extra virgin olive oil
3 tablespoon unsalted butter
¼ pound lardons (salted pork belly), chopped
1 pound button mushrooms, sliced
¾ cup pearl onions
1 small carrot, sliced
1 stalk celery, sliced
2 large shallots, minced
1 clove garlic, whole
2 tablespoons all purpose flour
2 tablespoons flat leaf parsley, minced
1 tablespoon fresh tarragon, minced
1 small bay leaf
½ teaspoon fresh thyme, minced
2 tablespoon brandy (optional)
1 ¾ cups dry red wine
2cups low sodium chicken stock
Sea salt to taste
Ground black pepper to taste

Lightly salt and pepper the chicken. In a Dutch oven or large casserole dish, heat the olive oil and melt the butter over medium high heat. Add the lardons to the Dutch oven and render out the fat until they are almost crispy. Remove lardons from pot and reserve; leaving the fat behind.

Reduce the heat to medium. Add the mushrooms and sear for 2-3 minutes; remove and reserve. Add the onions, carrots, celery and garlic and cook for 1 minute. Remove the vegetables leaving the fat behind. Add the chicken and brown both sides. Remove the chicken and reserve.

Reduce the Dutch oven heat to low. Add the

flour, parsley, tarragon, bay leaf and thyme. Incorporate the ingredients while cooking an additional minute. Return the vegetables and chicken to the Dutch oven. Add the brandy, wine and chicken stock. Stir together, cover the Dutch oven and simmer until the chicken is done- about 45 minutes to an hour.

For the last 5 minutes add the mushrooms. Remove the bay leaf and garlic clove, adjust the flavor with salt and pepper and serve.

**Note. Don't substitute chicken breasts in this dish. They will become dry and tasteless.

Let's talk about wine: This dish needs an old world wine if it is to reach its full potential. From France, you might use a less expensive red like a Bordeaux or Rhone as the add wine. For the pair wine we suggest **Chateau Druzac Margaux** (decant for 3-6 hours) or **Chateau Fonroque Saint-Emilion** (decant 3-6 hours). You could also use an Italian pair such as the **San Guido** (decant for 5+ hours) or **Vasco Sassetti Brunello 2003 (**decant for 2+ hours).

Veal Chops Sautéed with Wine and Tarragon

4 veal chops, 16-18 ounces each, cut 1 ¼ inch thick
2 tablespoon olive oil
2 tablespoon unsalted butter
3 large shallots, minced
1 clove garlic, whole
¾ cup dry white wine or French vermouth
½ teaspoon fresh basil, minced
½ teaspoon fresh tarragon, minced
¼ teaspoon fresh thyme, minced
¼ cup low sodium chicken broth
¼ cup heavy cream
Sea Salt to taste
Ground black pepper to taste

In a large sauté pan over medium high heat, add half the oil and melt half the butter. Lightly salt and pepper the chops and add them to the pan when hot. Cook to the desired doneness---about 5 minutes per side. When done, remove to a warm plate while you prepare the sauce.

Drain the residual fat from the pan. Add the remaining oil and butter to the pan; add the shallots and sauté 1 minute. Add the garlic clove and sauté an additional 30 seconds. Add the wine and the herbs and reduce by half. Add the chicken broth and reduce slightly again. Reduce the heat and add the cream stirring continuously. Remove the garlic.

Return the chops to the pan to heat up. Adjust the flavor with salt and pepper. Arrange chops on serving platter. Reduce the sauce a bit more to slightly thicken, and pour over the chops.

Variation #1: Before adding the wine, sauté ½ pound of sliced button mushrooms for 2 minutes and then continue with the recipe.

Variation #2: When sautéing the shallots, add 2 chopped anchovy filets and allow them to melt into the shallots before proceeding.

Let's talk about wine: At over $15 per pound, veal chops are an elegant extravagance and should be paired with a complimentary wine of equal extravagance. Stay with one of the outstanding *Pinot Noirs* such as: **Goldeneye**; **Etude**; **Pahlmeyer**; **Bell Gloss Clark & Tel.** or one of the wonderful **Ken Wright** Single Vineyard wines.

Filet of Sole Baked in Parchment

(Sole en Papillote)

4-8 ounce pieces of sole filet, pin bones removed
4 pieces parchment paper twice the size of each filet
1 pound fresh baby spinach
1 leek (white part only), well washed, sliced in half and thinly sliced
2 carrots, peeled, cut half, sliced thin on bias
1 fennel bulb cut in half, core removed, and shaved very thin
½ cup dry white wine

Zest of one lemon
Zest of one orange
4 tablespoons unsalted butter
4 drizzle of black truffle oil
Sea salt to taste
Ground white pepper to taste

Rub each piece of parchment paper on one side with ½ tablespoon butter. Place a handful of the fresh spinach on top of the parchment paper. Place a fish filet on the bed of spinach. Place the second ½ tablespoon butter on top of the sole.

Arrange the sliced leek on top of each filet. Arrange the sliced carrot and shaved fennel around the perimeter of the fish. Drizzle the fish with the truffle oil and the wine. Season the fish lightly with salt and ground white pepper.

Fold over the parchment paper and twist along the edge sealing each packet. Place each packet on a cookie sheet and bake in a pre heated 350° oven for about 20 minutes. Serve the packet sealed allowing each person to open their own packet.

Let's talk about wine: This is a very light dish and you do not want to overpower it with a full or complex wine. Stick to a wine such as: **Chateau Montet Blanc**, **Nobilus Vinho Verde**; **Roussanne** to add or pair.

Duck a L'Orange

1 whole 3-4 pound duck
Sea Salt to taste
Ground black pepper to taste
French 4 spice powder to taste
Zest of 2 oranges
Zest of 1 lemon
¼ cup Dijon mustard or whole grain mustard
1 cup fresh orange juice
1 cup Vouvray wine
¼ teaspoon French 4 spice powder
Sea salt to taste
Ground black pepper to taste

Wash the duck thoroughly and pat dry with a paper towel. Remove the wing at the elbow joint and discard. Sprinkle the inside and outside of the duck with salt, pepper and the French 4 spice blend. Message the duck with half of the lemon and orange zests. Place the duck on a baking pan with a rack and cook for 30-35 minutes at 350°, and then for another 25-30 minutes at 400°. While the duck is baking, make the A L'Orange sauce.

For the sauce:

In a sauce pot, combine the Dijon mustard, orange juice, wine, French 4 spice and the other half of the zests. Bring to a boil and then reduce the heat and simmer until the sauce is reduced by half. During the last 20 minutes of the duck's baking, baste the duck with the sauce.

When the duck is finished cooking, allow the duck to rest for 10 minutes before cutting it in half. Half a duck should serve one person, Serve with the remaining orange sauce on the side.

Let's talk about wine: We originally thought of doing this dish as a variation of the apricot glazed duck but decided to have it as a standalone. We suggest you look to that recipe and choose one of the wines recommended for that dish. This is also a perfect opportunity to venture out on your own and choose a wine you think would go well with this recipe.

Sliced Steak Provencal

1-4 pound flank steak
2 tablespoons extra virgin olive oil
1 teaspoon fresh rosemary, minced
1 teaspoon flat leaf parsley, minced
½ teaspoon fresh thyme, minced
½ teaspoon marjoram, minced
1/8 teaspoon ground cinnamon
Pinch of sea salt
Pinch of ground black pepper
2 tablespoons extra virgin olive oil
2 tablespoons unsalted butter
2 shallots, minced
1 clove garlic, minced

2 cups dry rose wine
3 tablespoons unsalted butter

Combine the oil, rosemary, parsley, thyme, marjoram, cinnamon, salt and pepper in a bowl and blend well. Spread the mixture over both sides of the steak, cover with plastic wrap and refrigerate 4-6 hours or overnight.

In a large sauté pan over medium high heat, add the olive oil and butter. Add the steak and sauté on both sides until the desired doneness. Baste the steak while cooking to enhance the flavor by spooning the oil/butter over the top of the steak during the cooking process. Remove and allow to rest.

In the same pan, pour off the residual cooking oil and discard. Over medium heat, add the oil and melt the butter. Add the shallots and garlic and sauté 1 minute. Add the wine and reduce by half. Remove the pan from the heat and add the cold butter to the pan, swirling constantly to incorporate it into the sauce. Cut the steak across the grain of the meat and serve with the sauce on the side.

Let's talk about wine: This is definitely a dish we want you to explore with. We have introduced a number of beef based dishes here in this chapter and in others. Think of those dishes. Look back at our suggestions. Learn from your own experience and choose a fabulous wine for this dish.

Herbed Veal Palliard with Cream

4-8 oz pieces of veal cutlets, pounded thin
2 tablespoons extra virgin olive oil
1 tablespoon fresh tarragon, minced
1 tablespoon fresh rosemary, minced
1 tablespoon flat leaf parsley, minced
¼ teaspoon fresh thyme, minced
2 tablespoons olive oil
2 tablespoons unsalted butter
1 shallot, minced
½ cup dry white wine
½ cup heavy cream
Sea salt to taste

Ground black pepper to taste

Lightly salt and pepper the veal cutlets. In a bowl combine the extra virgin olive oil and the herbs and blend well. Spread the mixed herbs evenly over both sides of the cutlets. Allow to sit and macerate for 15-20 minutes.

Preheat a grill to a high temperature. Sear the veal cutlets over the open flame 3-4 minutes on each side. Remove to a warm serving platter.

In a sauce pan over medium heat, add the oil and melt the butter. Add the shallot to the pan and sauté for 1 minute. Add the wine and deglaze the pan. Reduce wine by half, lower the heat, and add the cream. Adjust the flavor with salt and pepper. Allow the cream to slightly thicken, pour over the veal cutlets and serve.

Variation #1: Use 1 cup of wine and no cream. Reduce the wine by half before pouring it over the cutlets.

Variation #2: After cooking the shallots, add ½ pound of sliced mushrooms and sauté 2 minutes before adding the wine and the cream.

Let's talk about wine: There are some great blends that are a good of choice of wines to add or pair for this dish like: **Rustenburg**, **Tupungato**, **Cruz Alta Chairman's Blend**, **Avenel Napa Red**; **Pahlmeyer Red**. Choose one of these great wines and enjoy.

Veal with Ham and Gruyere

4-8 ounce size veal cutlets, pounded thin and
  then cut into 4 ounce pieces
4 thin slices of good quality ham
4 thin slices of Gruyere cheese
½ cup all purpose flour
6 eggs, beaten
2 tablespoons extra virgin olive oil
3 tablespoons unsalted butter
1 shallot, minced
1 cup dry white wine
2 tablespoons unsalted butter, cold

½ tablespoon flat leaf parsley, chopped
Sea salt to taste
Ground black pepper to taste

Lightly salt and pepper the cutlets. On 4 pieces of cutlet, lay one thin slice of ham and one thin slice Gruyere cheese on each. Top the veal with the other 4 halves of cutlet and press together firmly, making a "sandwich".

In a large sauté pan, over medium high heat, add the oil and melt the butter. Dredge each of the cutlet stack in the flour, and then in the egg. Place it in the frying pan. Cook until light golden in color--about 2-3 minutes per side. Remove to a warm serving platter.

In the same pan, place the minced shallot and sauté for 1 minute. Add the wine and reduce it by half. Remove the pan from the heat, and add the cold butter and swirl in the pan until completely incorporated. Add a bit of chopped parsley. Adjust the flavor with salt and pepper, pour over the cutlets and serve.

Variation #1: After reducing the wine, add ¼ cup cream to the pan, reduce slightly then add the cold butter and blend well.

Let's talk about wine: This rich dish calls for a wine that can stand up to it and add to the flavors: **Dr. Heidemanns Red or Qb A**; **Jean Albrecht Gewürztraminer**; **Bridgman Viognier** are all such wines. A Pinot Noir would also pair well if chosen carefully. We suggest the **River Road Sonoma**; **Truscott**; **La Crema**; or perhaps a Rhone blend like the **E Guigal Crozes Hermitage**.

Chapter 10:

Offal Isn't Awful At All

1. **Venetian Liver**

2. **Chicken Livers Lyonnaise**

3. **Calf's Liver with Mustard, Herbs and Breadcrumbs**

4. **Malaysian Spiced Braised Liver**

5. **Calf's Liver with Bacon and Onions**

   And 2 variations

6. **Calf's Liver in Cream & Mustard Sauce**

7. **Chopper Chicken Liver on Toast**

8. **Liver Tyrolesine**

9. **Southern Fried Chicken Livers**

10. **Chicken Liver Milanese**

    And 2 variations

11. **Pork Liver Wrapped in Caul Fat**

12. **Quick Liver Pate**

    And 1 variation

13. **Fioe Gras**

    And 4 variations

14. **Fried Lamb Sweetbreads**

15. **Sweet and Sour Sweetbreads**

16. **Sautéed Sweetbreads in Port Wine**

17. **Glazed Sweetbreads**

18. **Tripe with Onions, Olives & Tomatoes**

19. **Tripe Soup**

20. **Tripe in Meat Sauce**

21. **Sautéed Chicken Offal**

    And 2 variations

22. **Chicken Feet Asian Style**

    And 2 variations

23. **Pickled Pig's Feet**

    And 4 variations

24. **Grilled Pig's Feet**

    And 1 variation

25. **Aunt Helen's Pig's Feet & Sauerkraut**

26. **Pig's Feet Asian Style**

    And 1 variation

27. **Pig's Feet Italian Style**

    And 2 variations

28. **Pig's Feet Spanish Style**

29. **Sheep's Head**

30. **Braised Kidneys**

    And 3 variations

31. **Oxtail Stew**

Offal Isn't Awful At All

Let's talk about those things we really love, but don't really want to talk about. If you are first generation American you know what I am speaking of. If you are second or third generation, or even more, you may not, except if you were raised on a farm.

Sometimes we don't like to admit it, but when we eat meat, we are eating an animal. We, of the new generation, waste much of the animal because we take offense at the idea of eating certain "offal" parts. We must remember that the farmer and the peasant did not waste any part of the animal they have chosen to eat. They found uses for everything. Nothing was wasted. As a matter of fact, many of the parts that some consider offal, many other people consider a delicacy.

We of the second—third---fourth generation have lost touch with some of our more basic culinary roots. In a society where waste is almost endemic, we no longer consider the fact that "we must use every part of the animal" as important. Whatever part of the world your ancestors are from, when an animal was slaughtered, every part of that animal was used to benefit those who sacrificed it.

So, in this chapter, we will offer many suggestions for the use of those parts of the animal that many might not consider using. Sure we can all agree on the various ways to prepare and enjoy liver, but can you feel comfortable preparing dishes using heart, lung, kidney, brains, tails, feet etc?

Keep an open mind about the suggestions offered here. You should have little trouble finding most of the organ meats suggested here. If you have a markets specializing in Asian, Spanish, or other ethnic groups, we encourage you to explore these venues.

As you try the recipes suggested in this chapter, be prepared to experience both subtle and intense flavors and textures. Don't be thrown off by the fact that you are eating tongue or brain or blood. Try to move beyond the taboo that you may feel and into the realization that all of our ancestors looked forward to eating all of these "offal" with gusto and gratitude.

We would also like to comment on how we finally ended in choosing the wine suggestions for the dishes to Add/Pair in this chapter. Just as in the other chapters, we wanted to offer suggestions that yielded the "third layer of flavor" we spoke about---the flavor that is more than the sum of its parts---the flavor of the dish plus the flavor of the wine. Look to the general discussions about wine, beer and spirit pairing and understand that just as these dishes are difficult for many people to eat, their pairings are even more so.

* Please note:

Rather than pairing every recipe with wine, we have chosen to pair some and then have a general discussion for these recipes after each section. We do believe that the richness of liver pairs so very well with sparkling wines that we have included one sparkling wine suggestion after each recipe. In addition be sure to read the section after the "liver" section for additional suggestions.

NOTE: Be sure to read the entire liver/wine discussion at the end of this section.

Venetian Liver

1 pound calf's liver, sliced very thin
3 tablespoons extra virgin olive oil
5 tablespoons unsalted butter
2 large yellow onions, sliced very thin
4 cloves garlic, sliced very thin
4 tablespoons flat leaf parsley
Sea Salt to taste
Ground black pepper to taste

In a pan over medium high heat, add the olive oil and melt the butter. Add the onions. Season the onions with a bit of salt and fresh ground black pepper, and sauté until tender. Add the garlic and sauté an additional minute.

Increase the heat to high and add the liver. Sauté quickly, about 2 minutes per side. Adjust the flavor with salt and pepper. Remove the liver from the pan and serve over thin slices of Italian bread. Just before removing the onions from the pan, add ¼ cup balsamic vinegar. Toss the onions well and serve over the liver.

***Nino Franco Prosecco**

Chicken Liver Lyonnaise

12 chicken livers, cleaned of their membranes
1 cup buttermilk
1 cup all purpose flour
2 tablespoons unsalted butter
2 tablespoons extra virgin olive oil
2 tablespoons unsalted butter
2 tablespoons extra virgin olive oil
1 large yellow onion, sliced thin
1 clove garlic, minced
1 cup button mushrooms, sliced thin
¼ cup dry white wine
¼ teaspoon fresh thyme, chopped
Sea salt to taste
Ground black pepper to taste

Clean the chicken livers and remove the membranes. Pat livers dry with paper towel. Season the livers with a bit of salt and pepper and dredge in the flour. In a pan, over medium high heat, add 2 tablespoons olive oil and 2 tablespoons unsalted butter; add the livers and cook until just done, about 2-3 minutes. Remove and arrange on a serving plate.

In the same pan, reduce the heat to medium low, add an additional 2 tablespoons olive oil and 2 tablespoons of butter, and sauté the onions until they start to become golden brown. Add the garlic and sauté an additional minute. Add the mushrooms and sauté until crisp. Add the thyme and deglaze the pan with the white wine. Sauté the onions and mushrooms until all the liquid has evaporated. Adjust the flavor with salt and pepper. Pour the onion/mushroom mixture over the livers and serve with crusty bread.

Add/pair ***Nino Franco Rustico**

Calf's Liver with Mustard, Herbs And Breadcrumbs

4-6 ounce portions of calf's liver (4 ½ inch wide x ½ inch thick)
All purpose flour, seasoned with salt and pepper
2 tablespoons extra virgin olive oil
2 tablespoons unsalted butter
3 tablespoons Dijon mustard
2 large shallots, minced
1 clove garlic, minced
3 tablespoons flat leaf parsley, minced
2 teaspoons fresh thyme, chopped
1 tablespoon fresh basil, chopped
3 cups Panko breadcrumbs
8 tablespoons unsalted butter, melted
2 tablespoons extra virgin olive oil
Sea salt to taste
Ground black pepper to taste

Season the slices of liver with salt and pepper and then dredge in the seasoned flour. In a large pan over medium high heat, add the olive oil and butter. Add the liver to the pan and sauté briefly (30 seconds) on both sides. Do not cook through. Remove and reserve. In a large bowl, blend together the mustard, garlic, shallots, salt and pepper. Using a whisk, beating all the time, slowly add the drippings from the sautéed liver to the bowl to create a paste. Adjust the flavor with salt and pepper. Coat each liver slice liberally with the paste and then with the Panko breadcrumbs. Place the slices of liver on a broiling rack. Drizzle each piece with a blend of the melted butter and olive oil. Broil the liver until golden. Turn liver over and drizzle with some more butter and olive oil. Broil a bit more until golden once again. Remove and serve.

***Tokay 2009**

Malaysian Spiced Braised Chicken Liver

12 Chicken livers, cleaned of their membranes
4 tablespoons extra virgin olive oil
1 large yellow onion, minced
3 cloves garlic, minced
1 ½ teaspoons grated fresh ginger
2 teaspoons ground coriander
½ teaspoon ground cumin
½ teaspoon fresh ground black pepper
½ teaspoon ground white pepper
¼ teaspoon Sambal
3 tablespoons good quality soy sauce

Divide the livers into halves or thirds, depending on the size. In a wok, heat the oil over high heat. Add the onions and cook until tender. Add the garlic and cook stirring for an additional 2-3 minutes. Sprinkle the liver with the coriander, cumin, salt, ginger, and black and white peppers. Add the livers to the pan and cook on one side for one minute, then turn and cook on the other side for one minute. Add the soy and cook covered for an additional 2-3 minutes being careful not to overcook the livers. Serve immediately.

***<u>Freixenet Demi Sec</u>

Calf's Liver with Bacon and Onions

6 slices bacon
2 tablespoons extra virgin olive oil
2 large yellow onions, sliced thin
3 cloves garlic, sliced thin
4-6 ounce portions calf's liver, ½ inch wide
¼ cup red wine vinegar
Sea salt to taste
Ground black pepper to taste

In a large pan, over medium high heat, sauté the bacon in the olive oil until crisp. Remove the bacon and reserve. Add the onions to the pan and cook until tender. Then, add the garlic and cook an additional minute. Remove the onions and garlic and reserve. Add the liver to the pan and cook about 2 minutes per side. Return the onions and the bacon to the pan and cook together an additional minute. Add the vinegar and cook an additional 30 seconds. Serve immediately.

Variation #1: Use pancetta instead of bacon.

Variation #2: Use balsamic vinegar instead of red wine vinegar.

***<u>MUMM Napa Brut Rose</u>

Calf's Liver in Cream and Mustard Sauce

4-6 ounce portions calf's liver, ½ inch wide
All purpose flour, seasoned with salt and black pepper
3 tablespoons extra virgin olive oil
3 tablespoons unsalted butter
¼ cup dry red wine
½ cup heavy cream
½ cup beef stock
1½ tablespoons Dijon mustard
2 tablespoons unsalted butter
¼ cup fresh flat leaf parsley, chopped
Sea salt to taste
Ground black pepper to taste

Dredge the slices of liver in the seasoned flour. In a large pan over medium high heat, add the olive oil and melt the butter. Add the liver to the pan and sauté 1-2 minutes per side. Remove to a warm serving platter and reserve.

To the same pan, add the red wine and reduce by half. Then add the cream, beef stock and mustard to the pan. Whip together while cooking over low heat for 2 minutes or until the cream slightly thickens. Remove pan from the heat, and swirl small bits of "whole" butter into the pan until it is totally incorporated. Adjust the flavor with the salt and pepper. Pour over the liver and garnish with the chopper parsley.

***<u>Arthur Metz Cremant d' Alsace Brut</u>

Chopped Chicken Livers on Toast

Italian Bread, sliced on a bias ¾" thick
½ pounds chicken livers, cleaned of their membranes, coarse chop
3 tablespoons extra virgin olive oil
1 stalk celery with leaves, minced
1 small onion, minced
1 clove garlic, minced
¼ cup dry white wine
Sea salt to taste
Ground black pepper to taste
2 tablespoons capers, chopped
2 hard boiled eggs, chopped
1 tablespoon Italian parsley, chopped

Toast the thick slices of Italian bread drizzled with some extra virgin olive oil in a 350° oven until golden. Set aside to cool. Once cool, rub each slice of bread with a clove of garlic.

In a pan over medium high heat, add the olive oil and heat. Add the chicken livers and cook until done. Remove livers from pan and reserve. In the same pan, reducing the heat to medium, add the celery and onion and cook until onions start to caramelize. Then, add the garlic and sauté another minute. Return livers to the pan. Add the wine and reduce by half. Add the capers and mix. Cook for an additional 5 minutes. Remove livers from the pan and allow to cool. Once cool, place the livers in a food processor with the blade attachment and chop to a fine consistency. Remove liver from the processor and fold in the chopped egg and parsley. Adjust flavor with some salt and pepper. Serve the liver with the toasted bread.

Cristalano Brut Cava

Liver Tyrolesine

4-6 ounce portions veal or calf's liver, ½ inch slices
1 cup buttermilk
½ cup melted unsalted butter
2 tablespoons extra virgin olive oil
1 medium yellow onion, minced
2 cloves garlic, minced
2 slices pancetta
All purpose flour, seasoned with salt and pepper
¼ cup dry white wine
1 cup heavy cream
1 tablespoons capers, chopped
1 tablespoon Italian parsley, chopped
Sea Salt to taste
Ground black pepper to taste
Deep fried sage leaves as garnish

Place the liver and the buttermilk in a large bowl and allow to sit refrigerated for 2 hours. In a large pan over medium high heat, add the olive oil and melt the butter. Add the pancetta to the pan and render until almost crisp. Remove pancetta from the pan and reserve for later use.

Remove the liver from the buttermilk and pat dry. Discard the buttermilk. Dust the liver with the seasoned flour and sauté in a pan over medium high heat for about 3 minutes per side. Transfer the liver to a warm plate and keep warm. Add the wine to the pan and reduce by ½. Reduce heat to low and add the cream, stirring all the time. Cook at a low simmer for 10 minutes. Add the capers and return the pancetta to the pan; adjust the flavor with salt and pepper.

In a separate pan over medium high heat, add 3-4 tablespoons of extra virgin olive oil; fry 4-5 sage leaves until crisp in the oil. Pour the cream mixture over the liver and garnish with the crispy sage leaves and serve.

Matrell Prestige Extra Dry

Southern Fried Chicken Livers

2 pounds chicken livers, cleaned of all membrane and rinsed
1 cup all purpose flour
1 tablespoon onion powder
1 tablespoons garlic powder
1 teaspoon chili powder
½ teaspoon cayenne pepper
1 teaspoon fresh ground black pepper
1 teaspoon ground white pepper

Vegetable oil for frying
Sea s Sea salt to taste
Ground black pepper to taste
Sea salt to taste
Ground black pepper to taste
Chopped Italian parsley for garnish

Clean the livers and rinse them in cold water. Dry livers with some paper towel. Season the livers with a little bit of salt.

Combine the flour, black pepper, white pepper, onion powder, garlic powder, chili powder and cayenne in a large bowl. Dredge the livers generously in the seasoned flour and allow the livers to sit refrigerated for at least one hour, but overnight would be better.

Place the oil in a large pan, over medium high heat. Cook the livers for 5-7 minutes, turning them once or twice to assure even cooking. Cook until all the pink color is gone. Remove to a serving dish, sprinkle with the parsley and serve.

***Billecart-Salmon Brut**

Chicken Livers Milanese

1 pound chicken livers, cleaned of all membranes and rinsed
4 tablespoons extra virgin olive oil
1 clove garlic, minced
2 tablespoons Italian parsley, chopped
1 cup flour, seasoned with salt and ground black pepper
3 eggs, beaten
¾ cup dry seasoned breadcrumbs, blended with ¾ cup ground Romano cheese
2 tablespoons olive oil
2 tablespoons unsalted butter
Sea Salt to taste
Ground black pepper to taste

Place the cleaned chicken livers in a bowl with the extra virgin olive oil, minced garlic and parsley. Lightly season the livers with some salt and pepper refrigerate for 2-3 hours.

In three separate dishes, prepare the flour, eggs, and breadcrumb blend. Dredge the livers in the flour, shaking off the excess. Dip in the eggs and then cover with the breadcrumbs.

In a frying pan over medium heat, add the olive oil and melt the butter. Add the livers and cook until just done. Serve with lemon wedges.

Variation #1: Try using thin slices of calf's liver or veal liver instead of chicken livers.

Variation #2: Add 1 tablespoon fresh chopped basil and 1 teaspoon of fresh chopped oregano to the bread/cheese mixture.

*** **Louis Bouillet Blanc de Noirs Brut**

Pork Liver Wrapped in Caul Fat

2 pounds pork liver, cleaned of all sinew and cut into strips, 2 inches wide and 3 inches long
1 to 1 ½ pounds of *Caul fat
1 bay leaf for each packet produced
¼ tablespoon of Romano cheese for each packet produced
Pinch of cracked red pepper flakes for each packet produced
Sea salt to taste
Ground black pepper to taste

Lightly salt and pepper each piece of liver, then wrap in a piece of caul fat. Include inside each of the packets: one bay leaf, a pinch of crushed red pepper flakes and a ¼ tablespoon of Romano cheese. Wrap the packets tightly and then grill them until just cooked through -about 5-7 minutes. Serve.

*Note: Caul fat is the fatty membrane which surrounds internal organs of some animals, such as cows, sheep, and pigs, also known as the greater omentum. It is often used as a natural sausage casing.

*Remind your guests not to eat the bay leaf. If possible remove it before serving.

Add: This really goes well with beer. Try the Italian **Berra Moretti**

Quick Liver Pate

1 pound good quality liverwurst
2 shallots, minced
1 clove garlic, minced
1 tablespoon Italian parsley, minced
3 tablespoon good quality cognac or calvados

Combine all the ingredients in a food processor and process until smooth. Adjust flavor with the salt and pepper and place in a form pan or tureen. Chill at least 2 hours before serving.

Variation #1 Add 2-3 slices of crisp bacon or pancetta to the mix before processing.

**NOTE: Be sure to read the entire wine/liver discussion at the end of this section.**

Foie Gras

For our last liver dish, we wish to offer you some variations on this both wonderful and to some, controversial ingredient. For those who like liver, this is the penultimate enjoyment. To those who don't like liver, try this and you will become a convert. For those who find controversy in the way the animals are raised, we fully support your choice not to eat Foie Gras.

4-¾ inch slices of high quality foie gras
1 granny smith apple, cored, peeled and kept in
 water with the juice of ¼ lemon
Sea salt to taste
Ground black pepper to taste

Heat a frying pan over high heat. Season the slices of Foie Gras with salt and freshly ground black pepper. In the pan over medium high heat, sear the foie gras (no additional oil will be necessary; the liver will yield all you need.)

As the Foie Gras sautés and the fat has started to render, continue cooking while spooning the rendered fat up and over the pieces of foie gras.

Continue cooking and basting the foie gras until the pink center starts to fade. Turn the foie gras pieces over once for 10-15 seconds more, and remove to a warm plate leaving the rendered fat behind. Add the dry apple slices to the pan. Sauté the apple slices briefly until they begin to turn slightly tender, but still crisp. Add additional salt and pepper if necessary and serve the sautéed apples and rendered fat on top of the pieces of Foie Gras.

Variation #1: When you add the apple slices, also add 2 tablespoons Calvados to the pan and continue.

Variation #2: use fresh figs instead of apples. Remember, they need very little cooking.

Variation #3: Use slices of a hard pear instead of an apple. Use alone, or with 2 tablespoons of pear brandy.

Variation #4: Use wedges of fresh oranges alone or with orange brandy.

Note: Remember that the Foie Gras is the star and whatever you choose to add should compliment it in a minor way.

***<u>Krug Grand Cru</u>**

Let's Talk About Wine and Liver

As we sat down to discuss the individual dishes of liver, we began to realize quickly that we were going to have a difficult time. We spoke about the "love it or hate it" regard people have for liver, and the: "It's disgusting, but I've never tried it" attitude.

We then discussed the texture of properly cooked liver, and the taste qualities of the various types. We soon realized that it was far better to talk about liver as a whole, and to talk about types of wines that can add to or even subtract from the enjoyment of these dishes. Finally, we discussed the "King" of liver, Foie Gras, and what would go well with this delicacy.

We came to the realization that pairing wines

with liver is not simple. Once this Offal chapter was conceived and agreed upon, we really thought these peasant dishes of great flavor and richness would be easy to pair. It was anything but that. We soon realized that these dishes led to difficult wine selections.

We decided to offer a range or wines that we feel would pair well with the liver dishes we have selected to offer you. We believe they would blend well with some very high end wines such as: **Caymus Special Select 2006; 2007, 2008**; **Altamura 2006, 2007**; **Duckhorn Merlot Napa**; **Pahlmeyer Merlot**. If you wanted to go with some other great wines you might consider: **Sobon Estate, Paul's Vineyard Zin**; **Earthquake Petite Syrah** or **Earthquake Zin; Molly Dooker The Boxer**; You could also consider the **Offley 10 year old Tawny Port** or the **Graham's 20 year old.** For the Foie Gras you should seriously consider a great **sauterne or VIN Santo.** For any of the dishes a BRUT or Extra Dry sparkler would go very well: **Moet Brut**, **Veuve Clicquot Brut**, **De Margerie Grand Cru**, **Graham Beck Extra Dry**, and **Billecart-Salmon Extra Dry**.

SWEETBREADS
General Preparations of Sweetbreads for all Dishes

NOTE: Be sure to read the entire wine/sweetbreads discussion at the end of this section.

General Preparation Instructions:

Clean the sweetbreads of all membranes. In a large bowl of ice water, add 1 teaspoon salt and soak the sweetbreads for 2 hours. Change the water at least 3 times. Lay the sweetbreads out on a pan and flatten them using a meat mallet or side of a cleaver or knife.

Fried Lamb Sweetbreads

2 pounds "Prepared" Lamb Sweetbreads (see general preparations for sweetbreads)

2 ribs celery with leaves, coarse chop
2 carrots, coarse chop
4 cloves garlic, thinly sliced
1 yellow onion, coarse chop
3 cups chicken broth
1 large fennel bulb, sliced very thin
2 large yellow onions, sliced thin
1 teaspoon Dijon mustard
½ teaspoon cracked red pepper
1 bottle dry white wine
¼ cup white wine vinegar
1 cup all purpose flour, blended with one cup of coarse ground semolina flour, seasoned with 1 teaspoon salt, 1 teaspoon ground black pepper, ½ teaspoon cayenne pepper, and 1 teaspoon ground white pepper
1 large orange, thin wedges
2 lemons, thin wedges
Extra virgin olive oil for deep frying
Sea salt to taste
Ground black pepper to taste

In a large pot, combine the chopped carrot, celery, onion, garlic, chicken stock, wine, vinegar, salt, pepper, mustard, and red pepper. Bring the vegetable to a simmer for 30 minutes. Add the sweetbreads and simmer about 10 minutes until they are a creamy white color. Remove the sweetbreads and set aside.

In a large bowl, combine the sweetbreads, sliced onion, sliced fennel and seasoned flour. In small batches, deep fry the mixture in 350° olive oil. As each batch of sweetbread "fritters" is removed from the oil, season with a pinch of salt and pepper. Serve with wedges of fresh lemon and orange as garnish.

Sweet and Sour Sweetbreads

1 ½ pounds "Prepared" lamb or veal sweetbreads (see general preparation for sweetbreads)
4 tablespoons unsalted butter
2 tablespoons extra virgin olive oil
1 large yellow onion, chopped
1 large carrot, chopped
1 stalk celery with leaves, chopped

3 cloves garlic, sliced thin
2 ¼ inch thick slices of pancetta, coarse chop
¼ cup white wine vinegar
2 tablespoons granulated sugar
1/3 cup capers
6 tablespoons extra virgin olive oil
Sea salt to taste
Ground black pepper to taste

Prepare the sweetbreads as directed. In a large pot over medium heat, melt the butter in the olive oil. Add the onion, carrot, celery, garlic and pancetta, and sauté for 10 minutes. Add the sweetbreads and cook at a low simmer for 15 minutes. Remove to a serving plate.

In a separate pan, add the vinegar, sugar and capers and bring to a very low simmer for 4-5 minutes. Adjust the flavor with the salt and pepper. Pour over the sweetbreads and serve immediately.

Sautéed Sweetbreads in Port Wine

1 ½ pounds "Prepared" lamb or calf sweetbreads (see general preparation for sweetbreads)
4 tablespoons unsalted butter
1 tablespoon extra virgin olive oil
1 small yellow onion, thinly sliced
2 cloves garlic, sliced thin
½ cup good quality tawny port
½ cup heavy cream
Sea salt to taste
Ground black pepper to taste

Prepare the sweetbreads as directed. In a pan, melt the butter in the olive oil over medium heat. Season the sweetbreads with salt and pepper. Add the sweetbreads to the pan and sauté until they are a "milky" color-about 3-4 minutes per side. Remove and reserve.

Add the onion to the pan and sauté until tender. Add the garlic and sauté an additional minute. Add the port and reduce by half. Then add the cream while whisking. Allow the cream to thicken slightly. Pour over the sweetbreads and serve.

***ADD/PAIR: Illaparra 10 Year Old Tawny**

Glazed Sweetbreads

2 pairs of "Prepared" calf sweetbreads (see general preparation for sweetbreads)
4 tablespoons extra virgin olive oil
3 tablespoons unsalted butter
2 tablespoons shallots, minced
2 tablespoons celery, minced
2 tablespoons carrots, minced
1 clove garlic, minced
2 cups low sodium chicken broth
2 cups dry white wine or dry sherry
Sea salt to taste
Ground black pepper to taste

In a pan over medium heat, add the oil and melt the butter. Add the shallots, celery, carrots and garlic and sauté until the vegetables start to "sweat," being careful not to burn. Add the chicken broth, wine and sweetbreads and simmer covered for 25 minutes. Remove the sweetbreads to a baking pan. Season the sweetbreads with a bit of salt and pepper.

Continue to reduce the simmering liquid to the consistency of thick syrup. At this point, drizzle the reduced liquid equally over the sweetbreads and place them in a preheated 425° oven for 8-10 minutes. Baste 2-3 times with the pan juices. Serve.

Let's Talk About Wine and Sweetbreads

Here again with sweetbreads, our discussions revolved around the quality of the dishes and their creaminess, elegance, richness and texture. When the recipes are made as per directions, the final dishes have all of these qualities as well as a "full bodied" (borrowed from wine descriptions) mouth feel that must be experienced to understand.

As the discussion within the team dragged on, Joseph K. came up with the perfect reasons for choosing wines for such an experience. He explained that when faced with a dish that has such richness and fullness and such bounty in creaminess, he doesn't want the wine to get in the way. With these dishes, we have to let the dish speak for itself.

With this discussion, we soon realized the following recommendations for wines to ADD or PAIR with sweetbreads:

Mulderbosch Chenin Blanc; Nobilus Vinho Verdi; Bolla Orvieto or Bolla Soave; Bellini Orvieto or Bellini Soave; Niño Franco Prosecco; J. Albrecht Alsace Brut; Arthur Metz Alsace Brut; Osborne Fino Sherry; Taylor Fino Sherry.

TRIPE

General Preparation Instructions:

Generally, one can buy tripe that has been cleaned and cut into manageable pieces and partially cooked. Even though this may be true, there are some general preparation instructions to keep in mind._First, wash the tripe and blanch it in salted water for 15 minutes. Wash it again and cut it into pieces for cooking. Then, no matter the recipe, tripe must be cooked slowly over a very low heat. It will take on the characteristics of soft but still al dente sinew.

Remember, cooking will be *long and slow*!!!

Tripe with Onions, Olives & Tomatoes

2-3 pounds "Prepared" tripe cut into 2 inch x2 inch pieces (see general preparation for tripe)
3 tablespoons extra virgin olive oil
2 large yellow onions, sliced
4 cloves garlic, sliced
1-28 ounce can Italian whole tomatoes, hand crushed
½ bottle plus of dry white wine
1 cup Italian green olives, without pits
1 bay leaf
Sea salt to taste
Ground black pepper to taste

In a large pot over medium heat, add the olive oil.

Add the onions and sauté until tender. Add the garlic and sauté an additional minute. Add the hand crushed tomatoes and the tripe. **Reduce the heat to low.** Add enough wine to just cover the tripe. Add the bay leaf and the olives. Cook the tripe at a very low temperature until the tripe is done (soft but still slightly chewy). Add additional liquid to the pot as necessary during cooking. Adjust flavor with the salt and pepper. Remove the bay leaf and serve. Offer crushed red pepper flakes as a garnish.

Let's talk about wine: With this recipe, you would be wise to try a nice white like **the Mulderbosch Chenin Blanc** or the **Ratts Chenin Blanc**; the **Washington Hills Gewurztraminer** or the **Dr. Heidemanns Cabinet.**

Tripe Soup

2 pounds "Prepared" tripe cut into strips (see general preparation for tripe)
1 large yellow onion, cut in half
4 cloves garlic, cut in half
2 carrots, coarse chop
2 stalks celery with leaves, coarse chop
10 black peppercorns
1 bay leaf
4 cloves
1 teaspoon sea salt
2 tablespoons extra virgin olive oil
1/3 pounds pancetta, cut in small cubes
1 large yellow onion, coarse chop
1 stalk celery with leaves, coarse chop
1 clove garlic, minced
1 small head cabbage, shredded
10-12 fingerling potatoes, cut in half lengthwise
Sea salt to taste
Ground black pepper to taste

In a large pot, place the tripe, onion, garlic cloves, carrots, celery, peppercorns, bay leaf, and salt and cover with a generous amount of water. Bring to a boil and simmer very softly for 1 hour. Remove the tripe. Strain and reserve the liquid.

In another large pot over medium heat, add the

olive oil and pancetta and sauté gently until the fat is rendered and the pancetta is just slightly crisp. Add the onion and celery and sauté until tender. Add the garlic and sauté an additional minute. Add the reserved liquid, tripe, cabbage and potatoes and simmer gently until the tripe is cooked-as much as one additional hour. Adjust the flavor with salt and pepper and serve hot.

Let's talk about wine: this dish would pair well with the same wines suggested in the last recipe.

Tripe in Meat Sauce

Use the *Quick Meat Sauce* recipe as directed in the *"From the Heart"* chapter
2 pounds "Prepared" tripe, cut into strips
1 large yellow onion, cut in half
4 cloves garlic, cut in half
2 carrots, cut into large pieces
2 stalks celery, cut into large pieces
10 black peppercorns
4 whole cloves
1 bay leaf
1teaspoon sea salt
2 ounces extra virgin olive oil
1 pound Crimini mushrooms, sliced

In a large pot, place the tripe, onion, garlic cloves, carrots, celery, peppercorns, bay leaf, cloves and salt and cover with a generous amount of water. Bring to a boil and simmer very softly until done----at least 1-2 hours. Remove the tripe, strain and reserve the liquid.

In a large pot, over medium heat, sauté the mushrooms in the olive oil. After 3-4 minutes, add the tripe and the meat sauce. Add ½ cup of the reserved cooking liquid. Cook at a low simmer for 30 minutes, stirring often. Serve.

Let's talk about wine: This rich dish calls for a rich red like, **Madrone Knoll Cabernet Napa**; **Macchia Barbara or Sangiovese**; **Rudy Cabernet, Artesia Cabernet 2007, CH. De S. Casme Gigondas 2007**.

Sautéed Chicken Offal

You know that little bag you find inside the chicken from the supermarket? It usually contains the neck, liver, gizzards and the heart of the chicken. Most people just throw it away. You can also find whole packages of hearts, livers, and gizzards in lots of supermarkets today. Instead of throwing it away, try the following:

½ pound assorted chicken offal including necks, hearts, livers and gizzards
2 tablespoons extra virgin olive oil
4 tablespoons unsalted butter
½ small yellow onion, minced
1 clove garlic, minced
2 tablespoons Italian parsley, chopped
¼ cup cream sherry
Sea Salt to taste
Ground black pepper to taste

Clean the gizzards and cut into small pieces. Remove any membranes from the livers. In a pan over medium high heat, melt the butter in the oil. Place the necks in the butter and cook until golden. Add the onion and cook until soft. Then add the garlic and cook an additional 30 seconds. Add the gizzards, the hearts and the livers. Shake the pan well, tossing the ingredients a few times and then add the sherry. Cook just until the pink color is lost from the livers. Adjust the flavor with the salt and pepper and serve with toasted slices of French or Italian bread.

Variation #1 Hearts alone: Prepare a package of hearts along with your favorite fried chicken recipe. Dip into the buttermilk, dredge in the seasoned flour and drop a few into the pan with each batch of chicken you fry.

Variation #2 Gizzards alone: Prepare a package of gizzards as in variation #1.

Variation #3: In some olive oil, sauté an onion and 2 cloves of garlic. Dredge the gizzards in flour and add to the pan. Sauté until somewhat tender and add ½ cup of cream to the pan. Heat through and serve.

Let's talk about wine/beer: This is a rich dish

and deserves rich wine to add and pair. Use the **Osborne Cream sherry** as the add/pair wine for this dish. If you want to serve a separate pair wine then choose a full bodied chardonnay such as **Newton Unfiltered**, **DuMOL**. You might also turn to an old standard **Kendal Jackson Chardonnay Grand Reserve**. If you choose to serve a beer you might want to try a stout like **Murphy's.**

Chicken Feet Asian Style

Most supermarkets will carry packages of chicken feet that have been cleaned for preparation.

1 pound package of cleaned chicken feet
1 tablespoon peanut oil
1 tablespoon shallots, chopped
2 cloves garlic, chopped
1 tablespoon fresh ginger, minced
¼ cup soy sauce
2 tablespoon Hoisin sauce
2 tablespoon oyster sauce
1/3 cup low sodium chicken broth
1-2 teaspoon Sambal (optional)

In a wok or heavy pan, heat the oil over high heat. Add the ginger, shallots and garlic and sauté 30 seconds. Add the chicken feet and continue to sauté an additional 30-45 seconds, stirring all the time. Add the soy, Hoisin and oyster sauces and mix together well. Reduce the heat to a simmer and cook the chicken feet covered until very tender, about 20-30 minutes. Serve over rice or Asian noodles.

Variation #1: For a Thai curry twist, instead of the soy, oyster sauce and broth, add 1 tablespoon of red or green curry paste, the juice of 1 lime and 1 can coconut milk.

Let's talk about beer: This dish calls for a crisp lager like **Land shark** or **Yuengling**. You also might consider lighter ale such as **Monk in the Trunk.**

Pig's Feet

General Preparation Instructions:

Pig's feet are a great dish alone, or added to other dishes to enrich them. They should be simmered for 2-3 hours before any other preparation. The simmering liquid is:

6 pig's feet, split down the center
2 carrots, thinly sliced
1 large yellow onion, studded with 6 cloves
5 cloves garlic, crushed
12 black pepper corns, crushed
1 sprig fresh rosemary
1 sprig fresh thyme
1 sprig fresh Italian parsley
1 sprig fresh basil
2 bay leaves
2 teaspoons sea salt

Wrap each foot half in cheese cloth and tie in 2-3 places. Combine all the ingredients in a pan and bring to a boil. Add the pig's feet and bring to a very low simmer. Simmer for 2-3 hours. Remove the pig's feet; unwrap the feet and discard the simmering liquid.

Pickled Pig's Feet

6 half pig's feet halves (prepared as directed in the general preparation instructions)
5 cloves garlic, sliced
2 shallots, thinly sliced
2 tablespoons sea salt
1 tablespoon pickling spices
Red wine vinegar to cover

Place the pig's feet in a nonreactive container with the garlic, shallots, salt and pickling spice. Add just enough of the red wine vinegar to submerge the feet. Allow to marinate for at least 3 days refrigerated before serving.

Variation # 1: Add one chopped jalapeño pepper to the pickling liquid.

Variation # 2: Add half red wine and half red wine vinegar.

Variation #3: Add half white wine and half white wine vinegar.

Variation #4: Add half Riesling and half cider vinegar.

Let's talk about wine/beer: Intense vinegar taste is hard to pair with wine, so you might want to pair this recipe with beer, choose one that really stands up to the dish and the intensity of the flavors. You could also choose an intense brew such as **Arrogant Bastard** or Stout such as **Guinness's.**

Grilled Pig's Feet

6 pig's feet halves (prepared as directed in the general preparation instructions)

Seasoned flour

Dredge the pig's feet in the seasoned flour and grill on the stove or on the BBQ until a deep golden brown. Serve.

Variation #1: Rub the pig's feet generously with extra virgin olive oil; season with salt and pepper and grill on an indoor or outdoor grill.

Let's talk about wine: On thing we would like everyone to discover is that BBQ of almost any kind calls for a nice *GSM* from Rhone. Choose one of the **Don Presidente** or **Clos Saint Michel** wines.

Aunt Helen's Pig's Feet and Sauerkraut

6 pig's feet halves (prepared as directed in the general preparation instructions)
2 tablespoons extra virgin olive oil
1 large yellow onion, sliced thin
1pound sauerkraut
1 tablespoon caraway seeds
1 teaspoon fresh ground black pepper
½ cup dry or slightly sweet white wine

Combine all the ingredients in a covered pan and simmer over low heat for 30 minutes. Serve.

Let's talk about wine: While the team spoke about pairing this dish with a nice *Dornfelder*: **Dr. Heidemanns Red** also, **Dr. Heidemanns QbA or Kabinett.** You could also pair it with a nice **Hofbrau Muchen Hafe Wizen**.

When writing this recipe, my (Nick) mind drifted back to my days as a youth in Brooklyn and the person who inspired this dish my "Aunt Helen" (no blood relationship, next door neighbor, Mama's best friend). In those days we all had at least one Aunt Helen and her husband Uncle Phil---did you have one too? I know exactly what Aunt Helen and Uncle Phil would drink with this dish---a "Highball" (1 ½ oz rye whiskey, 3-5 oz Ginger Ale all over ice). And so in memory of you---Aunt Helen—I offer this as the perfect pairing to this wonderful peasant German Dish.

Pig's Feet Asian Style

6 pig's feet halves (prepared as directed in the general preparation instructions)
2 tablespoon peanut oil
1 tablespoon fresh garlic, minced
1 tablespoon shallot, minced
1 tablespoon fresh ginger, minced
¼ cup soy sauce
¼ cup oyster, Hoisin or black bean sauce
¼ cup low sodium chicken broth

In a wok or heavy pan over high heat, add the oil. Add the ginger, shallots, and garlic and sauté, stirring for 30 seconds. Add the pig's feet and stir an additional 30 seconds. Add the chosen sauce, and chicken broth and stir until well coated. Simmer for 1-2 minutes and serve.

Variation #1: Add 1-2 teaspoons Sambal to the mix.

Let's talk about beer: Bring on the Asian beers: **Singha**; **Chang, Tsingtao, Sapporo.**

Pig's Feet Italian Style

6 pig's feet halves (prepared as directed in the general preparation instructions)
4 tablespoons extra virgin olive oil
1 large yellow onion, minced
3 cloves garlic, minced
1-28 ounce can Italian tomatoes, hand crushed
1-8 ounce can Italian tomato paste
½ cup dry red wine
1 tablespoon fresh basil, chopped
Sea salt to taste
Ground black pepper to taste

In a large pan over medium high heat, add the olive oil and sauté the onion and garlic until tender. Add the crushed tomatoes, tomato paste and wine and bring to a simmer. Add the basil. Adjust the flavor with salt and pepper. Add the pig's feet and allow simmering for 30-40 minutes. Serve alone as an appetizer or over pasta or rice.

Variation #1: Add pig's feet to your Sunday Ragu for additional flavor.

Variation #2: Add 1-2 teaspoon of red pepper flakes to the sauce.

Let's talk about wine: Not just because the flavors are Italian but we really believe that this dish calls for a *Chianti* that is a Reserva. You might choose one of the following: **San Andrea**; **Trecciano**; **Da Vinci**; **Bellini**; **Reffino**

Pig's Feet Spanish Style

6 pig's feet halves (prepared as directed in the general preparation instructions)
2 tablespoons extra virgin olive oil
1 large yellow onion, sliced thin
3 cloves garlic, sliced thin
½ pound Spanish chorizo, cut into ½ inch chunks
1-28 oz can whole tomatoes, hand crushed
¼ cup dry red wine
1 teaspoon Spanish paprika
Sea salt to taste
Ground black pepper to taste

In a large pan, over medium high heat, add the oil. Add the chorizo sausage and cook to render out some of the fat. Add the onions and sauté until tender. Add the garlic and sauté an additional 45 seconds. Add the tomatoes and paprika. Add the pig's feet and mix well. Simmer the pig's feet for 30-40 minutes. Adjust the flavor with salt and pepper and serve.

Let's talk about wine: OK, since we stayed with Italian wines for the last recipe, let's stay with Spanish wines for this one. Try a good Spanish red: **LAN Rejoa**; **Tres Oros Tempranillio.** If we can convince you of nothing else please choose **Cleo** as the wine to pair with this dish.

Sheep's Head

It may be difficult to find this item, but if you are able to it is worth the effort. It is best and easiest to prepare when the head has been cut in half along the midline from front to back.

1 *sheep head, cut in half
¼ cup extra virgin olive oil
4 cloves garlic, minced
1 tablespoon fresh rosemary, minced
Sea salt to taste
Ground black pepper to taste

Combine the olive oil, garlic and rosemary and allow macerating for 1 hour. Brush the halves of the head inside and outside with the infused oil and sprinkle with salt and fresh ground black pepper. Place the sheep's head on a baking sheet, internal side down. Bake in a preheated 400° oven until the meat on the face is done, about 1 hour depending on the size of the head. You can also cook the head on a BBQ grill over indirect heat. Serve with lemon wedges.

Note: All the parts of the head except the bones can be eaten; face meat, tongue, brains, and of course, don't forget the eyes.

Let's talk about wine: The lamb and the richness of the parts of the head (brains, tongue, etc) call for a wine that can really cut through and compliment the richness. A great sparkler would go well here. Try the **Billecart-salmon Brut, Taittinger Rose**; or on the high end **Krug**. This peasant dish calls for a king wine.

Braised Kidneys

4 tablespoons extra virgin olive oil
2 veal kidneys, sliced very thin
4 ounces unsalted butter
4 tablespoons red wine vinegar
1 large red onion, chopped
3 cloves garlic, chopped
2 tablespoons Italian parsley, chopped
3-4 tablespoons dry red wine
Sea salt to taste
Ground black pepper to taste

Heat the oil in a pan over medium heat. Once hot, gently sauté the kidneys 2-3 minutes. Add 2 tablespoons red wine vinegar and cook an additional 3 minutes. Remove the kidneys and drain on paper.

In a second pan over medium heat, add the butter to melt. Add the onion, garlic and parsley and sauté until very soft and the onion starts to caramelize. Add the kidneys and increase the heat to high. Continue cooking until the mixture is almost dry. Add the remaining vinegar and red wine and cook an additional 3-5 minutes. Adjust the flavor with the salt and pepper and serve.

Variation #1: Use lemon juice instead of vinegar and white wine instead of red wine

Variation# 2: Add ½ pound sliced mushrooms when cooking the onions.

Variation #3: Sprinkle the completed dish with 3 coarsely chopped plum tomatoes before serving.

Let's talk about wine: Although rich in some ways, this dish calls for a crisp cold white to pair with it. A sparkler such as **Moet** or **Montaudon** is a good option.

Oxtail Stew

5 pounds of oxtails
2 large yellow onions, 1 inch
2 carrots, 1 inch dice
2 ribs celery, 1 inch dice
4 whole cloves garlic
6 black pepper corns
2 bay leaves
2 tablespoons extra virgin olive oil
1 cup pancetta, ¼ inch dice
½ cup fresh ham, ¼ inch dice
½ cup dry white wine
1-28 oz can whole Italian tomatoes, hand crushed
Pinch ground cloves
Pinch ground cinnamon
Sea salt to taste
Ground black pepper to taste

In a large pot, place the oxtails, one of the onions, one carrot, a celery stick, the garlic, black pepper corns and bay leaves. Cover with water and bring to a boil. Simmer over low heat for 60 minutes, making sure to skim the top of the liquid every 4-5 minutes. Remove the oxtails and drain the cooking liquid into another pot discarding all the vegetables and spices.

Chop the remaining onion, celery and carrot. In a large pan over medium high heat, sauté the vegetables in the olive oil along with the oxtails, pancetta and ham for 10-12 minutes. Add the wine and reduce until there almost no liquid remaining. Add the tomatoes. Cover and cook at a low simmer for about 3 hours until the meat is very tender. Add some of the reserved cooking liquid from time to time as necessary. Add the pinch of ground clove and pinch of ground cinnamon. Stir to blend; adjust flavor with the salt and pepper and serve.

Let's talk about wine: The richness and the gelatinous nature of this soup goes well with a fruit forward merlot. Pair it with the **Courtney Benham Merlot,** or the **Dominican Oaks Cabernet Napa;** or the **Elderton Friends.**

Chapter 11:

COME FLY WITH ME

Come Fly with Me---Chicken and Their Wings From Around the World

Is it me, or is the entire world obsessed with chicken wings? The claim to who has the best wings around is endless. From sports bars, to restaurants, to one's own kitchen, many try to claim to have the best. While we will give you a number of recipes for the "BEST" Buffalo wings, we really don't want to stop there. We will be offering you a series of recipes for wings seasoned with spices and prepared so that you can experience the world wide flavors of this little delectable part of the chicken.

It is unfortunate that we confine ourselves to the wonderful flavors of well cooked wings coated with some combination of butter and our own special hot sauce. While great, we need open ourselves to the worldwide flavors that can impart whole new experiences to our enjoyment of wings.

In this section we will not be confining ourselves to wine parings only. The Monday night football fan would say---What about beer? So this is one of the sections in which we will be offering both beer and wine suggestions.

We will be offering recipes that span the globe in spices and preparations. Once again we encourage you to use all of these as a basis to move beyond them and experiment with your own variations.

After the correct preparation of the wings, everything is dependent upon the spices used in coating the cooked wings. So let's first talk about the preparation and cooking of the wings.

Not only will we concentrate on wings in this chapter, we have also included other recipes for chicken that do not appear in other chapters of the text. We will offer a wide variety of roasting and braising recipes and of course using left over chicken for pot pies and croquets. But let's start with that all time favorite chicken wings.

Cooking the Wings:

The following recipes are designed to provide a serving of 12 pieces and can be adjusted as necessary for additional wings.

To begin, it is best to separate the wings from the drumettes to make for easy handling and even cooking. (Drumettes tend to take longer to cook).

Lightly salt and pepper the chicken pieces. Very lightly dust the wings and drumettes with self rising flour (this will add a slight crispness to the chicken). Deep fry the wings at 350° for 2-3 minutes. Remove and drain on paper towels. Let the oil return to temperature, then deep fry the drumettes for 4-5 minutes. Remove and drain.

When ready to eat, drop both the wings and/or the drumettes in the 350° oil for 2-3 minutes more to completely cook through.

The hot wings should now be tossed in a large bowl that contains the butter or olive oil and seasoning and served immediately. You may have to prepare the coating ahead of time so that it is ready when the wings are ready.

***Note:** Instead of wings or drumettes, all these recipe varieties can be made with chicken tenders.

French Wings

5 tablespoons melted butter
1 tablespoons lemon juice
1 teaspoon Herbs de Provence
1/8 teaspoon white pepper
1/8 teaspoon black pepper
1/8 teaspoon sea salt
¼ teaspoon cayenne pepper

Combine all the ingredients in a large bowl. Add the cooked wings and toss well to coat. Serve immediately.

ITALIAN Wings

½ cup extra virgin olive oil
1 clove garlic, minced
1/8 teaspoon crushed dry oregano
1/8 teaspoon crushed dry basil
1 teaspoon red wine vinegar
½ teaspoon crushed red pepper flakes
2 tablespoons Romano or Parmesan cheese

Combine all the ingredients in a large bowl. Add the cooked wings and toss well to coat. Serve immediately.

MEXICAN Wings

4 tablespoons olive oil
1 shallot, minced
1 clove garlic, minced
1 small Serrano chili, minced (or pick your heat)
1/8 teaspoon dry cumin
1tablespoon fresh cilantro
1 ounce tequila
4 tablespoons unsalted butter, softened

In a sauté pan over medium heat, cook the shallot, garlic and chili in the olive oil until tender. Add all the other ingredients except the butter and cook an additional minute. Remove from the heat. Add the butter. Place in a large bowl and add the wings. Toss to coat and serve.

Wings from ARGENTINA & CHILI Chimichurri Dipping Sauce

1 cup extra virgin olive oil
4 tablespoons fresh lemon juice
2/3 cup flat leaf parsley, minced
2 cloves garlic, minced
2 teaspoons fresh basil, finely chopped
1 teaspoon fresh thyme, finely chopped
1 teaspoon fresh oregano, finely chopped
Sea salt to taste
Ground black pepper to taste
1 teaspoon cayenne

Combine all the ingredients and let stand at least 2 hours before serving. Toss the wings with the sauce or serve on the side.

GREEK Wings

4 tablespoon extra virgin olive oil
1 teaspoon dried Greek oregano, crushed
1 tablespoon red wine vinegar
½ cup crumbled feta cheese
3 pepperoncini pepper, chopped
1 teaspoon fresh ground black pepper

Combine all the ingredients in a large bowl. Add the cooked wings and toss well to coat. Serve immediately.

RUSSIAN Wings

4 tablespoon sour cream
2 tablespoons vodka
1 teaspoon fresh dill, minced
1 small shallot, minced
Sea salt to taste
Ground black pepper to taste

Combine all the ingredients in a large bowl. Add the cooked wings and toss well to coat. Serve immediately.

Wings from INDIA

4 tablespoons melted, unsalted butter
1 teaspoon curry powder
¼ teaspoon cayenne
1 teaspoon fish sauce

Combine all the ingredients in a small saucepot and warm. Place the ingredients in a large bowl and add the cooked wings. Toss to coat wings and serve.

Wings from JAPAN

2 tablespoons soy sauce
1 tablespoon seasoned rice vinegar
2 scallions, split and chopped thin
½ teaspoon fresh, grated ginger
1 tablespoon hot Asian chili oil

Combine all the ingredients in a large bowl. Add the cooked wings and toss well to coat. Serve immediately.

CHINESE

2 tablespoons soy sauce
1 tablespoon oyster sauce or hoisin sauce
2 tablespoons Chinese rice wine
2 tablespoons hot Asian chili oil

Combine all the ingredients in a large bowl. Add the cooked wings and toss well to coat. Serve immediately.

BBQ

1 tablespoon extra virgin olive oil
1 shallot, minced
1 clove garlic, minced
Pinch dry oregano
Pinch dry basil
Pinch ground cumin
Pinch chili powder
Pinch cayenne
¼ cup cream sherry
1 teaspoon sherry vinegar
1 teaspoon soy sauce
1 teaspoon fish sauce
¼ cup ketchup

In a sauté pan over medium heat, cook the shallot and garlic in the olive oil until tender. Add in the spices and heat through. Add the sherry and let the liquid evaporate by half. Add the remaining ingredients and mix thoroughly. Place in a large bowl and add the cooked wings. Toss to coat and serve.

Thai

1 tablespoon peanut oil
1 shallot, minced
1 clove garlic, minced
2 Thai chilies crushed (more to taste)
Juice of one lime
1 teaspoon soy sauce
1 tablespoon Nam Pla
½ cup coconut milk unsweetened
1-2 teaspoons red or green curry paste

In a sauté pan, heat the oil over medium heat. Add the shallot and cook for 1 minute. Add the garlic and sauté an additional 30 seconds. Add the crushed chilies, limejuice, soy, Nam Pla, coconut milk and curry and blend well. Heat through and combine with the wings in a large bowl. Toss to coat and serve.

Buffalo Wings

And finally we come to the bee all and end the entire infamous buffalo wing. I wish I could give you the one and only one recipe for the American standard, but they are as varied as the bars and restaurants that serve them. So I will just give you my favorite recipe and some suggestions for others, and let you decide how to best experiment with them.

4 ounces melted butted
2 cloves garlic, minced
1 tablespoon fresh ground black pepper
1 teaspoon ground white pepper
¼ cup your favorite hot sauce

Combine all the ingredients in a bowl and add the cooked wings. Toss the wings in the mixture and serve.

Variation #1: I have found using the green jalapeño hot sauce (sweeter and milder) tends to be a good choice for those who don't like a lot of heat.

Variation #2: Add 1 tablespoon of good quality soy sauce to the hot sauce to lend a depth of flavor.

Variation #3: When you melt the butter, add 2-3 chopped anchovy filets. Don't tell your guests, but they will be sure to ask what that wonderful deep flavor is.

Let's talk about Wine and Beer and Chicken Wings:

Since you might be serving a number of styles of wings at a party, it would be very difficult to provide you with specific wines to serve. Based on past experience, I have found that the vast majority of people enjoy a good beer with a stack of wings. But if you are to serve wine alone, it is best to remember the motto: **The more heat---the more sweet.** As we have discussed in a number of other place in the book, when offering spicy foods, it is best to offer some sweeter wines to help cut the heat. A *Late Harvest Riesling* like **Washington Hills** or **Ch. San Michele** would go well as would as a *Viognier* like **Spier, Gassier,** or **Oak Grove** would stand up to the heat in the spicier wings. I have also enjoyed Chenin Blanc with some spicy foods and would recommend **Ratts** or **Mulderbosch.** Reds would be a bit harder, but certainly a *Dornfelder* like **Dr. Heidemanns** from Germany would do. As for beer, you might like to stick to a nice *IPA* such as: **Pikes, Dog Fish Head,** or **Harpoon** or an *amber beer or ale* like **Monk in a Trunk**, **Sam Adams**, or **Yuengling. Sam Smith's Organic Larger** would also pair well with the spices of these wings.

French Roasted Chicken

1 3-4pound roasting chicken
2 shallots, sliced
1 lemon, quartered
1 sprig fresh rosemary
2 sprigs fresh flat leaf parsley
1 sprig thyme
3 tablespoon extra virgin olive oil
1 clove garlic, minced
1 teaspoon fresh rosemary, minced
1 teaspoon fresh flat leaf parsley, minced
1/8 teaspoon fresh thyme, minced
1 shallot, minced
3 tablespoons unsalted butter
1 cup dry white wine
¼ cup heavy cream
Sea salt to taste
Ground black pepper to taste

Place a rack in the baking pan and place the chicken on the rack. Into the cavity of the chicken, place the shallots, lemon, rosemary, parsley and thyme sprigs.

In a bowl, combine the 3 tablespoons olive oil, minced garlic, minced rosemary, minced parsley and minced thyme. Blend well. Lightly salt and pepper the outside of the chicken. Rub the blended herbs over the entire chicken. Place the chicken in a pre heated 350° oven, and bake for 45 minutes to one hour. Remove the chicken from the oven and drain any juices that have accumulated in the cavity of the bird into the pan. Place the chicken on a serving platter.

Place the roasting pan on the stove top and heat the juice on a low heat. Add 1 minced shallot and cook for 1 minute. Add the wine and simmer the pan sauce while scraping all the brown bits off the bottom of the pan. Reduce the heat to low. Then add the butter. Add the cream and blend well. Adjust the flavor with the salt and pepper. Serve the chicken with the pan created gravy on the side.

Let's talk about wines: A nice wine to ADD to the pan would be a *dry rose* like **Mulderbosch, Travel,** or **Province**. If you wanted to add a bit of sweetness, you could add a *cream sherry*. Try **Osborne**. A more traditional addition might be a **Macon Villages Chateau de la Tour** or a unoaked *chardonnay* like **Dominican Oaks**. When considering wines to pair, you could serve the wine you add to the dish as the pairing wine as well. You could also consider a light *Pinot Noir* like **Angeline California**, **Mark West**, or **La Crema.** For this dish, I might consider a high end *chardonnay* such as **Newton Unfiltered.**

Italian Roasted Chicken

1 3-4 pound roasting chicken
1 small red onion, quartered
3 cloves garlic, crushed
10 fresh basil leaves
2 tablespoons extra virgin olive oil
2 cloves garlic, minced
1/8 teaspoon sea salt
½ teaspoon ground black pepper
1 teaspoon dried basil, crushed
½ teaspoon dried oregano, crushed
¼ cup grated Romano cheese
2 tablespoon extra virgin olive oil
1 red onion, minced
2 cloves garlic, minced
2 cups dry white wine
Sea salt to taste
Ground black pepper to taste

Place the chicken on a rack in a baking pan. Into the cavity of the chicken, stuff the red onion, crushed garlic, and basil.

In a bowl, combine the olive oil, minced garlic, dried basil, dried oregano and Romano cheese. Blend well, and then rub the entire chicken with the mixture, coating the chicken completely. Bake the chicken in a pre heated 350° oven for 45-60 minutes. Remove the chicken from the oven and drain all the juices from the cavity of the bird into the pan. Set the chicken aside.

Over low heat on the stove top, place the roasting pan. Add 2 tablespoons of olive oil and the sliced red onion. Sauté the onion 2 minutes, then add the garlic. Sauté an additional minute, then add the wine. Reduce the liquid by ½ and serve the chicken with the pan juices gravy on the side.

Let's talk about wines: If we want to stay with the Italian theme, you could ADD a *Pinot Grigio* like **Barone Fini, Armani Venezia,** *or* **Cavit**. Some richness can be added by adding **Vasco Sassetti Rosso** or, *Macchia Barbara.* You might also consider adding dry *Marsala.* As with all other dishes, you can PAIR the wine you ADD with the dish. Additional suggestions might be a *Riesling such as :(* **Bridgeman, Silver Wing,** or **Chateau Saint Michelle**. Don't hesitate serving a light red such as a *Chianti* like **Trecciano** or a *Pinot Noir like* **Castle Roc; River Road Reserve, or Sonoma Cuvee**.

Chinese Roasted Chicken

1 3-4 pound roasting chicken
3 tablespoons soy sauce
2 tablespoons oyster sauce
1 tablespoon sesame oil
1 small yellow onion, quartered
2 large slices fresh ginger
2 cloves garlic, mashed
1 tablespoon canola oil
1 teaspoon onion powder
1 teaspoon onion powder
1 tablespoon soy sauce
1 tablespoon fish sauce
1tablespoon oyster sauce
1 tablespoon sesame oil
2 tablespoons extra virgin olive oil
1 yellow onion, sliced thin
½ cup low sodium chicken broth
½ cup dry white wine
Sea salt to taste
Ground black pepper to taste

Place the chicken on a rack in a baking pan. In the cavity of the chicken, place the soy sauce, oyster sauce and sesame oil. Using your hand rub the entire inside of the chicken with the mixture. Into the cavity, stuff the yellow onion, ginger and garlic. In a separate bowl, combine the canola oil, onion powder, garlic powder, soy sauce, fish sauce, oyster sauce and sesame oil. Blend well. Rub the entire outside of the chicken with the mixture and place in a 350 degree preheated oven for 45-60 minutes. Remove the chicken from the pan and drain all the cavity juices into the pan. Over a low heat on the stove top, place the roasting pan. Add the olive oil and the onions and cook until the onions are tender. Add the chicken broth and the wine and simmer until the liquid is reduced by 1/3. Serve the chicken with the pan gravy.

Let's talk about wines: Here it might be best to ADD a very light white like a **Vinho Verde Grazela** or a *Pinot Grigio* **Conte Fini**. To add richness to the dish you could ADD a full bodied *chardonnay* like **Muirwood or Sonoma Loeb Reserve.** As always use the wine you ADD as the wine you PAIR. In addition you might choose to pair a Torrentes like **Mendoza Station** or a full bodied *Albarino*. A nice red that would complement the dish would be a fruity *Shiraz* like **Gumdale Reserve, Jip Jip Rocks, or Yellowtail**. This would also PAIR with a *beer* such as Dogfish **Head** or a **Hafwissen** from Germany.

Spanish Roasted Chicken

1 3-4 pound roasting chicken
1 tablespoon extra virgin olive oil
1 tablespoon Spanish paprika
½ teaspoon sea salt
1 teaspoon ground black pepper
¼ cup Spanish dry sherry
1 small yellow onion, quartered
5 cloves garlic, crushed
2 tablespoons extra virgin olive oil
1 tablespoon Spanish paprika
Sea salt to taste
Ground black pepper to taste
1 yellow onion, minced
2 cloves garlic, minced
¼ pound Spanish chorizo, grated
½ cup dry red or white wine
½ cup low sodium chicken broth
Sea salt to taste
Ground black pepper to taste

Place the chicken on a rack in a baking pan. In a bowl, combine the olive oil, paprika, salt, pepper and sherry. Blend well and coat the inside of the chicken cavity with the mixture. Place the quartered onion and the crushed garlic into the cavity of the bird.

Rub the outside of the chicken with 2 tablespoons of olive oil. Season the chicken with some more paprika, salt and pepper. Bake the chicken in a preheated 350° oven for 45-60 minutes. Once done, remove the chicken from the roasting pan, draining the cavity juices back into the pan. Place the roasting pan on the stove top. Set the chicken aside.

Over medium heat, add the onion to the pan and sauté 2 minutes. Add the garlic and sauté an additional minute. Add the ground chorizo and sauté 30 seconds. Add the wine and chicken broth and reduce by 1/3. Adjust the flavor with the salt and pepper. Serve the pan gravy on the side with the chicken.

Let's Talk about Wines: ADD: Even though it is chicken, this is a bold dish and you should not be fearful of adding bold wines. A big bold *Spanish red* like **Clio** or a Bold Zinfandel such as: **Rosenblum ,** or **Sobon Paul's Vineyard.** or even a *cabernet* like **Coastline, Dominican Oaks, Montoya, or Liberty School** would add much to the dish. If you choose a white you might want to stick with a *Bordeaux Blanc* like **Rothschild,** or **Chateau Bonnet.** When choosing wine to PAIR with this dish, you could stick with the ADD wine or select a complimentary wine such as a nice ***Rioja; Crianza, or* Monte Buena** or an elegant *merlot* like **Duckhorn, Elderton,** or **Bridgeman.** As for a white, try a nice *Albarino* or *Viognier*.

Greek Roasted Chicken

1 3-4 pound roasting chicken
1 yellow onion, quartered
4 cloves garlic, crushed
3 sprigs fresh oregano
3 sprigs fresh flat leaf parsley
1 lemon, quartered
Juice of one lemon
Zest of one lemon, grated
1 clove garlic, minced
1 tablespoon fresh oregano, crushed
Sea salt to taste
Ground black pepper to taste
1 red onion, minced
2 cloves garlic, minced
1 cup dry white wine

Sea salt to taste
Ground black pepper to taste

Place the chicken on a rack in a baking pan. Stuff the cavity of the chicken with the quartered onion, crushed garlic, quartered lemon, fresh oregano and fresh parsley.

In a bowl, combine the olive oil, lemon juice, lemon zest, minced garlic, dry oregano and a pinch of salt and ground black pepper. Blend well. Rub the entire outside of the chicken with the mixture. Bake the chicken in a preheated 350° oven for 45-60 minutes. Remove the chicken from the roasting pan, draining the cavity juices into the pan. Place the pan on the stove top over medium heat. Set the chicken aside.

Add the red onion and garlic to the roasting pan and cook until translucent. Add the wine and reduced by 1/3. Adjust the flavor with salt and pepper and serve with the roasted chicken.

Let's talk about Wines: With the lemon undercurrent in this dish, it might be best to ADD a *Sauvignon Blanc* like **Adler Fels, Kim Crawford,** or **Gordon Brothers** as this will enhance the sauce and the lemon. You could also try a *dry rose* such as: **Mendoza Station** or **Beaulieu Vineyards** as this will add another layer of flavor to the pan gravy. When choosing wine to PAIR with this dish, you could stick with the ADD wine. In addition, you could choose a **Pinot Grigio** like **Santa Margarita, Barone Fini,** or **Kupelwieser.** A *Bordeaux Blanc* would also work very well with the dish. Try **Rothschild Blanc.** As for Greek wines, you could PAIR the dish with **Domestica Red or White.** You could even try one of the **Retsina** wines.

Indian Roasted Chicken

1 3-4 pound roasting chicken
¼ cup coconut milk
1 tablespoon curry paste
1 yellow onion, quartered
4 cloves garlic, crushed
2 large slices fresh ginger

2 tablespoon canola oil
½ teaspoon garlic powder
½ teaspoon onion powder
1 teaspoon curry powder
Sea salt to taste
Ground black pepper to taste

Place the chicken on a rack in a baking pan. In a bowl combine the coconut milk and curry paste and blend well. Coat the entire inside cavity of the chicken with the mixture. Stuff the cavity with the quartered onion, mashed garlic and slices of ginger.

In a bowl, combine the canola oil, salt and pepper, onion powder, garlic powder and curry powder. Blend together and coat the entire outside of the chicken with the mixture. Bake in a 350° preheated oven for 45-60 minutes and serve.

Let's talk about wine: This very aromatic dish calls for a wine that can compliment it like a *dry Riesling* or a *Gewürztraminer* like **Rene Sparr, Albrecht,** or **Washington Hills**. Or try a nice rich *pinot noir* such as: **Meiomi, Pahlmeyer Jayson,** or **Patz & Hall**.

Chicken Kiev

4-8 ounce skinless, boneless chicken breasts, pounded thin
8 tablespoons cold unsalted butter, cut into small cubes
4 scallions, finely chopped
4 teaspoons fresh flat leaf parsley, finely chopped
½ cup all purpose flour
4 eggs, beaten
1 cup plain dry breadcrumbs
4 tablespoons extra virgin olive oil for frying
Sea salt to taste
Ground black pepper to taste

Pound the chicken breasts between sheets of plastic wrap, being careful not to break through the breasts. Season the pounded breasts lightly with salt and ground black pepper. On each breast, place 2 tablespoons of the cubed butter, 1 chopped scallion and 1 teaspoon of chopped parsley. Roll the breasts, folding in the sides, to make a tight roll, encasing the butter and scallions. Roll each chicken breast in the flour, then in the egg and finally in the breadcrumbs. Place them seam side down on a plate, and refrigerate for 2 hours.

When ready to cook, remove the chicken from the refrigerator. In a large sauté pan over medium heat, add the olive oil. Cook the chicken until a deep golden color on all sides. Be careful not to handle the chicken rolls too roughly. You want to keep the butter from leaking from the inside of the rolls. Serve as is or with some cooked rice. If done correctly, when you cut into the chicken, the butter and herbs will flow out making their own butter gravy.

Variation #1: Stuff the chicken with grated mozzarella and chopped ham.

Variation #2: Lay a slice of prosciutto on the chicken breast and some crumbled gorgonzola before rolling.

Variation # 3: Use either veal cutlets or chicken cutlets instead of chicken in any of the variations.

Let's talk about wine: This dish calls for a rich *chardonnay* like La **Crema, Newton Unfiltered, Chalk Hill, Mer Soleil Gold, Lloyd, Sonoma Loeb Reserve** or **Martin Ray RRV Reserve**

Chicken with Tomatoes and Onions

4 skinless boneless chicken breasts
4 Tbs extra virgin olive oil
1 large sweet onion sliced thinly
2 cloves garlic sliced thinly
1 28oz can San Marzano Tomatoes hand crushed
1 Tbs fresh basil chopped
Salt and pepper to taste

Heat the oil in a frying pan. Lightly salt and pepper the chicken breasts. Place in the pan and sauté until just done. Remove and reserve. Add the onions to the pan and sauté until tender. Add the garlic and sauté an additional minute. Add the hand crushed tomatoes and stir well. Add the basil. Continue sautéing for 3-4 minutes. Adjust the salt and pepper and return the chicken breasts to the pan. Heat the breasts through and serve.

Let's talk about wine: This is a simple and somewhat light dish. It should be paired with a like wine. A nice Sangiovese would go well like the **Macchia** or the **Sobon** from California or the **Il Ginepro** from Italy. You could also go with a somewhat richer wine like the **Courtney Benham Merlot** or the **Rudy Cabernet**.

Chicken Putanesca

4 skinless boneless chicken breasts
4 TBs extra virgin olive oil
1 large sweet onion sliced thinly
2 cloves garlic sliced thinly
6 anchovy filets chopped
1 28oz can San Marzano Tomatoes hand crushed
½ cup assorted cured Italian olives sliced
1 Tbs cappers
1 pinch crushed red pepper flakes
Salt and pepper to taste

Heat the oil in a pan. Lightly salt and pepper the breasts and add them to the pan. Sauté the chicken breasts until just done. Remove and reserve. Add the onions to the pan and sauté until tender. Add the garlic and sauté an additional; minuet. Add the anchovy filets and allow to melt. Add the tomatoes and stir well. Add the olives and the capers and cook together 2-3 minutes. Return the chicken to the pan and heat through. Serve.

Let's talk about wine: This is a rich dish with complex flavors and calls for a wine to match it. An excellent pair would be the **Rocca Felice Dolcetto de Alba** as would the **Villa Malfi Valpolicella Repasso**. You might want to go high end with a full Amarone such as the **Zenato Amarone.**

Chicken with Apricot Glaze

This is a very simple chicken dish that produces outstanding results.

4 chicken breasts bone in and skinned
Salt and pepper to season
1 8oz jar good apricot preserves
3 Tbs good quality soy sauce
1 Tbs good quality hot sauce

Pre heat an oven to 400 degrees. Lightly season the chicken breasts and brush with half the soy sauce. Combine the remaining soy with the apricot preserves and the hot sauce in a bow; blend well and reserve. Place on a pan and place in the over bone side down. Bake at 400 degrees for 30 minutes. Baste the breasts with half the glaze and bake an additional 10 minutes. Baste with the remaining glaze and bake an additional 5 minutes. Serve.

Let's talk about wine: The sweet/spicy nature of this dish calls for wines such as: **Washington Hills Riesling; Dr. Heidemanns QBA**; **Jean Albrecht Gewürztraminer.** The **Mulderbosch Chenin Blanc** would also pair well as it also has a slight bit of sweetness.

Chapter 12:

OCEANS, RIVERS AND STREAMS

OCEANS RIVERS & STREAMS

The earth is over three quarters water--oceans, rivers, and streams. There is more life in the waters than on land or in the sky. We have plundered the resources of the great bodies of water to near exhaustion but recently we have learned that we can get more from careful management and farming than we can get from wholesale plunder.

Some countries don't agree with our desire to manage these resources but they will eventually have to side with us as these resources diminish. We really can live in harmony with the natural resources of the water, but we all need to agree to cooperate.

This chapter is devoted to some of the great dishes from the waters of the earth. These seafood dishes are in addition to the various fish and shellfish dishes that you can fined in other chapters of this text.

Chef Joe is one of the most renowned seafood chefs in South Florida having been an executive chef for Legal Seafood, in addition to a TV personality demonstrating the ease of preparation of great seafood dishes at home, for the TV audience.

Here we provide you with many great seafood dishes with the hope you enjoy them, and the wine pairings that we have suggested.

Clams Casino

24 middle neck clams
6 strips bacon, ¼ inch strips
½ cup red pepper, ¼ inch diced
½ cup green pepper, ¼ inch diced
2 garlic cloves, chopped
¼ cup green onions, ¼ inch chop
2 tablespoons Italian parsley, chopped
¼ cup sherry

½ cup seasoned breadcrumbs
½ stick unsalted butter, cut into small cubes
Ground black pepper to taste

are fully open the clams with a clam knife. (Be sure to use a protective glove or towel to hold the clam when trying to open). Scrap all the meat into one side of the clam and place on a cookie sheet. Discard the empty other half of the clam.

In a sauté pan over medium heat, render down the bacon until almost crispy. Remove the bacon pieces from the pan and set aside. Add the red and green peppers to the bacon fat and cook for 1 minute. Add the garlic and green onions and cook for one minute more. Add the parsley and season with some ground black pepper. Deglaze the pan with the sherry; reduce the liquid by half and remove from the heat. Blend in the reserved bacon pieces and the breadcrumbs to make the stuffing.

Stuff each clam with the stuffing. Top off each clam with a small cube of butter. Bake in a pre-heated 350° oven for 15 minutes. Serve with wedges of lemon.

Let's talk about wine: We feel that clams are one of those dishes that cries out sparklers whether they are raw or cooked. Try the **Montaudon Brut Rose**, **Rondel Rose Cava**, **Moet,** or the **Graham Beck Brut Rose.** If you wanted to stay with a still wine we certainly would suggest a *dry rose* such as a **Travel,** or **Muga**, or **Mulderbosch**.

Clams Posillipo

¼ cup extra virgin olive oil
4 garlic cloves, sliced
1 yellow onion, chopped
½ cup white wine
2-28 ounce cans San Marzano style plum tomatoes, hand crushed
2 tablespoons fresh oregano, chopped
2 tablespoons fresh basil, chopped
2 tablespoons Italian parsley, chopped
24 little neck clams
¼ cup extra virgin olive oil

½ cup white wine
Sea salt to taste
Ground black pepper to taste

In a saucepot over medium heat, add the olive oil. Add the garlic, cook for 30 seconds or until golden, then add the onions and cook until the onions are translucent, but not brown. Add the white wine, reduce by half, then add the tomatoes, oregano, basil, parsley and the salt and pepper to taste. Simmer for 30 minutes.

In a separate pot with a lid, over medium high heat, add the olive oil. Wait until the oil is very hot, then carefully add the clams and then the wine to the pot, and close the lid. Steam the clams for 3-4 minutes, then add the reserved sauce to the clams, close the pot lid again, and allow the clams to steam completely open; another 4-6 minutes. Serve with some crusty Italian bread.

Let's talk about wine: see suggestions after recipe#1

Stuffed Baked Clams Oreganata

24 little neck clams
3 tablespoons extra virgin olive oil
3 garlic cloves, minced
¼ cup dry white wine
½ cup dry seasoned breadcrumbs
¼ teaspoon fresh basil, chopped
¼ teaspoon fresh oregano, chopped
½ teaspoon green onions, chopped
4 tablespoons grated Romano cheese
½ stick unsalted butter, cut into small cubes

In a large sauté pan over medium high heat, add the olive oil. Once the oil is hot, add the garlic, cook for 30 seconds or until the garlic is golden. Then, add the wine. Reduce the wine by half and remove from the heat. Blend together the breadcrumbs, basil, oregano, scallions, garlic, cheese and olive oil, and add it to the pan. Mix well until the breadcrumbs have soaked up all the liquid. Divide the mixture evenly into each clam. Top off each clam with a small cube of butter.

Bake in a preheated 350° oven for 15 minutes. Serve with wedges of lemon.

Let's talk about wine: see suggestions after recipe #1

Fried Clams

1 pound Ipswich clams, shucked from shell, tail cleaned and rinsed well
or
24 cherry stone clams, shucked from shell, rinsed well
2 ½ cups cornmeal
1 cup cake flour
1/2 cup Panko breadcrumbs
2 teaspoons garlic powder
2 teaspoons onion powder
1 teaspoon old bay seasoning
2 eggs, beaten
2 cups buttermilk
Oil for deep frying

In a bowl, combine the eggs and buttermilk. Add the shucked clams to the batter and allow the clams to sit for at least two hours before use. In a separate bowl, blend the flours, panko, onion powder, garlic powder and old bay seasoning in a bowl. When ready to cook, drain the excess buttermilk from the clams using a sieve until well drained. Add the clams to the flour mix and coat well. Be careful not to cook too many clams at one time, causing them to stick together. Deep fry the clams until golden in 350° oil. Serve with lemon and/or cocktail sauce or tartar sauce.

Let's talk about beer: Somehow fried clams just go best with a cold beer. Suggested beers would be: **Long Hammer IPA** or **Pikes IPA.** Also **Bass Ale** would pair well as would **Kirin.**

*Note: Recipes 1-4 can be made using oysters as well as clams.

Oysters Rockefeller

12 large oysters, shucked and returned to half a
  shell (Blue Point oysters preferably)
6 ounces baby spinach, stems removed
4 ounces unsalted butter
2 ¾ cups yellow onion, minced
¼ cup celery, minced
2 each garlic cloves, minced
2 tablespoons Pernod liqueur
½ cup Ritz Crackers, crushed
6 ounces gruyere Swiss
Sea salt to taste
Ground black pepper to taste

Place the oysters on a cookie sheet and set aside.
Bring 1 quart of water to a boil in a medium pot.
Add the spinach and cook until very tender and
the water is green--5 to 6 minutes. Drain the
spinach in a colander set over a large bowl and
reserve 2 3/4 cups of the cooking liquid. Let the
spinach sit until cool enough to handle; squeeze
spinach well and then finely chop; set aside.

Melt the butter in a medium pot over medium
high heat. When the butter is foamy, add the
onions, celery and garlic and cook, stirring until
soft and translucent, but not brown, about 3
minutes. Add the reserved spinach water, bring
to a boil and cook for 1 minute. Add the chopped
spinach, liqueur, salt and pepper and simmer,
stirring occasionally, until the mixture reduces
slightly, about 10 minutes. Remove from the heat,
add the crackers and stir well to combine. Cool
completely before using.

Divide the spinach mixture among the oysters.
Top each oyster with a ½ounce of the Swiss
cheese. Bake in a preheated 475° oven for 10
minutes and serve.

Let's talk about wine: This very rich, high end
dish calls for a high end sparkler like one of the
following *champagnes*: **Billecart-Salmon Brut
Reserve or Brut Rose**; **Moet Rose**; **Montaudon
Classe M**; **Krug Brut**.

Crispy Soft-Shell Crab with Lemon-Pepper Remoulade

1 cup cornmeal
1 cup all purpose flour
2 tablespoons Old Bay seasoning
2 eggs, beaten
2 cups buttermilk
1 cup all purpose flour
6-8 soft-shelled crabs, cleaned of the gills and
  skirt flap
Canola oil to deep fry
Sea salt to taste
Ground black pepper to taste
Fresh lemons as garnish

In a large bowl, combine the cornmeal, flour, and
Old Bay seasoning and set aside. In another bowl,
beat the egg and add the buttermilk and set aside.
In a third bowl, place some flour.

Dust the crabs lightly in the flour and then
dip them in the egg. Immediately, dredge the
crab in the cornmeal blend. Place the crab in a
preheated 350° deep fryer until very crisp-- about
4-5 minutes. Remove from fryer and allow the
crabs to drain a bit on some paper towel. Season
lightly with salt and fresh ground black pepper
and serve with the lemon-pepper Remoulade and
lemon wedges on the side.

Lemon-Pepper Remoulade:

1cup mayonnaise
1 tablespoon Dijon mustard
1 tablespoon small capers
½ oz lemon juice
½ teaspoon lemon zest
1 garlic clove, minced
1 each anchovy, minced
1 teaspoon horseradish, drained
Sea salt to taste
1 teaspoon coarse grind black pepper

Combine all ingredients in a mixing bowl and
blend well. Allow the Remoulade to sit for about
an hour before using.

Let's talk about wine: The overall taste of the dish

would be greatly complimented by a California Style *Sauvignon Blanc* such as: **Amici; Adler Fels; Courtney Benham ; Robert Mondavi Fume Blanc** or one of the lighter *New Zealand Styles* such as: **Nobilo** or **The Crossings**.

with a rich flavor that can stand up to wine such as a *light pinot noir*: **La Crema**; **Truscott**; **Angeline California**; **Cruz Alta** or *a rich chardonnay* from California such as: **Mer Soleil Gold**; **Sonoma Loeb Reserve**; **Muirwood Single Vineyard** or **Lloyd.**

Herb Breadcrumb Encrusted Blue Fish

2-8 to 9 ounce each, blue fish filets, skin on
1 cup Panko breadcrumb
2 cloves garlic, minced
2 green onions, minced
2 tablespoon Italian parsley, minced
¼ cup Romano cheese
¼ cup extra virgin olive oil
Juice of half a lemon
Sea salt to taste
Ground black pepper to taste
Fresh lemons wedges as garnish

In a bowl, blend together the Panko, garlic, green onion, parsley, Romano cheese, olive oil and lemon juice. Adjust the flavor with a bit of salt and pepper. On a baking sheet, coated with a bit of olive oil, lay the blue fish filets, skin side down on the baking sheet. Divide the breadcrumb mixture on top of the filets evenly. Bake the filets in a preheated 350° oven until done----about 20-30 minutes. Place the filets under the broiler for 2-3 minutes to brown the crust. Serve with the lemon wedges.

Variation #1: Mix ¼ cup chopped fresh mushrooms with the breadcrumb mixture.

Variation #2: Add ¼ teaspoon chopped fresh rosemary to the breadcrumb mixture.

Variation #3: Add 1 tablespoon grated lemon zest to the breadcrumb mixture.

Variation #4: Add ½ teaspoon cayenne pepper to the breadcrumb mixture.

Variation #5: Substitute snapper, grouper, or flounder for the bluefish.

Let's talk about wine: Bluefish is a very oily fish

Red Snapper with Olives and Tomatoes

4 –9-10 ounce Red Snapper filets, skin and pins bones removed
¼ cup seasoned flour
3 tablespoons extra virgin olive oil
2 anchovy filets, chopped
¼ cup Cerignola green olives, sliced
¼ cup Gaeta black olives, sliced
2 plum tomatoes, coarse chop
1 tablespoon Italian parsley, chopped
Sea salt to taste
Ground black pepper to taste
Crushed chili flake to taste
1 tablespoon fresh basil, chiffonade

Dredge the snapper filets in the seasoned flour, shaking off the excess. In a large sauté pan over medium high heat, add the oil in a pan. Place the fish, skin side down first in the pan and cook for 1-2 minutes. Carefully turn the filets over and cook the snapper for another 1-2 minutes. Remove the fish from the pan and set aside on a warm platter.

Reserving the oil in the pan, add the chopped anchovy filets and allow them to melt in the oil. Add the olives and the tomatoes and heat through. Adjust the flavor with the salt, pepper and the chili flake. Simmer for 5 minutes. Add the fresh basil to the pan, stir and pour over the fish.

Variation #1: Add ¼ cup sautéed mushrooms to the pan when you add the olives and tomatoes.

Variation #2: Add ¼ cup sliced marinated artichokes to the pan when you add the olives and tomatoes.

Variation #3: Add 2 tablespoons balsamic vinegar when you add the olives and tomatoes.

Let's talk about wine: As with the previous dish, you have one that can be best complimented by a light *pinot noir* or rich *chardonnay*. You might choose one of the wines suggested there or perhaps a *chardonnay* such as: **Chalk Hills**; **Groth** or **Patz and Hall.**

Classic Shrimp Scampi

12 large shrimp, 13/15 size, peeled and deveined, tail on
2 tablespoons extra virgin olive oil
3 tablespoons unsalted butter
½ cup flour
4 cloves garlic, minced
¼ cup dry white wine
Juice of half a lemon
½ cup low sodium fish or chicken stock
1 tablespoon unsalted butter, cold
1 tablespoon fresh basil, chopped
1 tablespoons Italian parsley, chopped
Lemon wedges for garnish
Sea salt to taste
Ground black pepper to taste

In a sauté pan over medium high heat, add the olive oil and the butter. Dust the shrimp with some flour and add the shrimp to the pan and cook them about 2 minutes on each side; or until the shrimp are slightly opaque.

Immediately, add the garlic to the pan; continue to sauté the shrimp with the garlic for about 30 seconds. Then immediately deglaze the pan with the wine and lemon juice. Remove the shrimp from the pan and place on a warm serving plate. Reduce the wine by 1/2. Add the stock and bring to a simmer. Reduce the liquid a bit more. Remove the pan from the heat; swirl in the cold butter until completely incorporated. Adjust the flavor with salt and pepper. Finish the pan sauce by adding the fresh basil and parsley to the sauce. Immediately, pour over the shrimp. Serve with some lemon wedges on the side.

Let's talk about wine: With this classic we suggest you stay with one of the *classic light Italian whites*: **Kupelwieser Pinot Grigio; Barone Fini Pinot Grigio, Bellini Soave; Bolla Orvieto Classico; Kupelwieser Pinot Blanco.**

Salmon Carpaccio

1 pound fresh Alaskan salmon filet, chilled and sliced very thin at a 45 degree angle*
4 tablespoons extra virgin olive oil
2 tablespoons fresh lemon juice
2 green onions, minced fine
3 tablespoons small capers
3 cups arugula
2 tablespoons fresh lemon juice
3 tablespoons extra virgin olive oil
Drizzle of Mustard Aioli (see recipe), optional
Sea salt to taste
Ground black pepper to taste

Slice the salmon filets very thinly and place on a serving plate in a single layer. Drizzle the 4 tablespoons of olive oil and the 2 tablespoons of lemon juice over the sliced salmon. Season the salmon lightly with the salt and pepper. Sprinkle the scallions over the salmon along with the capers. Cover the salmon with plastic wrap and allow the salmon to macerate for 1-2 hours refrigerated.

In a bowl, add the arugula, lemon juice, olive oil and salt and pepper to taste and toss gently. Remove the salmon from the refrigerator. Place the arugula salad in the center of the salmon. Drizzle a bit of the mustard sauce over the salmon and the salad and serve.

*****Note:** You may also take the slices of salmon and place them between two pieces of plastic wrap and gently pound them thin.

Mustard Aioli:

1 ½ ounces champagne vinegar
2 ounces Dijon mustard

1 small shallot, minced
2 garlic cloves, minced
Juice of 1/2 a lemon
1 egg yolk
2 cups olive oil
Sea salt to taste
Ground black pepper to taste

In a food processor, add the vinegar, mustard, shallot, garlic, lemon juice and egg yolk. Turn processor on and whip ingredients for 30 seconds; then begin to add the oil slowly to the processor. Adjust the flavor with a bit of salt and pepper.

Let's talk about wine: This appetizer calls for a *dry Prosecco* such as the **Santi Nello** or the **Niño Franco.** You could also try a *dry to medium dry sherry* such as the **Sandmen** or **Taylor.**

Shrimp Fra Diavolo

1 ½ pounds jumbo shrimp, 13/15 size, peeled and deveined, tail off
¼ cup extra virgin olive oil
4 cloves garlic, crushed
½ teaspoon crushed red pepper flakes
¾ cup white wine
1-28 ounce can San Marzano plum tomatoes, hand crushed
4 large basil leaves, torn into large pieces
Sea salt to taste
Ground black pepper to taste
¼ cup extra virgin olive oil

In a saucepan over medium high heat, add the oil. Add the crushed garlic and cook until a light golden color. Add the crushed red pepper flake; cook for 10 seconds, then add the white wine, the hand crushed tomatoes, basil, salt and pepper. Cook for 30 minutes. Add the shrimp, and allow to poach in the sauce until the shrimp becomes opaque. (Be careful not to overcook the shrimp). Serve as is, or over your favorite pasta.

Variation #1: Instead of shrimp, use the meat taken from 3-4 lobster tails cut into large chunks.

Variation #2: Instead of shrimp, use 2 dozen cleaned little neck clams and cover the pan once all the ingredients are in. Cook until all the clams are open being sure to discard any that don't open.

Let's talk about wine: A great southern Italian red such as the **Calea Nero d'Avola** would pair well as wood a *Chianti Reserva* such as the **Bellin**i or **Ruffino.** You could also move to California for a great Italian such as the **Macchia Sangiovese** or the **Macchia Barbera.**

Shrimp & Chicken Jambalaya

1 pound jumbo shrimp, 16/20 size, peeled and deveined
1 pound chicken tenderloins cut into 1 inch cubes
¼ cup Creole seasoning* (see recipe)
4 tablespoons olive oil
½ cup celery, ½ inch chop
½ cup yellow onion, ½ inch chop
½ cup sweet red pepper, ½ inch chop
2 garlic cloves, chopped
1 cup plum tomato, coarse chop
3 green onions, ¼ inch chop
3 tablespoons all purpose flour
¼ cup fresh lemon juice
2 tablespoons Worcestershire
2 tablespoons whole grain mustard
2 cups water

Generously season the shrimp and chicken with the Creole seasoning. In a large skillet style pan, over medium high heat, add the oil. Carefully place the chicken in the skillet and allow the chicken to sear on one side. Do not shake the pan or move the chicken. After about 2-3 minutes, turn the chicken over and complete the cooking process. Remove the chicken from the pan and reserve.

Using the same pan, and following the same cooking procedure as the chicken, sear the shrimp. The cooking time for the shrimp will be slightly less than the chicken. Remove the shrimp from the pan and reserve.

In the same pan, reducing the heat to medium, add the celery, onion and red pepper. Cook the vegetables until just tender. Add the garlic and cook an additional minute. Add the flour and cook stirring all the time until the flour takes on a light golden color. Add the tomato, green onions, lemon juice, Worcestershire and mustard and mix well. Add the water and stir until thickened. Add the chicken and shrimp back to the pan and heat through. Adjust flavor with salt and pepper if needed and serve over white rice.

Creole Seasoning:

3 tablespoons sea salt
5 tablespoons paprika
2 tablespoons onion powder
2 tablespoons garlic powder
2 tablespoons dried oregano
1 tablespoon dried thyme
1 tablespoon cumin
1 tablespoon black pepper
1 tablespoon white pepper
1 tablespoon cayenne pepper

In a mixing bowl, combine all the ingredients and mix well.

Let's talk about Beer: Good Cajun food calls for a good beer. Serve one of the following: **Yuengling Lager**, **Land shark**, **Dog Fish Head**, or **Magic Hat #9** for great pairings. This dish would pair with a rich wine such as a *petite syrah* such as **Martin Family**; **Earthquake** or my personal favorite **Macchia.**

Cornmeal Crusted Ruby Red Trout with Raspberry-Jalapeno Compound Butter

2-9-11 ounces each, butterfly ruby red trout,
1 cup rice flour, seasoned with some salt and pepper

2 eggs, beaten
1 tablespoon milk
1 cup white cornmeal
2 ounces canola oil
2 tablespoons unsalted butter
1 ounce Raspberry-Jalapeno Butter*(see recipe)
Sea salt to taste
Ground black pepper to taste

Trim the trout of any belly fat that may remain, along with the dorsal fin. Rinse the trout with water and pat dry with paper towel. Set aside.

Next, in one dish, place the rice flour and season with salt and pepper. In another dish, combine the eggs with the milk. In a third dish, place the cornmeal. Following a standard breading procedure, dust the trout with the seasoned rice flour and then dip it into the egg batter, then into the cornmeal flour. Be sure to coat completely. (It's not necessary to bread the skin side of the trout.) Let the trout sit for 10 minutes before cooking.

In a large non-stick sauté over medium high heat, add the oil and melt the butter. Once hot, sear the trout, cornmeal side down, for two to three minutes, or until the trout is a deep golden brown. Turn the trout over to cook the skin side for one or two minutes more and plate immediately. Top the trout with a couple of slices of the raspberry-jalapeno compound butter.

*Raspberry-Jalapeno Compound Butter:

1 stick (4 ounces) unsalted butter, room temperature
1 teaspoon fresh jalapeno, seeds and membrane removed, minced
2 tablespoons fresh raspberry puree
1 teaspoon lemon juice
Pinch of sea salt

In a mixing bowl with the paddle attachment, place the room temperature butter. On low speed, start to break the butter up into a paste. Once the paste has formed, add the remaining ingredients to the bowl and blend until incorporated, but not over whipped. Using a sheet of wax or parchment paper, place the blended butter at one end of the paper across the length of the paper. Carefully roll the butter inside the paper to form a tube, about 1 inch in diameter. Place the stick of butter on a flat surface and refrigerate until solid.

Let's talk about wine: We don't do it too often but sometimes we like to treat ourselves with a great wine to compliment a very nice dish. This dish would pair well with a complex merlot and if we wanted to go high end we would suggest a merlot such as the **Duckhorn Estates** or **Pahlmeyer** or **Twomey.**

Cedar Smoked Wild Alaskan King Salmon

4-5 pound side of wild salmon, skin on, pin bones removed, trimmed of some belly fat
Aluminum foil sheet long enough to hold the salmon
1 cup light brown sugar
3 tablespoons sea salt
2 teaspoons ground black pepper
2 garlic cloves, minced
2 tablespoons fresh basil, chopped
2 tablespoons green onion, chopped
1 tablespoon fresh tarragon, chopped
1 tablespoon fresh thyme, chopped
1 tablespoon Italian parsley, chopped

Place the side of salmon on top of the foil sheet. Begin to evenly sprinkle the brown sugar over the entire surface of the salmon. In a mixing bowl, combine the salt, pepper, garlic, basil, green onion, tarragon, thyme, and parsley, and mix well. Evenly distribute the herb mix over the top of the salmon.

To smoke the salmon, build a smoker with smoldering hardwood chips, keeping the temperature inside the smoker between 150° and 160°. (Apple wood or cherry wood chips are a nice selection.) Smoke the salmon until the thickest part of the fish registers 150°, (about 1 ½ hours). Serve immediately or serve at room temperature. Can also be wrapped tightly and refrigerated for up to 4 days.

Let's talk about wine: This would be a perfect dish to pair with a light to medium *pinot noir* such as: **Angeline RRV; Belle Gloss Meiomi;** or one even lighter like **Mark West.** Another *light red* that would go well might be the **G&D Beaujolais.** You could also try a *richer rose* like **Pigmentum; Muga** or **Mulderbosch.**

Grilled Mojo Marinated Halibut Steak with Red Onion Jam

4-16-20 ounces each, halibut steaks, center bone intact
1 ½ cups Mojo marinade*(see recipe)
1 cup red onion jam**(see recipe)

Marinate the Halibut steaks in the Mojo marinade for at least three to four hours before grilling.

*Mojo Marinade:

3 garlic cloves, coarse chop
¼ cup yellow onion, diced
½ cup orange juice
¼ teaspoon orange zest
¼ cup lime juice
¼ teaspoon lime zest
½ teaspoon cumin
½ teaspoon fresh oregano, fine chop
¼ teaspoon ground black pepper
½ teaspoon sea salt
1 tablespoon fresh cilantro, fine chop
½ cup olive oil

In a blender, add the garlic, onion, orange juice and orange zest, the lime juice and the lime zest, cumin, oregano, pepper, salt, and cilantro. Pulse the blender to incorporate the ingredients, then slowly begin to add the olive oil to the blender to complete the marinade. Blend until smooth.

**Red Onion Jam:

2 tablespoons olive oil
2 each red onions, thinly sliced
¼ cup granulated sugar
1 tablespoon fresh thyme, fine chop
½ cup tawny port
½ cup balsamic vinegar

½ teaspoon sea salt
¼ teaspoon ground black pepper

In a large sauté pan over medium heat, add the oil. Making sure that the red onion slices are completely separated from each other, add the onions to the oil and begin to cook them until they start to turn brown, but not burnt. Remember to toss the onions occasionally for even cooking. Add the sugar, thyme, port, balsamic, salt and pepper. Continue to cook the onion until no liquid is apparent in the pan. At this point, be careful not to burn the onions. Spread the onions out on a cookie sheet and allow the jam to cool to room temperature. May be made a week in advance.

Let's talk about wine: Four very nice *tawny ports* that could be you ADD and PAIR wines are: **Taylor**; **Graham**; **Osborne** or **Offley.** A nice idea would be to use the regular tawny port as your add wine and then use an aged one (10 years) as the PAIR wine.

Seared Ahi Tuna with Sweet & Spicy Ginger Sauce

4-9-10 ounces each, Ahi tuna steaks, skin off, no blood line
Sea salt to taste
Ground black pepper to taste
1 ounce olive oil
Drizzle of Sweet & Spicy Ginger sauce*(see recipe)

In a skillet style pan, over high heat, add the oil. (It is important to have the pan at a high temperature to obtain a crisp crust on each steak.) Season four slices of center cut tuna steak, at least 1 inch thick, with a bit of salt and pepper. Sear each tuna steak for about 45 seconds, to a minute on each side. This procedure should allow you to maintain a rare temperature for the tuna steak. Cook the tuna longer if you desire the fish to be cooked more. Remove tuna from the pan and allow to rest.

Using a very sharp knife, slice each steak into

¼ inch slices, and fan out over a serving plate. Drizzle a bit of the Sweet & Spicy Ginger Sauce and serve.

*Sweet & Spicy Ginger Sauce:

2 ounce fresh ginger, minced
6 garlic cloves, minced
1 each fresh Thai chili pepper, minced
2 tablespoon fresh cilantro, minced
3 tablespoon sweet soy sauce
1 ounce white vinegar
2 ounce granulated sugar
Sea salt to taste
½ tablespoon sesame oil

Combine ginger, garlic, Thai Chile, and cilantro in a food processor and chop well. Add the soy, vinegar, sugar, salt to taste and sesame oil and blend well.

Let's talk about wine: We haven't really suggested any of the fine sakes from Japan. One of the *milky sakes* would go well: **Divine Droplets** for example. You could drink it either slightly chilled, room temperature, or slightly warm but not hot.

Chipotle-Orange Glazed Grilled Shrimp

2 pounds jumbo prawns, U-8 size, peeled and deveined, tail on
2 cup orange juice
1 tablespoon orange zest
4 tablespoon lemon juice
4 garlic cloves, minced
2/3 cup olive oil
½ cup soy sauce
2 tablespoon chipotle in adobo, chopped
2 tablespoon fresh basil, chopped
1 teaspoon sea salt
2 teaspoon ground black pepper

Combine the orange juice, orange zest, lemon juice, garlic, soy, chipotle, basil, salt and pepper in a blender. Turn blender on high and slowly add the oil until well incorporated. Place the prawns in a large mixing bowl. Add almost all of the marinade to the prawns, reserving about a cup, and allow the prawns to marinate for at least 2-3 hours. After marinating, skewer the shrimp to help with the cooking procedure.

Preheat the grill to an extreme high temperature. Brush and oil the grates to prevent sticking. Grill the skewered shrimp for about 4-5 minutes on each side. Plate the shrimps on a warm serving platter. Place the reserved marinade in a saucepan and bring to a boil. Reduce the marinade to a thick consistency. Drizzle the glaze over the shrimp and serve.

Let's talk about beer: Let's stay with the Mexican themes of the dish and pair it with a Mexican beer. We suggest a Mexican beer with this dish: **Dos XX lager or dark** or the **Mondello lager or dark**.

Chef Joe's Famous Ceviche

½ pound raw shrimp, cut into ½ inch cubes
½ pound yellowtail snapper, cut into ½ inch cubes
½ pound small bay scallops, about ½ inch in size
(If small scallops are not available, cut larger scallops in to ½ inch cubes)
1 small red onion, diced
1 each cucumber, peeled and seeded, diced
¼ cup red pepper, diced
1 cup yellow pepper, diced
¼ cup fresh cilantro, chopped
2 Serrano peppers, seeds removed (or not), minced
Juice of 6 limes
3 tablespoon orange juice

Mix all ingredients in a large mixing bowl and allow to macerate for at least 3-4 hours, tossing the ingredients every once in a while. Serve with plantains chips, sweet potatoes chips, or tortilla chips.

Let's talk about beer and wine: Remember the high acid nature of the dish. First we suggest you consider one of the *beers from Mexico* suggested in the last recipe. If you want to pair the dish with a

wine, we suggest a California *chardonnay* such as: **Mer Soleil Gold**, **Angeline RRV**, **Martin Ray Reserve**; **DuMOL**; or **Newton Unfiltered**.

Herb Crusted Diver Scallops with Lemon Oil

2 pounds "dry packed" Jumbo "diver" sea scallops, about 8 per pound, any cartilage removed
3 tablespoon extra virgin olive oil
2 tablespoon fresh basil, chopped fine
2 tablespoon fresh thyme, chopped fine
2 tablespoon fresh tarragon, chopped fine
3 tablespoon Italian parsley, chopped fine
Sea salt to taste
Ground black pepper to taste
Drizzle of Lemon oil*

Rinse and pat the scallops dry with paper towel. Combine the basil, thyme, tarragon, and parsley in a small bowl and blend together. Season the scallops with some salt and pepper. Generously coat the scallops on all sides with the fine herb mix. Gently press down on the scallops so the herb mix adheres to the scallops. Allow the scallops to rest a few minutes. In a large sauté pan over high heat, add the extra virgin olive oil. Once hot, carefully add the scallops to the oil and sear them on both sides for 2-3 minutes each. Check for doneness. Plate the scallops on warm serving plates and drizzle with the lemon oil and serve.

*Lemon Oil:

1 cup extra virgin olive oil
Zest of 2 lemons
Sea salt to taste
White pepper to taste

Combine the olive oil, zest, salt and pepper and mix well. Ideally, allow the oil to sit for about a week to allow the flavors to infuse. Strain the infused oil through a fine sieve.

Let's talk about wine: A crisp *sauvignon blanc* would bring out the citrus flavors in this dish. Try:

Kim Crawford, **Cottesbrook**; **Framingham Hawke's Bay**; or **Veranda.**

Backyard BBQ Clam Bake

4 pieces aluminum foil 24x24
4 pounds seaweed*
4-1 lb live Maine lobsters
2 pounds Ipswich clams, purged before use
2 pounds Prince Edward Island mussels
2 ears fresh corn, shucked, cut in half
8 each red bliss potatoes
4 each Linguica Portuguese sausage, par grilled and cut in half
1 bottle dry white wine
2 lemons cut in half
Melted butter for garnish
Coarse sea salt for garnish
Lemon wedges for garnish

*Note: Seaweed can usually be obtained from your local fishmonger. Maine lobster usually come delivered packed in it.

Place a sheet of the aluminum foil on a work surface. Place 1 pound of the seaweed in the center of the foil. Place one of the lobsters on top of the seaweed. In any random fashion, surround the lobster with a ½ pound of the clams and a ½ pound of the mussels. Place a piece of corn on top of the shellfish along with a couple of potatoes. Finally, place a couple of pieces of the sausage on top of the lobster and a half piece of lemon. Begin to seal the package tightly so the contents may steam within. Place the "package" on the preheated grill at an extreme temperature, and cook for about 45 minutes, to an hour. Serve with melted butter, some coarse sea salt, and some lemon wedges.

Let's talk about beer: Since this sounds like a party, this may be the right time to get a *¼ keg* of your favorite beer. Bottle beer is very good but there is nothing quite like tap beer fresh from the keg. **Yuengling** would be a very good choice along with a New England brew such as **Harpoon** or **Sam Adams.**

Miso Glazed Sea bass with Yuzu-Ginger Glaze

4 each 9-10 ounce Chilean sea bass, center cut, no skin
1 ½ cups Miso Marinade*(see recipe)
2 ounce olive oil
Drizzle of the Yuzu-Soy Glaze**(see recipe)

*Miso Marinade:

½ cup Sake
½ cup Mirin
8 tablespoon white Miso paste
2 tablespoon honey
2 tablespoon granulated sugar
White pepper to taste

In a large mixing bowl, combine the Miso, honey, sugar, pepper, vinegar and water. Blend well. Place the sea bass filets in the marinade and allow to sit for at least 3-4 hours before preparation.

In a skillet style pan, over medium high heat, add the oil. It is important to have the pan at the desired temperature to obtain a crisp crust on each sea bass filet. Allow the fish to cook for 4-5 minutes on each side. Based on how thick the piece of sea bass is will determine how long it should be cooked for. You may pan sear the fish on both sides, and then finish it in a preheated oven to cook to the desired doneness. (The internal temperature of most fish is 150-155°). Once done, place the fish on warm serving plates and drizzle with the Yuzu-Ginger Glaze.

**Yuzu-Ginger Glaze:

1 ½ cups Yuzu juice
½ cup light soy sauce

Juice of 1 orange
1 tablespoon fresh ginger, minced
½ tablespoon Chile garlic paste (Sambal)
½ cup granulated sugar
1 tablespoon water
4 tablespoon cornstarch

In a small saucepan over medium high heat, combine the Yuzu juice, soy sauce, orange juice, ginger, and chili garlic paste. Bring to a simmer.

At the same time, in a medium saucepan over medium high heat, combine the sugar and the water. Bring to a boil and cook the mixture until it starts to turn a dark golden color, about 8-10 minutes. (Be careful not to walk away during this process. The syrup will burn very quickly.)

Once the sugar water has reached the desired color, carefully add the Yuzu sauce to the syrup. Return all the contents to a simmer once again.

Combine the water and cornstarch in a small bowl to form "slurry." Add the slurry, a little at a time to the Yuzu mixture, and allow the sauce to come to a boil once again in order to allow the sauce to thicken to a glaze. (All of the slurry may not be needed to obtain the desired thickness of the glaze.)

Let's talk about beer and wine: One of the great *Japanese beers* such as **Kirin**; **Sapporo** or the new **Sapporo Reserve** would add much to this dish, as would cold *sake* such as **Divine Droplets**.

Chapter 13:

THERE'S ALWAYS ROOM FOR DESSERT

New York Cheesecake

1. **Atlanta Pecan Pie**

2. **Christmas Nut Rings & Stuffed Cookies**

3. **Mom's Ricotta Cheese Cake**

4. **Zeppole de San Giuseppe**

5. **Ricotta Crepes with Mascarpone Topping**

6. **Pear Pie**

7. **Zabaglione with Raspberries & Blueberries**

8. **Hot Buttered Rum**

9. **Cheese Platter**

10. **Italian Ambrosia**

11. **Panettone French Toast**

12. **White Chocolate & Hazelnut Bread Pudding**

13. **Sweet Crepes with Cinnamon Sugar**

And 4 variations

14. **Crème Brulee**

15. **Rice Pudding**

And 2 variations

16. **Baklava**

17. **Pears Poached in Wine**

18. **Key Lime Pie**

And 2 variations

19. **Captain Joe's Bananas Foster**

And 2 variations

20. **Tiramisu**

And 1 variation

21. **Carrot Cake**

And 1 variation

22. **Oranges in Orange Syrup**

23. **Italian Version of an English Trifle**

And 2 variations

24. **Peaches Poached in Wine**

And 1 variation

25. **Peach Pizza**

And 2 variations

26. **Rita's Apple Pie**

There's Always Room for Dessert

Americans are obsessed with sweet desserts like no other group of people. No matter how big the meal we are served, our host will say at some point: "Be sure to save some room for dessert." And, once the meal is finished, no matter how stuffed we are, the table will soon be filled with all sorts of desserts. It matters little that the dessert course we are served may have as many calories as the rest of the meal. Once it is served, we all dive in with gusto.

Our host pleads, "Please just a little piece." Our answer, "Ok, but just give me a little sliver serving of each (perhaps 2—3—4)." Yes, this is what we crave and so we now bring you a chapter devoted to those sweet and decadent morsels with which we end our meals.

I must admit, growing up, I was not served a lot of these kinds of desserts. At home, at the end of the meal, my mother would bring out fresh fruit, celery, nuts, fresh fennel, fresh dandelions, and maybe a bit of cheese. This was "dessert" because it was something to aide in the digestion of the meal. Would you consider a plate of excellent cheeses and some croutons dessert? How about an excellent Port with some strawberries or a small piece of sweet chocolate on the side? What would you think of a very nice brandy? What about a glass of Sambucca with two or three espresso coffee beans?

There are many dessert wines that can be served alone or with some sweet or not so sweet dessert. We will be offering many choices in this chapter and we hope you have saved some room for the desserts suggested here.

Let's talk about wine: For the dessert chapter, we have provided a variety of classic and not so classic desserts. Pairing wines with dessert is perhaps the most difficult. Do you pair a dry wine with a sweet dessert? Yes. Do you pair a sweet wine with a sweet dessert? Yes. Should I serve a sparkler? Why not? A Port with some chocolate? ---MMMMMMMMMM!! We encourage you to read each of the dessert recipes that you are going to try and think of the flavors. Are they sweet? Complex? Creamy? Rich? At the end of the recipe section we will be offering some general suggestions about pairings that we hope are helpful when you choose your wines for pairing. We will also be offering some spirits suggestions because certain desserts really go very well with spirits.

Again, read each recipe---think of the flavors---think of what would compliment them---remember the dish plus the wine equals a third flavor, and if chosen properly that flavor will be greater than the sum of its parts.

When we think of a must use wine for a particular dessert we will suggest that particular wine after the recipe as we did in the in other places in the book.

NOTE: Be sure to read the entire wine/dessert discussion at the end of the chapter.

New York Cheesecake

¼ pound butter
1 all butter pound cake, crust removed and sliced into ¼ inch slices
4-8 oz packages regular cream cheese, room temperature
1 2/3 cups granulated sugar
¼ cup cornstarch
1 tablespoon pure vanilla extract
2 extra-large eggs
3/4 cup heavy whipping cream
9 inch spring form pan

Use the butter to grease a 9 inch spring form pan. Layer the sliced pound cake in the bottom of the pan, making sure to cover the entire bottom of the pan. In a mixing bowl, with the paddle attachment, place 1 package of cream cheese, 1/3 cup sugar and the cornstarch. Beat the mixture at low speed until creamy. Continue beating the cream cheese as you add the remaining packages. Increase the speed to high, and beat in the remaining sugar, vanilla extract and the eggs (one at a time). Gently spoon the mixture into the spring form pan.

Place the spring form pan in a water bath that comes up the sides about 1 inch. Bake in a preheated 350° oven for about 1 hour, or until the center of the cake barely moves when you shake the pan.

Cool the cake on a wire rack for 90 minutes. Cover the pan with plastic wrap and cool in the refrigerator overnight.

To remove the cake from the pan, with a sharp knife, score the perimeter of cake between the cake and the pan. This is to prevent any sticking that may have occurred. Remove the spring form ring, leaving the cake on the bottom section of the pan, which can then be placed on a plate for serving.

***De Margerie Grand Cru Rose

Atlanta Pecan Pie

1 homemade or good quality store bought piecrust
5 extra large eggs
1½ cups packed light brown sugar
1 cup dark corn syrup
1 stick unsalted butter, melted
1 teaspoon pure vanilla extract
½ teaspoon kosher salt
¼ teaspoon ground white pepper
1 ½ cups fresh pecans

Butter a 9 inch Pyrex plate and place the piecrust in it, making sure to press it lightly to the bottom and the sides. In a mixing bowl with the wire whip attachment, beat the eggs at high speed until frothy. Reduce the speed to medium, and add in the sugar, corn syrup, butter, vanilla, salt and pepper.

Remove bowl from the mixer. Using a spatula, fold the pecans into the bowl. Pour the batter into the unbaked pie shell. Bake in a preheated 375° oven for 40-50 minutes. The center should move just slightly when the pan is shaken. Allow to cool on a rack for about an hour. Serve.

***A Jack Daniels Old Faison or Manhattan

Christmas Nut Rings and Nut Stuffed Cookies

The traditional way to make this dish may be very expensive for most. When I was young, my father would make his own wine. He would take 5 gallons of the new wine and give it to my mother to boil down into a little less than one gallon of syrup. It was rich and sweet. You can try to make the syrup this way with gallons of Primitivo wine but after much experimentation I have found a very reasonable substitute for the original.

Syrup: Place 6 liters of prune juice with pulp and 2 pints good quality honey in a large pot and boil it down to 3 liters of syrup.

Here are two traditional recipes that my family makes at Christmas. One is for traditional Christmas Cookies and the other is for a Nut Ring. I hope you will try them. Traditional baked goods are a good way of passing on a tradition.

½ cup unsalted walnuts
½ cup unsalted cashews
½ cup unsalted hazel nuts
½ cup unsalted Brazil nuts
½ cup unsalted pine nuts
½ cup unsalted almonds
½ cup unsalted peanuts
Homemade or good quality store bought piecrust
Oil for deep frying
Multi colored nonpareil sprinkles

Make the syrup as directed above. In a large pot, keep the syrup hot and close to boiling. Coarsely chop all the nuts and combine them well in a bowl. Remove about 2/3 cup of the nut mixture, chop finely and set aside.

Nut Ring:

In a large sauté pan on medium heat, add 1 cup of the hot syrup and 1½ cups of the coarsely chopped nuts. Mix and stir continually until the mixture is almost dry. Turn the mixture onto a plate.

*WARNING: Be careful. The syrup glazed nuts will be very hot and will stick to your skin and burn you.

Once the nuts cool a bit, but before they begin to "set," begin to shape the mixture into a ring. (The best procedure to follow when making the nut ring is to wet you hands with ice water and shape the ring by hand). Press the nuts firmly together---moisten your hands again—repeat and repeat until a nice ring is formed. Once it is shaped, sprinkle the top with the nonpareils and set aside to dry and set. After about 2 hours it can be covered with aluminum foil for later use. Serve it sliced into thin wedges.

Nut Stuffed Cookies:

In a large sauté pan, place 1 cup of the hot syrup and 1 cup of the reserved finely chopped nuts. Mix and stir the nuts in the syrup as they cook, until they are medium dry. Remove and set aside. Roll out the pie dough thinly. Cut into 2-3 inch circles. Place a teaspoon of the reserved nut mixture on each. Fold each circle over and seal tightly with a fork. Deep fry the stuffed dough pouches at 350° until golden. Remove and drain. Dip each into the hot syrup, remove and drain. Sprinkle each with the nonpareils. Allow to cool and serve. They can be stored covered for several days. Any of the remaining syrup can be used as simple syrup. Let your imagination be your guide.

***Sambucca on the rocks with Coffee Beans

Grandma's Ricotta Cheese Cake

Chef Joe and I had a discussion about the lack of a crust on this cheesecake since all cheesecakes have some sort of bottom crust. As I explained---this is Grandma's (his grandmother my mother) recipe and she never used a crust. You will find that the cake is so moist that no crust is necessary. I must admit that I do use a non stick spring form pan and also put a piece of parchment paper on the bottom of the pan (Sorry Mama).

12 extra large eggs
¾ cup granulated sugar
2 pounds low moisture ricotta
1 ounce anisette
Grated zest of one lemon
Grated zest of one orange
1 ounce orange juice
¼ cup milk chocolate, coarsely grated
12 maraschino cherries cut in half

In a mixing bowl, beat the eggs at high speed until they become frothy. Continue beating as you add the sugar. Beat until the mixture is a pale yellow. Reduce the speed to slow, and add the ricotta, a bit at a time until well incorporated. Add the anisette, orange juice, lemon zest and orange zest. Pour the mixture into a greased 9 inch spring form pan. Bake in a preheated 350° oven for 1 hour in a water bath. After one hour gently drop the halved cherries on the top of the cheesecake. Bake an additional 30-45 minutes until the center of the cake barely wiggles when the pan is shaken. Allow the cheesecake to cool on a rack for 1 hour, then cover with plastic wrap and refrigerate overnight.

***Espresso Coffee with some Sambucca and lemon peel and also with Sambucca on the rocks with coffee beans.

Zeppole di San Giuseppe

8 cups all purpose flour
2 packs dry yeast
2 ½ cups warm whole milk
¼ teaspoon kosher salt

3 eggs
Grated zest of one lemon
Grated zest of one orange
1/3 cup granulated sugar
¼ teaspoon kosher salt
6 tablespoons unsalted butter
Canola oil for frying
Powdered sugar

Dissolve the yeast in the warm milk. In a large bowl, combine the flour, salt, and the milk/yeast mixture and knead into a ball. Allow the dough to rise for one hour. Knead the orange and lemon zest and sugar into the dough ball. Melt the butter and knead it into the dough until it is totally incorporated. Beat the eggs and knead into the dough until fully incorporated. Knead the dough well until the dough is uniform and slightly sticky. Flour a board and roll out the dough. Cut the dough into 2 inch circles and place on a sheet to rise until double in size. In a deep fryer, drop the dough rounds 2 or 3 at a time until golden. Remove the fried dough from the fryer and place into a "double" bagged paper bag. Dust the Zeppole with the powdered sugar; close the bag tightly and shake the bag to coat the Zeppole completely with sugar. Open the bag of goodies and enjoy. Ahh, heaven!

***<u>**Bellini Lemoncello**</u> or their <u>Vin Santo</u>

Ricotta Crepes with Mascarpone Topping

12 eggs
½ cup granulated sugar
2 pound low moisture ricotta
½ cup heavy cream
1 teaspoon kosher salt
1 teaspoon vanilla extract
1 teaspoon orange extract
Zest from one orange
Seeds from half a vanilla bean*
¼ pound unsalted butter

In a mixing bowl on high speed, whip together the eggs and the sugar. Whip until the mixture turns a pale yellow, about 2 minutes. Reduce the mixer speed to medium; add the other ingredients except for the butter to the bowl; blend until well incorporated. Using a 6" nonstick sauté pan, brush the pan lightly with a bit of butter in the pan. Preheat the pan over medium heat and pour about 2 ounces of the egg mixture into the pan. Tip and rotate the pan to coat the bottom with a thin layer of the batter. Cook until just dry on top then roll the crepe out of the pan onto a dish. The crepes may be served warm, cool, or at room temperature. Top or roll the crepes with fresh fruit or drizzle with some syrup, or the topping suggested below.

***Note:** To remove the seeds from a whole vanilla bean, use a very sharp and pointy little knife. Cut the bean lengthwise down the middle using the point of the knife. Hold the split bean on one end with the interior exposed. Scrape the seeds from the inside by sliding the tip of the knife along the length of the bean. This should yield thousands of "speck" size seeds.

Mascarpone Topping:

2 cups mascarpone cheese
1 teaspoon orange extract
1 teaspoon vanilla extract
Grated zest of one orange
Seeds from half a vanilla bean
1/3 cup or more of honey to taste
1 cup heavy cream

Mix together all the ingredients with a kitchen mixer until well blended, fluffy and smooth. Check for sweetness; add additional honey if you wish.

****<u>**Galliano and Orange Juice (add some vodka and you have a Harvey Wallbanger---OH my ---am I really that old??)**</u>

Pear Pie

5 cups pears, peeled and sliced thin into wedges
½ cup sugar
1 cup sour cream
2 tablespoons all purpose flour

½ teaspoon orange extract

½ teaspoon almond extract

½ teaspoon vanilla extract

¼ teaspoon kosher salt

1 homemade or good quality store bought piecrust

In a large bowl, add the sliced pear, sugar, and flour and toss together. Add the sour cream, extracts, salt and toss to combine. Pour into the pie shell and bake in a preheated 350° oven for 45-60 minutes or until done. Serve.

***Martel Cordon Blu

Zabaglione* with Raspberries & Blueberries

Zabaglione:

1 cup heavy cream

1 teaspoon vanilla extract

4 egg yolks

1/2 cup Vin Santo

2 tablespoons cream sherry

Combine the cream and the vanilla extract in a large mixing bowl and whip into hard peaks using a "fine wire" whisk. Set aside.

Over a double boiler, on medium to high heat, place a large bowl; add the egg yolks, Vin Santo and Sherry. Wisk the yolks continuously, until the custard base starts to change color and become thick. (Be careful the temperature isn't too high, otherwise you'll get scrambled eggs.) Simply remove the bowl intermittently from the heat to temper the yolks. Fold the mixture into the whipped cream and set aside. Chill 45 minutes.

Fruit:

1 pint fresh raspberries

1 pint fresh blueberries

½ cup Vin Santo

½ cup honey

3 tablespoons granulated sugar

In a pan combine the raspberries, blueberries, Vin Santo, honey and sugar. Heat over low

heat and stir until well incorporated. Place the berry mixture in a dish and top with the chilled zabaglione and serve.

*Note: Zabaglione can be used in almost an infinite number of ways as a dessert in and of itself, or as part of other desserts, or as a sauce for desserts.

***Add and Pair Bellini VIN Santo

Hot Buttered Rum

Although not really a dessert, we thought this recipe was worthy of inclusion in the dessert section of the text. Enjoy!

8 cups of water

5 tea bags (your choice of flavors)

1 large cinnamon stick

6 whole cloves

¾ cup granulated sugar

3 tablespoons vanilla extract

1½ cups dark rum

1 sticks unsalted butter

Heat the water to boiling in a pan with the cinnamon stick, cloves, sugar and vanilla. Steep the tea bags for 5 minutes. Add the butter and the rum. Stir until the butter is melted and serve.

***If you can find it use Seven Tiki Rum.

NOTE: Be sure to read the entire wine/dessert discussion at the end of the chapter.

Cheese Platter

In America, most would not consider the following a dessert, but in Europe and elsewhere, this would be the correct way to top off a meal. Try it sometime, and you may just feel the same. The following is a suggestion, and you can make variations to the cheeses, fruits and fresh vegetables, based on what you find in the market when you go shopping.

2 wedges Asiago cheese

1-3 inch chunk of Danish or Maytag blue cheese
3-4 chunks Romano
2 slices Gruyere Swiss
3-4 chunks goat cheese feta
2-3 slices ricotta Salada
1 thick slice port salute
1 large chunk extra sharp cheddar
1 granny smith apple, sliced and mixed with the juice of a ¼ lemon
Bunch of white seedless grapes
Bunch red seedless grapes
1 small head fennel, sliced
1-2 kohlrabies, sliced
Thin slices of French style baguette, toasted

Assemble the above ingredients on a platter. It should serve 4 people for dessert.

***__Martel Cordon Blu__

__Italian Ambrosia__

1 cup dried pineapple chunks
1 cup dried apricots, sliced
1 cup dried figs, sliced
1 cup dried strawberries, sliced
½ cup semi-sweet chocolate chips
½ cup plain walnuts, coarse chop
¼ cup pecans, coarse chop
¼ teaspoon cinnamon
¾ cup honey
3 tablespoons balsamic vinegar
¼ cup brandy
1 ½ cups whipped cream
3 cups ricotta
½ cup heavy cream
Zest of one orange, grated
Zest of one lemon, grated
Zest of one lime, grated
Zest of one lemon, sliced very thin
Zest of one orange, sliced very thin
Zest of one lime, sliced very thin
3 tablespoons water
¾ cup water
½ teaspoon vanilla

In a large bowl combine all the dried fruits, nuts, cinnamon, honey, vinegar and brandy. Mix together and set aside. Fold the whipped cream together with the ricotta and the grated zests. Peel the other lemon, orange and lime of their zests, being careful not to cut into the white pith below the zest. (A potato peeler is good for this task.) Cut the zests into very thin strips. In a pan, over medium heat, combine the water, sugar and vanilla and heat until sugar has dissolved. Heat for ten minutes then add the sliced zests. Continue heating for an additional ten minutes. Remove the zests from the pan and allow to cool and dry.

Fold the ricotta/whipped cream mixture together with the macerating fruit/nut mixture. Serve with a sprinkle of the caramelized zests as a topping.

__Panettone French Toast__

You know that big box of Panettone you get for Christmas and don't know what to do with it? It makes great French toast that can be used for an elegant dessert.

4 slices Panettone, 1-2 inch thick slices
6 eggs
Zest of 1 orange
3 tablespoons orange brandy
1 tablespoon frozen orange juice concentrate
¼ teaspoon salt
1/8 teaspoon ground white pepper
1 tablespoons ground cinnamon
6 tablespoons unsalted butter

In a bowl whisk together the eggs, orange zest, orange brandy, orange juice concentrate, salt, pepper and cinnamon. Using a large nonstick pan over medium-high heat, melt one tablespoon butter. Dip the Panettone in the egg mixture and place in the pan. Cook until the egg is cooked and golden brown. Serve with maple syrup or honey.

***__Krug Brut or Martell Extra Dry__

White Chocolate & Hazelnut Bread Pudding

3 cups heavy cream
10 ounces white chocolate
8 ounces whole milk
2 eggs
8 egg yolks
½ cup granulated sugar
¼ teaspoon salt
20 ounces brioche bread, 1 inch cubes
2 tablespoons cold unsalted butter
¾ cup coarsely chopped hazelnuts

Place the cream in a large mixing bowl, then, place on top of a pot filled with water over medium heat; creating a double boiler. Begin to heat. Add the chocolate to the cream and begin to whisk. Remove from the heat when the chocolate has melted and the cream is smooth. Set aside.

In another large mixing bowl, combine the milk, eggs, egg yolks, sugar and salt. Heat the milk mixture on the double boiler. Whisk to combine ingredients. Once the milk has warmed, remove from the double boiler and slowly add to the chocolate cream mixture.

Grease a 9x12 baking dish with the unsalted butter. Distribute the cubed brioche bread evenly in the dish. Evenly distribute the hazelnuts in the dish. Pour the cream base into the dish. Shake the dish a few times to fill all the gaps. Allow the dish to sit a few minutes to allow the bread to soak up the cream. Cover the baking dish with foil; place in a preheated 300° oven for about 1 hour. Remove the foil and check the pudding to make sure the bread and cream has set. Bake the bread pudding uncovered for another 15 minutes, or until golden. Place on a cooling rack for at least 30 minutes before serving.

***__Graham's 20 Year Old Port__**

Sweet Crepes with Cinnamon and Sugar

1 cup all purpose flour
4 eggs
1 cup whole milk
2 tablespoons granulated sugar
½ teaspoons vanilla extract
½ teaspoon orange extract
Pinch of salt
¼ pound unsalted butter
3 tablespoons granulated sugar blended with 1 teaspoon ground cinnamon

In a blender, add the flour, eggs, milk, vanilla and orange extracts, sugar and salt. Blend until well incorporated. Using an 6 inch nonstick sauté pan over medium heat, lightly butter the pan, and add about 2 ounces of the egg mixture into the pan. Turn the pan; coating the entire bottom with the egg mixture. Cook for about 30-45 seconds, turn the crepe over and cook an additional 10 seconds. Turn the crepe out onto a dish and sprinkle with the sugar/cinnamon mixture. Add a dollop of freshly whipped cream on top of the crepe and serve.

Variation #1: Drizzle some chocolate syrup on top of the crepe.

Variation #2: Serve with a scoop of vanilla ice cream.

***__Osborn Cream Sherry__**

Crème Brulee

2 cups heavy cream
4 eggs
2 tablespoons granulated sugar
½ cup light brown sugar

In a mixing bowl with the wire whip attachment, whip the eggs on high until they become light yellow in color. Immediately add the heavy cream slowly, continuing to whip the whole time. Add the sugar while continuing to whip. Once incorporated, add the custard to a large mixing bowl and place on a double boiler. Whip the egg mixture constantly over boiling water until the mixture thickens and easily coats a spoon.

Once the custard is done, place the mixture into buttered crème Brulee ramekin cups. Cover the cups with plastic wrap and chill at least 8 hours.

Finally, place the ramekins in a shallow pan surrounded with water. Place in a cold oven and heat to 275°. Bake for 30 minutes. Remove from the oven and sprinkle the top with a bit of brown sugar. Flame the sugar with a small kitchen torch until the top of the Brulee is light brown on top. Return to the refrigerator and cool completely. Serve.

***<u>Moet Nectar Imperial Rose</u>

Rice Pudding

2 cups cooked basmati rice
1 ½ cups half and half
7 tablespoons granulated sugar
¼ teaspoon salt
2 tablespoons soft unsalted butter
1 teaspoon vanilla extract
1 vanilla bean seeds, extracted
4 eggs
1 tablespoon orange juice
1 tablespoon grated orange

In a mixing bowl, blend together the half and half, salt, sugar, butter, vanilla extract, vanilla seeds, eggs, orange juice and zest. Add the rice and blend well. Pour into a buttered baking pan, and place in a pre heated 325° oven until the pudding is set---about 45-60 minutes. Remove and serve warm or chilled with a dollop of whipped cream.

Variation #1: add ½ cup golden raisins to the mixture before baking.

Variation #2: Add 1 tablespoon cinnamon to the mixture before baking.

***<u>Billecart-Salmon Rose</u>

Baklava

1 pound phyllo dough sheets
¾ pound unsalted butter, melted
3/4 pound unsalted walnuts, fine chop
¾ pounds unsalted almonds, fine chop
¼ cup granulated sugar
1 ½ teaspoons ground cinnamon
½ teaspoon ground cloves
¼ teaspoon ground nutmeg
¾ cup plain dry breadcrumbs

For the syrup:

4 cups granulated sugar
2 cups water
1 lemon cut in half
2 cinnamon sticks

In a small saucepan over medium heat, melt the butter; be careful not to let the butter turn brown. Set aside for later use.

Place the walnuts and almonds in a mixing bowl together with the sugar, cinnamon, cloves and nutmeg. Set up a work area with the butter, breadcrumbs, nut mixture and a 9x12 baking pan. Lightly butter the bottom of the pan with some of the melted butter. Place one sheet of the phyllo pastry on the pan, and lightly butter that. Repeat the process until you have placed 6 or 7 sheets of phyllo in the pan. Lightly dust with the breadcrumbs, and then sprinkle a thin layer of the nut mixture over the dough. Place one sheet of phyllo on top; lightly butter it and place another sheet on and lightly butter it. Sprinkle a light layer of breadcrumbs and then a thin layer of the nut mixture. Repeat the process until you have used up all the nut mixture. Once at the top, place a sheet of phyllo pastry on the baklava. Lightly butter it, and place another sheet on and lightly butter it. Repeat until you have 6-7 phyllo layers on top of the baklava. Cut the completed work into thirds; down the length of the pan and then make diagonal cuts to form a diamond pattern. Place in a preheated 350° oven, and bake for about 1 hour or until it turns a deep golden color. During the baking, brush the baklava 3-4 times with the remaining butter. While the baklava is baking, make the syrup.

The Syrup:

In a pan, place all the ingredients and slowly bring to a boil stirring until all the sugar is melted. Boil the mixture for 10 minutes. Remove the cinnamon sticks and any lemon seeds that may have gotten into it. After removing the baklava from the oven, immediately pour the prepared syrup over it. Allow the baklava to cool for 2-3 hours before serving. Can be stored covered at room temperature for 3-5 days.

NOTE: Be sure to read the entire wine/dessert discussion at the end of the chapter.

Pears Poached in Wine

6 firm Bosc or Bartlett pears
2 cups tawny port
¼ cup brandy
3 slices of orange
2 slices of lemon
1/8 teaspoon ground cinnamon
1/8 teaspoon ground cloves

Peel the pears completely. Slice the pears in half and starting at the bottom, carefully scoop out the core of the pear using a melon baler. In a saucepot with a lid, place the port brandy orange slice, lemon slice, cinnamon and clove, and bring the pot to a slow boil. Boil for about 10 minutes; then reduce the heat to the lowest possible setting. Add the pears and cook covered until tender--- about 45 minutes to 1 hour. Remove the pears to a serving dish.

Continue to reduce the remaining liquid to a boil and reduce by ¼. Strain and cool the syrup. Drizzle the syrup over the pears, and top with a dollop of fresh whipped cream.

***Use the poaching port—Illaparra 10 year Old is excellent.**

Key Lime Pie

1 homemade or good quality, store bought pie shell
5 egg yolks
½ cup soft, unsalted butter
½ cup granulated sugar
½ cup brown sugar
4 tablespoons key limejuice
2 teaspoons key lime zest (regular lime will do)
½ teaspoon salt

In a mixing bowl, beat the egg yolks until pale yellow in color. As you continue beating the yolks, add the butter, then both sugars, the limejuice, zest and salt. Beat for 2 minutes. Fill the pie shell with the custard and bake in a preheated 325° oven until set----about 30-35 minutes. Remove and allow the pie to cool completely. Serve with fresh whipped cream.

Variation #1: Use lemon juice and lemon zest.

Variation #2: Use orange juice and orange zest.

Captain Joe's Bananas Foster

4 ounces unsalted butter
½ cup brown sugar
4 firm bananas, peeled and sliced into 1 inch slices, on the bias
¼ cup Captain Morgan's original spiced rum

Melt the butter over medium heat in a large sauté pan, then add the brown sugar and incorporate with the butter. Add the bananas to the pan and cook until the bananas start to caramelize over medium high heat. Remove the pan, away from any open flame and add the rum. Carefully catch a flame off the gas stove or use a BBQ lighter to light the rum and "flambé" the bananas. Be careful, the flame will shoot up above the pan. Allow the flame to burn itself out. Serve over ice cream and/or a slice of buttered and toasted pound cake.

Variation #1: Instead of Captain Morgan's original spiced rum, add a flavored brandy of your choice.

Variation #2: Try using sliced apples or pears, instead of bananas.

***Seven Tiki Rum** on the Rocks

Tiramisu

1-16oz package of ladyfingers cookies
1 pound mascarpone cheese
1 cup heavy cream
1 teaspoon vanilla extract
¼ cup granulated sugar
1 cup double strength espresso, room temperature
½ cup high quality coffee liqueur
¼ cup unsweetened cocoa powder

In a mixing bowl, whip the mascarpone until soft and creamy. In a separate mixing bowl, combine the heavy cream, vanilla extract and sugar and beat until soft peaks are formed. Gently fold the whipped cream into the whipped mascarpone until incorporated.

In a 9x12 serving dish, layer the ladyfingers evenly on the bottom. Brush the cookies with the espresso/coffee liquor blend, or dip the fingers into the coffee and assemble as you go. Spread a thin layer of the mascarpone cream on top of the cookies. Sprinkle lightly with the cocoa powder. Place another layer of the ladyfingers in the dish, and repeat the process until all the mascarpone cream is used up. Final result will have a layer of the mascarpone cream on top. Sprinkle the tiramisu with a bit more cocoa powder. Chill for 3-4 hours and serve.

Variation #1: after each layer of cream, add a layer of fresh raspberries.

***Bellini VIN Santo**

Carrot Cake

1 cup unsalted butter, room temperature
1 cup granulated sugar
1 cup brown sugar

½ teaspoon ground nutmeg
1 teaspoon ground cinnamon
½ teaspoon orange zest
½ teaspoon lemon zest
4 large eggs
1 ¾ cups carrot, finely grated
1/3 cup walnuts, fine chop
2 ½ cups all purpose flour, sifted
3 teaspoons baking powder
½ teaspoon sea salt
1/3 cup warm water

In a bowl, whip the butter until creamy. As you continue to whip the butter, add the sugars, nutmeg, cinnamon, orange zest and lemon zest. Add in the carrot and the walnuts. Continue beating as you add the eggs, one at a time.

In a separate bowl, sift the flour, baking powder and salt together. Add the water and mix together. Fold the flour mixture into the carrot mixture.

Grease and flour three 9 inch cake pans. Divide the batter equally among the pans. Bake in a pre heated 350° oven for 25 minutes. Remove the cake from the oven and cool about 20 minutes before removing the cakes from the pans.

Serve alone with whipped cream or use your favorite icing and build a three layer cake.

Variation #1: instead of carrots use Granny Smith apples.

NOTE: Be sure to read the entire wine/dessert discussion at the end of the chapter.

Oranges in Orange Syrup

6 large navel oranges, separated in sections
Zest of 3 oranges
1 cup granulated sugar
½ cup water
¼ teaspoon ground cinnamon
¼ cup orange brandy

Peel the oranges and break into individual sections. Arrange in a serving bowl. In a pan, add the sugar and the water and bring to a boil.

Add the orange zest and cinnamon. Cook about 5-10 minutes. Add the orange brandy and stir well. Pour the syrup over the orange wedges and chill well. Serve alone or with whipped cream or ice cream.

***Martel Cordon Blu**

Italian Version of an English Trifle

1 store bought, all butter pound cake cut into ¼ inch slices
½ cup apricot jam
¼ cup strawberry jam
¾ cup Vin Santo
2 ½ cups chocolate cannoli cream*
1 pound low moisture ricotta
¾ cup confectioners' sugar
¼ cup unsweetened cocoa power
½ teaspoon vanilla extract
1 cup whipped cream*
1 cup heavy cream
1 teaspoon vanilla extract
¼ cup sugar
Fresh strawberries for garnish
Fresh raspberries for garnish
Shaved chocolate for garnish

*Cannoli cream:

Combine the whole milk ricotta, confectioners' sugar, unsweetened cocoa powder, and the ½ teaspoon of vanilla extract in a bowl and blending them until smooth. Reserve.

*Whipped cream:

Combine the heavy cream, 1 teaspoon of vanilla extract, and the sugar in a bowl and whip until soft peaks are formed. Reserve.

In a large bowl, place a layer of the pound cake slices to cover the bottom and brush them with the Vin Santo. Spread a thin layer of the apricot preserves over the cake and follow it with a thin layer of the chocolate cannoli cream, and then a thin layer of the whipped cream. Place another layer of the pound cake slices on top and brush

with Vin Santo once again. Repeat the layering process with the strawberry preserves, the cannoli cream, and finally the whipped cream. Continue the process until all the ingredients are used up.

Decorate the top of the trifle with some fresh sliced strawberries, raspberries, and shaved chocolate. Cover and chill 3-4 hours and then serve.

***Bellini VIN Santo**

Peaches in Wine

6 fresh peaches or nectarines, peeled, pitted and sliced into quarters
¼ cup granulated sugar
2 tablespoons orange zest
4 black peppercorns
1 cinnamon stick
1 bottle red wine (Preferably, a Chianti or even better, a Primitivo would be nice. A Cotes du Rhone would also be a nice choice.)

Place ½ the peaches in a large storage jar that can be sealed tightly. Add the sugar, orange zest peppercorns, and cinnamon stick. Add the remaining peaches.

Pour the wine into the jar, shaking it a couple times to remove any air pockets. Make sure the peaches are completely submerged. Seal tightly and allow the peaches to macerate in the wine for at least 3 days.

Variation #1: Macerate the peaches in white wine instead of red.

***San Andria Chianti Classico; Layer Cake Primitivo; Don Presidente Cotes du Rhone**

Peach Pizza

1 pound pizza dough, store bought or fresh *(See the pizza dough recipe in the "From the Heart" chapter of the book.)

3 cups fresh peaches, peeled and pitted, thinly sliced

½ cup sugar

1 teaspoon vanilla extract

½ teaspoon ground cinnamon

½ cup apricot preserves

¼ cup cream sherry

Spread the dough out on a buttered cookie sheet. In a bowl, combine the peaches, sugar, vanilla and cinnamon. Mix the peaches well, and allow them to sit for 5 minutes. In a second bowl, mix the apricot preserves and cream sherry together.

Lay the peach slices in a single layer on top of the pizza dough. Brush the peaches and the dough with the apricot mixture. Bake in a pre-heated 350° oven until the crust is golden brown on the bottom. Serve warm or chilled.

Variation #1: Instead of peaches, use sliced granny smith apples, mixed with ½ cup sugar and ½ teaspoon of apple pie spice. Brush the apples with some apple butter blended with Calvados on the top.

Variation # 2: Use 2 cups sliced, fresh strawberries mixed with ½ cup sugar. Glaze the strawberries with strawberry preserves blended with brandy.

***Osborne Cream Sherry**

Rita's Apple Pie

1 homemade or good quality store bought piecrust

Topping:

6 tablespoons all purpose flour

¼ cup brown sugar

¼ cup granulated sugar

½ teaspoon cinnamon

¼ teaspoon nutmeg

¼ teaspoon salt

6 tablespoons cold unsalted butter, cut into pats

¾ cup macadamia nuts, coarsely chopped

Place the flour, sugars, cinnamon, nutmeg and salt in a food processor and pulse to combine.

Add the cold butter, and pulse the processor until the consistency of the flour is like coarse oatmeal-about 8-12 times. Add the nuts and pulse an additional 4-6 times. Reserve refrigerated until ready to use.

Filling:

2 tablespoons all purpose flour

6 large granny smith apples, peeled, cored and sliced thin

2 tablespoons lemon juice

1 teaspoon lemon zest

¾ cup granulated sugar

¼ teaspoon nutmeg

½ teaspoon cinnamon

1/8 teaspoon allspice

1/8 teaspoon ground ginger

½ teaspoon kosher salt

1/8 teaspoon white pepper

Peel, core and slice the apples and toss with the lemon juice and zest in a large bowl. Add the sugar, nutmeg, cinnamon, allspice, ginger and salt. Toss again. Line the pie plate with the crust. Add the apple mixture. Top with the crumb/nut mixture. Bake in a preheated 350° oven for 1 hour. Check after 30-40 minutes; if the edge of the pie is getting too brown, cover the edge with aluminum foil.

Variation #1: Instead of apples, use an equal amount of peeled and cored seckel pears.

Variation #2: Instead of the crumb topping, use a second piecrust and crimp the edges before baking.

Let's talk about wine, spirits and desserts:

As we stated in the introduction of the chapter, we feel that wine, and sometimes spirit selections for desserts are very difficult. We would find ourselves suggesting 10-20 different pairings for each dessert depending on what you, as the chef hoped to accomplish.

For that reason we will be making some general suggestions about the selections of pairings with the expectation that you will be able to use them in your selection process.

There are very widely accepted criteria regarding the selection of dessert/wine or spirit pairings. If you follow these simple rules you can't go wrong:

- Serving rich chocolate---pair with a nice tawny port.

Illaparra 10 Year Old; Graham 10 or 20 Year Old; Taylor 40 Year Old

- Serving something creamy rich--- pair with a sparkler.

De Margerie Grand Cru; Montaudon Brut Rose; Crystal; Krug; Rondel Cava Brut or Semi Seco; Thorn Clark Brut

- Serving a cheese platter---pair with a good cognac.

Martel Cordon Blu; Hennessey XO; Louis XIII

- Serving espresso---pair with **Sambucca.**

- Serving ricotta cheesecake---pair with a Vin Santo or anisette.

Bellini VIN Santo; Marie Brizzard

- Serving something rich in nuts---pair with a medium dry sherry, calvados, cognac or sauternes.

- Serving fruit-----pair with Sauternes.

- Serving pie----compliment the flavor of the filling.

- Sparklers—Sparklers—Sparklers!!

Remember a good sparkler will compliment any dessert.

Now that we have given you these general "rules", you should feel free to disregard them if you think that some other pairing would accomplish what you want to accomplish for the last course you will be serving your guests.

This is really an excellent opportunity to give your guests a choice. Provide some suggested pairings from above, and allow your guests to choose what they would like to end the meal with. They know best what they feel would be the best ending to the meal you have served. It is adventuresome but worth the chance.

For the One You Love

Chapter 14:

FROM THE HEART

Joseph K's Section

13. **Joe's Famous Meatloaf**

14. **Grilled Chicken**

15. **Maple Salmon**

16. **Italian Salmon**

17. **Five Alarm Chili**

18. **Joe's Death by Chocolate**

Chef Joe's Section

19. **Hog Snapper Pepe**

20. **Yellow Gazpacho with Poached Rock Shrimp**

21. **Chicken Scarpariello**

And 1 variation

22. **Mesa Verde Green Chili**

23. **Herb Crusted Rotisserie Pork Loin Cooked Over Lobelville Cedar**

24. **Famous Chef Joe's Baby Back Ribs**

25. **Hoisin Ginger Glazed Pork Loin Rib Chops**

Nick's Section

1. **Mom's Marinara Sauce with Spaghetti**

   (plus 5 variations)

2. **Pizza Dough and How to Use It**

3. **Sunday Ragu from Puglia alla Nick**

4. **Christopher's Chicken Cutlets with Mustard and Capers**

5. **Herbed Chicken Radicchio**

6. **International Chicken Soup**

7. **Italian Sausage with Swiss Chard**

8. **Maria's Oven Roasted Chicken with Lemon and Garlic**

9. **A Quick Meat Sauce**

10. **Chunky Fresh Tomato Sauce**

11. **Septembers Tomato Salad**

12. **Spinach with Mashed Potatoes**

From the Heart

Here we are, near the end of the first of what we hope will be a number of wine pairing journeys. We have introduced you to not only great recipes from around the world, but also the use of wines, beers and spirits in the preparation of these foods to enhance the flavor, as well as pairing wines to compliment the recipes. Hopefully, you will now feel confident to move beyond this book, and be daring enough to make your own selections of wines, beers and spirits.

In this book, we have devoted much time to more traditional recipes because we believe you have to understand them in order to understand the new dishes being presented. Additionally, we have chosen to concentrate on American, Italian and French cuisines because of our backgrounds and the belief our readers will be more familiar with them.

We did foray into various other world cuisines and In future editions, we will be looking to expand your knowledge by devoting more time to in depth discussions of other cuisines from around the world along with suggestions for wines to Add and Pair.

And so, now, in our final chapter, we devote some special recipes that have been developed by our authors for their families and friends, called, *"From the Heart."*

Each of us will offer you a number of recipes that they believe send the love we feel for wine, food and you. They may not have special names and they may not be recognized as dishes that are on the menus of world famous or even local restaurants, but they will express our love for tradition and our love for food and wine.

Many will be the traditional family recipes we grew up with and others will be ones we have developed over the years as we have explored the food and wine spectrum. We hope you enjoy them as much as our families and we have enjoyed them.

As for the wine selection for each of the dishes, each of us made our own special selection to pair with each of our dishes.

Nick's Section

As the lead writer, I will be the first to offer some of my family recipes brought from Puglia, Italy from my immigrant parents. I have chosen to include them in this section rather than the Italian section because they are so personal. Most of these recipes are really my interpretations of my mother's dishes that were handed down through the generations, blended with those of my father's family. Others are ones that I have developed over the years and I hope you will like.

As for the recipes for these dishes, when I asked my mother how much of each item I should put in she would always say "enough." I would ask, "What is enough?" Without fail, her response would be an emphatic **"enough!"**

Likewise, when I asked how long I should knead the dough; she would say, "Until it feels right." At this point, I gave up asking and came over the house and watched her make all those wonderful dishes. As I watched, I learned what "enough" was and what "until it feels right" actually felt like.

In the following recipes, just like my mother did over the years, and as her mother had done, lead with your heart and soul and put your touch on them.

After 94 wonderful years, my mother is now gone. As the youngest of her children, I am the only one who still makes all the "old dishes." It is my hope that these wonderful dishes may find a new life with you and your family. Enjoy—Enjoy—Enjoy!!

Mom' Spaghetti Marinara

You (Chef Joe did) are going to tell me that I never sautéed the garlic in the olive oil. Well, I did that for years and it never tasted like Mom's sauce. Finally I watched Mom make the sauce and she did it just as described below so that is how I present it to you.

1 pound spaghetti or linguini
½ cup extra virgin olive oil
10 cloves garlic, coarse chop
1 8 ounce can tomato paste
3-28 oz cans whole tomatoes, hand crushed
¾ cup Italian parsley, coarse chop
1 teaspoon sea salt
10-20 grinds of fresh black pepper
Cracked red pepper for garnish

Add the hand crushed tomatoes and paste to a large pot and stir together. Add the raw garlic, olive oil, parsley, salt and pepper and bring to a boil. Reduce the heat and simmer 15-20 minutes and serve.

Bring to a simmer and cook for at least 30 minutes. Adjust the flavor with salt and pepper.

In a large pot of salted boiling water, cook the pasta until it is al dente. Drain pasta very well. Toss the pasta with a generous amount of the sauce and serve.

Variation #1: Serve the pasta with cracked red pepper as a garnish.

Variation #2: Add 1 ½ cups frozen peas to the sauce

Variation #3: add a can of drained and rinsed cannellini beans to the sauce

Variation #4: add a can of drained garbanzo beans to the sauce

Variation #5: add 4 chopped anchovy filets to the sauce

Let's talk about wine: Use the **San Andria Chianti Reserva** for the add wine. I would pair this with a rich Italian wine such as **San Guido** or the **Paulo Scavino Barolo.**

"Potato" Pizza Dough and How to Use It

2 pounds all purpose flour
1 large baking potato, boiled then mashed (save the water)
3 tablespoons extra virgin olive oil
1 tablespoon sea salt
1 packet dry yeast
1 cup reserved potato water (thank you Mom!)

Combine the yeast with the reserved potato water. Add the remaining ingredients to a mixing bowl with a dough hook and begin to blend. Gradually add some of the reserved potato water with the yeast slowly to the bowl, so that the dough forms a ball that is slightly sticky, but not wet. Once obtaining the desired result, removed the dough to an oiled bowl and cover. Allow the dough to proof (rise" for 1-2 hours in the refrigerator. When nearing time for preparation, remove dough from the bowl and "punch down" the dough to proof a second time at room temperature. This will allow the dough to be stretched when ready for use.

Deep Dish Focaccia:

In a 9x14 baking pan, spread 2-3 tablespoons of olive oil. Take the dough and spread it out in the pan, turning at least twice so both sides are covered with the oil. Use one 28 oz can of Italian tomatoes. Hand tear the tomatoes into halves or "filets," and squeeze out some of the juice. Press the tomato filets into the dough at about 3-4 inch intervals. Sprinkle the top with 1-2 tsp of Sea salt. Bake at 350° until golden.

Variation #1: Instead of tomatoes, sprinkle the top with 1 teaspoon of hand crushed dry rosemary and coarse salt. Brush with a bit of extra virgin olive oil when finished baking

Variation # 2: Before spreading out the dough, knead into it, 1 cup of sliced olives, such as Gaeta or Calamata; then spread and bake. No additional salt is necessary.

Variation # 3: Instead of olives, knead 1 cup sliced sun dried tomatoes packed in olive oil. Spread and bake.

Variation # 4: Knead ¼ cup grated Romano cheese, ¼ cup Parmigiano-Reggiano and ¼ cup grated provolone into the bread with ¼ cup extra virgin olive oil.

Pizza:

Spread ½ the pizza dough recipe on a deep cookie sheet covered with 2-3 tablespoons of olive oil. Distribute a ½ pound of low moisture mozzarella over the top of the dough, pressing it into the dough. Evenly spread one 28 oz can of Italian tomato filets over the dough. Sprinkle one tablespoon of fresh basil, one teaspoon oregano, ½ teaspoon freshly ground pepper and ½ cup Romano cheese over the surface. Bake at 350° until golden on the bottom.

General Pizza:

On a deep-dish cookie sheet, add 2-3 tablespoons of olive oil. Spread out ½ the dough recipe turning over at least once. Add your favorite sauce and cheese and bake at 350° until bubbly and golden on the bottom.

Onion Calzone (an old family recipe):

Sauté 3-4 sweet yellow onions in extra virgin olive oil over medium heat, season with salt and pepper. Cook onions until golden brown and well caramelized. Spread ½ the dough mixture out onto a pan greased with 2-3 tablespoons of olive oil. Spread the onions over the top of the dough. Add 1 cup sliced, Italian green olives. If desired, add a few anchovy filets. Bake in a 350° oven until golden on the bottom.

Let's talk about wine: When you think about pizza, you must think about hearty Italian reds either from Italy or you might try some new ones from California using "Italian" grape varietals: **Il Ginepro Sangiovese**, **Ruffino Chianti Ducale**, **Vasco Sassetti Brunello**, **Arcordini Valpolicella Repassa**, **Zenato Amarone**, **Macchia Barbera or Sangiovese**

Sunday Ragu from Puglia alla Nick

Sauce:

3 tablespoons extra virgin olive oil
1 large yellow onion, minced
4 cloves garlic, minced
2 cups hearty Italian red wine
2-8 ounce cans tomato paste
3-28 ounce cans tomato puree
1 cup water
1 cup Romano cheese
3 tablespoons fresh basil, chopped
1 tablespoon fresh oregano, minced
Sea salt to taste
Ground black pepper to taste

Meat:

6 Italian Sausage links (sweet and/or hot)
Put a tooth pick in the hot so people can tell the
   difference
6 large country style spear ribs

Braciole:

6 thin slices flank steak, pounded flat 3 inches
   wide by 6 inches long
4 cloves garlic, chopped
¾ cup Romano cheese
½ cup Italian parsley, chopped
Sea Salt to taste
Ground black pepper to taste
2 tablespoons pine nuts (optional)

Meatballs:

1 pound chopped chuck
1 pound chopped pork
1 cup seasoned breadcrumbs
1 cup Romano cheese
4 cloves garlic, minced
1 medium yellow onion, minced
2 tablespoons fresh basil, chopped (or 1 tablespoon
dried basil)

1 tablespoon fresh oregano, chopped (or ½ tablespoon dried oregano
2 tablespoon Italian parsley, minced (or 1 ½ tablespoon dried parsley)
2 eggs, scrambled
Sea salt to taste
Ground black pepper to taste
Extra virgin olive oil for frying

Sauce: In a large pot over medium high heat, sauté the onion and garlic in the olive oil until tender. Be careful not to burn the garlic. Add the tomato paste to the pot and sauté for 3-4 minutes. Add the red wine to the pot and bring to a simmer. Reduce heat and add the tomato puree, water, Romano cheese, basil and oregano. Bring to a slow simmer.

Meats: In a large pan, over medium high heat, add 2-3 tablespoons of olive oil. Cook the sausage until brown and add them to the sauce. In the same pan, cook the spare ribs until brown and add them to the sauce.

Braciole: Lay each pounded piece of flank steak out on a flat surface. Season each piece with a bit of salt and pepper. Sprinkle each one with the Romano cheese, garlic and parsley. Roll each slice into a roll and secure with twine or toothpicks. In the same pan used for the meats, cook the braciole until brown on all sides and add to the sauce.

Meatballs: In a large bowl, combine and blend well all the ingredients for the meatballs. Roll the meat into 2-3 inch balls and cook them in the same pan until they are brown. Add them to the sauce.

Once all the meat has been cooked scrape all the browned bits off the bottom of the pan along with a bit of the residual fats into the sauce and mix in. Cook the "ragu" at a low simmer for 1-3 hours and serve with your favorite pasta. Rigatoni works well with this sauce.

Let's talk about wine: Here again, bold reds are the thing. In addition to those mentioned in recipes #1 and #2, I would suggest the following: **Madrone-Knoll Cabernet** (2-3 hours to open);

Pahlmeyer Red Merlot; **Muga Rioja**; **Barnett Vineyards Cabernet** or **Merlot**; **Paul's (Sobon) Vineyard Zinfandel**; **Titus Cabernet** (1-2 hours to open). Or you can stay Italian with **Tignanello 2007** (3-4 hours to open); **Rocca Felice Borolo Reserva 1997**; **Allegrini Amarone 2006** (3-4 hours to open).

Christopher's Chicken Cutlets with Mustard and Capers

2-8 ounce skinless, boneless chicken cutlets cut in half
Sea salt to taste
Ground black pepper to taste
Flour for dusting
2 tablespoons extra virgin olive oil
1 large shallot, minced
1 clove garlic, minced
½ cup dry white wine
¼ cup Dijon mustard
2 tablespoon small capers

Pound the cutlets thin between sheets of plastic wrap. Season the cutlets with a bit of salt and pepper. Dust lightly with flour and sauté in the olive oil over medium heat until almost done. Remove and reserve.

In the same pan, add the shallot and garlic and cook until tender being careful not to burn the garlic. Add the wine and mustard and blend. Then, add the capers. Return the chicken and any collected juices to the pan and cook until done.

Let's talk about wine: When making this dish, my ADD/PAIR wine is almost always a *white burgundy* or *unoaked/slightly oaked chardonnay* from California. Try one of the following: **Edna Valley Chardonnay.**; **Martin Ray RRV Chardonnay.**; **Dominican Oaks Unoaked Chardonnay.**

Radicchio Herbed Chicken

2-8 ounces skinless, boneless chicken breasts cut in Half

4 tablespoons extra virgin olive oil

1 tablespoon unsalted butter

2 green onions, minced

2 teaspoons Italian parsley, minced

2 teaspoons fresh basil, minced

1 teaspoon fresh thyme, minced

1 teaspoon fresh rosemary, minced

1 head radicchio, sliced thin

4 tablespoons extra virgin olive oil

1 tablespoon balsamic vinegar

Sea salt to taste

Ground black pepper to taste

4 plum tomatoes, coarse chop

2 green onions, chopped

1 clove garlic, minced

1 tablespoon fresh basil, minced

4 tablespoons extra virgin olive oil

Sea salt to taste

Ground black pepper to taste

In a sauté pan over medium high heat, place the olive oil and butter. Combine all the herbs and press them into both sides of the chicken cutlets. Careful sear the cutlets until done and drain the oil. Reserve the chicken and keep warm.

In the same pan, over medium high heat, add the extra virgin olive oil. Once hot, place the radicchio in the pan and toss continuously. Add the balsamic and adjust flavor with a bit of salt and pepper. Cook radicchio until slightly wilted. Set aside.

In a bowl, combine the plum tomato, green onions, garlic, basil, extra virgin olive oil, salt and pepper. Allow to macerate for 30 minutes. To assemble the dish, make a bed of the wilted radicchio; place a chicken cutlet on top of the radicchio and then top the cutlet with the tomato salad.

Let's talk about wine: This rich and complex dish can stand up to and be complimented by one of the lighter *Pinot Noirs*: **Mark West**, **La Crema Sonoma**, **Angeline California**, or **Truscott.** A full-bodied *chardonnay* would complement the dish as well. Try on e of the following *chardonnays*: **Newton Unfiltered**, **Pahlmeyer**, **Jayson**, or **Mer Soleil Silver.**

"International" Chicken Soup

The basic recipe is Mom's but I added to it from contact with other cultures. Chicken Soup is the universal antibiotic so I just kept adding to mine and it turned out pretty good.

1 whole chicken (4-5 pounds), cut into pieces including the back

Cold water to cover by 2-3 inches

1 large yellow onion, coarse chop

4 cloves garlic, chopped

4-5 carrots, cut into rounds or half moons, (depending on size)

3-4 stalks of celery, plus center leaves, cross cut

2 medium size tomatoes, coarse chop

3 large slices of fresh ginger

¼ cup Italian parsley, chopped

1 teaspoon dry dill

1/3 cup extra virgin olive oil

1 teaspoon sea salt (more if desired)

1 teaspoon ground black pepper

1/8 cup good quality soy sauce

1/8 cup fish sauce

1 pound small pasta like Ditalini or broken thin spaghetti

In a large pot, combine the chicken pieces and enough water to cover them by 2-3 inches. Bring the water to a boil and skim the surface as necessary. Simmer for 20 minutes. After the initial simmer, add all the other ingredients to the pot, except for the pasta and return to a boil. Reduce heat to low and simmer for 45 minutes. Turn off the heat and let stand 15 minutes. Remove the chicken from the pot and allow cooling. Remove the ginger slices and discard.

Once cool enough to handle, pull the meat from the chicken parts and return the meat to the pot. Discard the bones and skin. Adjust the flavor with salt and pepper as necessary. Cook the pasta in a separate pot to the desired doneness and serve with the soup.

*NOTE: Some will say that it is healthier to chill the soup after making it to remove the layer of chicken fat that coagulates on the top. While it may be healthier, it will also remove about 80% of the flavor and what every mother knows is the best part for making you feel better when you have a cold.

Let's talk about wine: Chicken Soup is comfort food for a cold winter evening or when you are sick with a cold and need that warm good feeling and all the good things that are in the soup. I will leave the wine selection up to you.

Mom's Italian Sausage with Swiss Chard

3 tablespoon extra virgin olive oil
3 pounds sweet (or hot) Italian sausage
1 large yellow onion, coarse chop
5 cloves garlic, sliced thin
2-28 ounce cans Italian whole tomatoes, hand crushed
2-8 ounce cans tomato paste
½ cup hearty red wine
2 large bunches of rainbow or regular Swiss chard, center rib removed
Any type of pasta (optional)
Grated cheese (optional)
Crushed red pepper (optional)

Tear the leaves of the Swiss chard into pieces; discard the center rib. Rinse the Swiss chard well and set aside. In a large pot over medium high heat, add the extra virgin olive oil. Remove the sausage from the casing and crumble into the oil; cook until done. Remove and reserve the sausage pieces. Leave the sausage renderings in the pot.

After reducing the heat to medium, add the onion to the pot and cook until tender. Add the garlic and cook an additional minute until the garlic is golden. Deglaze with the wine and reduce by half. Add the tomatoes and tomato paste to the pot and bring to a simmer. Return the sausage

to the pot. Add the Swiss chard and mix. Cook covered until the Swiss chard is tender, stirring 2-3 times during the cooking process. Adjust the flavor with pepper (there should be enough salt). Serve alone, or with pasta, cheese and crushed red pepper as garnishes.

Variation #1: Use hot Italian sausage, or cheese/parsley sausage instead of sweet.

Variation #2: To prepare the dish as a side, leave out the sausage and just sauté onions and garlic; add the tomatoes and the Swiss chard and cook until tender.

Let's talk about wine: A nice *merlot* would pair well with this dish even as you increase the heat a bit. Hot Italian sausage is just a bit spicy and would not overwhelm a rich wine. Try one of the following: **Chateau Montet Merlot; Blackstone Merlot; Courtney Benham Merlot; Twomey Merlot** or you could go high end with the **Duckhorn Estates Merlot**.

My Sister's Maria's Roasted Lemon Chicken with 15 Cloves of Garlic

1 large roasting chicken, cut into 8 pieces
Zest of one lemon
Juice of 2 lemons
1 cup dry white wine
15+ cloves of garlic, coarse chop
2-3 tablespoons extra virgin olive oil
Sea salt to taste
Ground black pepper to taste
1 tablespoon fresh oregano
1 cup dry white wine or chicken stock

Combine the zest, lemon juice, wine, garlic, and olive oil in a baking pan and roll the chicken in the juices. Allow the chicken to macerate skin side down for about 30 minutes. After the chicken has macerated, turn the chicken skin side up. Sprinkle with the salt, pepper and oregano. Roast the chicken at 350° until the chicken is done, about 45-55 minutes and the internal temperature is 160°. Place under the broiler for the last 5 minutes to crisp the skin. Serve with the pan juices as gravy. A side of rice with the juices goes very well.

Let's talk about wine: For this recipe, I like to use **Martini & Rossi Dry Vermouth** for the ADD wine. I feel it adds so much to the dish. As I mentioned in the introduction, I believe that this great wine can be added to any dish that calls for the addition of a Dry White Wine. This will keep the wonderful memory of the great Julia Childs alive. As for the PAIR wine, try a nice *Pinot Grigio* such as: **Kupelwieser; Barone Fini; Conti Fini** or **Cavit.**

Quick Meat Sauce

Don't have time to simmer for hours? Need a quick hearty sauce for pasta? Try the following:

3 tablespoons extra virgin olive oil
1 large yellow onion, chopped
4 cloves garlic, chopped
1 pound ground chuck
1 pound lean ground pork
1 tablespoon ground black pepper
1 ½ tablespoons hand crushed dry basil
¾ tablespoon hand crushed, dry oregano
¾ cup grated Romano cheese
2-28 ounce cans Italian tomato puree
1-28 ounce can water
1-8 ounce can Italian tomato paste
Sea salt to taste
Ground black pepper to taste

In a large pot over medium heat, add the oil. Add the onions and sauté until tender. Add the garlic and sauté an additional minute being careful not to burn it. Crumble the meat into the pot along with the black pepper. Stir constantly until the meat is cooked through.

Add the dry basil and stir-add the dry oregano and stir-finally add the cheese and stir. Add the puree, water and paste and blend all together. Bring to a simmer and cook for 30 minutes or longer. If it is too thick, you can add water as necessary. Adjust the flavor with the salt and pepper and serve with your favorite pasta.

Let's talk about wine: This dish calls for a nice Chianti: **Bellini**; **Gabbiano**; **San Andrea**; **Trecciano;** or a *Sangiovese*: **Il Ginepro**; **Sobon**; **Macchia**.

Chunky Fresh Tomato Sauce

6-8 pounds vine ripened, beefsteak or heirloom tomatoes *(save the seeds and juice for the next recipe)
4 tablespoons extra virgin olive oil
1 large yellow onion, minced
4 cloves garlic, sliced thin
1 small can tomato paste
1/3 cup fresh basil, minced
¼ cup flat leaf parsley, minced
¼ cup grated Romano cheese
Sea Salt to taste
Ground black pepper to taste

Score the tomatoes in a crisscross pattern on the bottom of the tomatoes, opposite side of the core. (Try not to cut too deep into the tomato). Drop the tomatoes into a large pan of boiling water. Remove the tomatoes from the hot water when the skin starts peeling away from the tomato. Plunge the tomato into an ice bath. Allow to sit for a couple minutes to cool.

Once the tomatoes are cool enough to handle, peel the skin away from the tomatoes and discard. Cut the tomatoes in half and squeeze all the seeds and juice out of the tomatoes into a bowl. Cut the tomatoes in large pieces.

Add the olive oil to a pan over medium heat and sauté the onion until tender. Add the garlic and sauté an additional minute. Add the cut tomatoes and tomato paste to the pan. Blend well; then add the basil and parsley to the pan. Add the grated cheese and adjust the flavor with salt and pepper. Serve.

Let's talk about wine: See the suggestions for the Chiantis in the previous recipe.

Insalata di Settembre "Tomato Juice" Salad from My Youth

Every September my family would turn 20 bushels of plum tomatoes into, puree, packed whole tomatoes, diced tomatoes, etc. The products produced would provide us with all our tomato needs for the year. From all of the tomatoes, the raw juice and seeds were salvaged and turned into "La Salada de Pomadoro" Whenever I make a large fresh tomato sauce, as in # 6 above, I saved all the reserved seeds and juice from the above recipe and turned them into a wonderful memory.

Reserved juice and seeds from recipe #10

4 ripe plum tomatoes cut into bite size pieces
1 large red onion, cut in half and sliced very
  thin
¼ cup extra virgin olive oil
Sea Salt to taste
Ground black pepper to taste

Combine all the ingredients in a large bowl and refrigerate for 2-3 hours until very chilled. Serve in bowls, with chunks of Italian Bread. This is a hand food. Break off pieces of bread-dip-soak-grab some onions & tomatoes---ENJOY. (Bibs are recommended but not required).

Let's talk about wine: OK-OK you want me to say it but I won't. I can think of no better wine to serve with this dish but the great homemade G---- Red wine I made with my father in the basement he dug out by hand in the Flatbush section of Brooklyn, New York. Look to the introduction regarding that. There is one Italian Restaurant in Queens, New York that still serves homemade Italian wine. Every time I visit NYC, I eat there and have the "house" red wine. Tears come to my eyes. If homemade wine is not an option for you, good *Chianti* will do nicely.

Mom's Spinach and Mashed Potatoes

So you might be asking yourself how these two dishes might go with each other. It started out with my working class immigrant family starting dinner with a "filling" dish--a large bowl of greens, soup, or pasta, all served with lots of great crusty bread. I guess it was my mother idea to create this "filling" dish. She would make a big bowl of spinach sautéed in garlic and olive oil and an equally big bowl of fresh mashed potatoes. Both items would be served to us in separate bowls, but we would eat them together with bread--- WOW!!

4 pounds fresh baby spinach, cleaned
4 tablespoons extra virgin olive oil
5-6 cloves garlic, sliced thin
1 cup water
Sea Salt to taste
Ground black pepper to taste
Extra virgin olive oil to drizzle
4 large Idaho Potatoes
½ cup milk
¼ cup extra virgin olive oil
Sea salt to taste
Ground black pepper to taste

Spinach:

In a large sauté pan over medium high heat, add the olive oil and then the garlic. Cook the garlic until it turns a very light golden color, then add the spinach and stir well. Season the spinach lightly with salt and pepper. Add the water and cover. Cook until wilted. Adjust the flavor with salt and pepper and place in a large serving bowl.

Potatoes:

Peel the potatoes and cut them into chunks. Place them in a pot of boiling water and cook until fork tender. Strain the water from the potatoes. Return the potatoes to the pot. Mash well. Add the milk and olive oil and mash again. Add salt and pepper to taste. Place in a serving bowl. Serve each person two small bowls, one with the spinach and one with the potatoes. Drizzle a bit of extra virgin olive oil on each dish. Serve with crusty Italian bread and crushed red pepper as garnish.

Let's talk about wine: Please see the discussion after the last recipe.

Joseph K's Section

Joe's Famous Meatloaf

1 pound ground chuck
½ cup ketchup
1/8 teaspoon crushed hot red pepper
¼ teaspoon fresh ground black pepper
1 egg, beaten
¼ cup seasoned breadcrumbs
2 tablespoons diced yellow onion
¼ cup tomato juice
¼ cup ketchup
1 teaspoon yellow mustard
¼ cup brown sugar

Pre heat the oven to 400°. In a large bowl, combine the beef, ketchup, black pepper, red pepper, egg, seasoned breadcrumbs and onion. Mix well. Be careful not to overwork the meat. Line a loaf pan with foil and place the meat mixture into it.

In a separate bowl combine the remaining ketchup, mustard and brown sugar until smooth. Brush the top of the meat with mixture and bake in the oven for 45 minutes until the meat is no longer pink inside with an internal temperature of 155°. Glaze the meatloaf with any remaining sauce and serve.

Let's talk about wine: There are some wonderful inexpensive merlots that would go very well with this dish. You would do well serving the **Bridgeman Merlot** or the **Courtney Benham**. If I were forced to choose the one reasonably priced red wine to drink with a dish like this, there would be no doubt that I would choose the Spanish wine **Clio.** It is one of my favorite reds at any price. So I offer this to you.

Grilled Chicken

2 cups chili sauce
¾ cup red wine vinegar
2 tablespoons prepared horseradish
4-6 ounce chicken breasts

Combine the chili sauce, vinegar and horseradish in a large bowl. Place the chicken breasts in the bowl and mix well. Marinate the chicken for at least 30 minutes, but no more than 2 hours. Grill the chicken, while continually brushing the chicken breasts as they cook. Cook until the internal temperature of the chicken is 160°. Serve.

Let's talk about wine: When drinking a white with this dish I would prefer a full bodied chardonnay such as the **Dominican Oaks; Pahlmeyer; Jayson's; Newton Unfiltered; Lloyd; Patz and Hall**. Their full bodied nature and rich mouth feel would each stand up to and add to the complex flavors of this simple dish.

Maple Salmon

1 pound salmon filets
¼ cup maple syrup
2 tablespoons soy sauce
Ground black pepper to taste

In a bowl, blend together the maple syrup, soy and black pepper. Place the salmon filets in a shallow baking dish. Coat the salmon with the syrup mixture and bake in a 350° oven until done-about 15-20 minutes.

Let's talk about wine: A nice simple pinot noir would best bring out the flavors of this dish and compliment it very well. I would suggest the **Alterra Napa** or the **Estancia.**

Italian Salmon

1 ounce high quality, low sodium Italian dressing
2 tablespoons lemon juice
8 ounces sliced mushrooms

1 pound salmon filets

In a bowl, combine the dressing, lemon juice and mushrooms. Place the salmon in a shallow baking dish and coat the salmon with the mushroom mixture. Bake in a preheated oven at 350° until done---about 15-20 minutes.

Let's talk about wine: We have said time and time again in the text that salmon is one of the fish that pairs so well with Pinot Noir. This dish and the one that precedes it are no exceptions. There are many great Pinots but **Goldeneye**; **Pahlmeye**r; **Jayson**'s and **Patz and Hall** are my very favorites and I offer them to you for consideration to pair with these two dishes.

Fire Alarm Chili

1 pound ground chuck
2-8 ounce cans of Pinto or Red Kidney beans, drained and rinsed
24 ounces, low sodium tomato juice
48 ounces, high quality beef stew
1 large yellow onion, chopped
Cayenne pepper to taste
Additional hot sauces as garnish

In a pan over medium high heat, brown the beef and drain off the excess grease. Add the beans, beef stew, onions and cayenne pepper. Simmer for 20 minutes and serve. You can add additional spice to the dish or serve a variety of hot sauces.

Let's talk about wine: If you wanted to go with a slightly sweet wine I would suggest the **Louis Bouillet Extra Dry** or the **Montaudon Extra Dry**. I addition, we have spoken about the use of sweeter wines for spicy dishes but here I would like to offer an alternative, a super big and bold red to pair with this dish. Try one of the following all of which need some hours to open: **Madrone Knoll Cabernet** (3-4 hours to open); **Pahlmeyer Preparatory Red** (1-2 hours to open); **Dominus 2006** (4-5 hours to open); **Zenato Amarone** (3-4 hours to open); **Concha y Toro Don Melchor 2007** (3-4 hours to open) or **Ch Brane Contenac Margaux 2003** (4-6 hours to open)

Joe's Death By Chocolate

2 boxes of prepared chocolate mousse
2 boxes of Instant chocolate pudding
6 bars of crunchy nutty candy like Snickers or Butterfingers, or both
Large tub of Cool Whip
1 large package of Oreo Cookies, ground

This should be prepared in a large punch bowl or it's equal. Prepare the chocolate mousse and the chocolate pudding according to package directions and set aside. Break the package of Oreo cookies into small pieces and set aside. Break the candy bars into very small pieces and set aside.

Sprinkle about a ½ inch of the broken Oreos on the bottom of the bowl. Cover with the prepared chocolate pudding and smooth out evenly. Sprinkle with ½ of the broken candy bars. Cover with the prepared mousse spread evenly. Sprinkle the top of the mousse layer with half the remaining Oreos and half the remaining candy crumble. Cover with the cool whip and sprinkle the top with the remaining Oreo and candy crumbles. Refrigerate for 3-4 hours and serve.

Let's talk about wine: We have spoken often of the marriage of the taste of food and wine creating a third flavor; well nowhere is that marriage more successful than that of chocolate and a good port. It is almost unreal how the two go together. Choose a great Vintage Port such as the **Osborne 2003** or the **Grahams 2007**. In addition consider an ager tawny port such as the **Illaparra 10 year old** or the **Quinta 20 year old**. If you want to go all out then choose the **Taylor 40 year old**.

Chef Joe's Section

As a chef for nearly thirty years, one can only imagine the number of recipes that I've created over that time span. Consequently, as with most chefs, and individual epicureans, I've been exposed to quite a few individuals who have had a great deal of influence on my style of cooking, and the ideas I come up with.

One thing is for sure. I've learned to truly appreciate the opportunity I've had to share my knowledge with the people who eat the food I prepare.

As for the following recipes, each was created with a story behind it. Each recipe has been tried and true. I hope you enjoy.

Hog Snapper alla Pepe

4 8-9oz Hog Snapper filet, skin and pin bones removed; (may substitute yellowtail snapper)
2 ounces olive oil
2 tablespoons unsalted butter
All purpose flour
4 fresh artichoke bottoms, quartered
2 tablespoons sun dried tomatoes, cut into strips
2 tablespoons capers
½ cup dry white wine
¾ cup low sodium fish or chicken stock
Juice of half a lemon
2 tablespoons unsalted butter
8 ounces jumbo lump crabmeat
1 tablespoon fresh basil, chiffonade
1/2 tablespoon Italian parsley, chopped
Sea salt to taste
Ground black pepper to taste

In a large sauté pan over medium high heat, add the olive oil and melt the butter. Dust each piece of the snapper with flour and place in the hot pan, skin side up. Cook the snapper for 3-4 minutes on each side, being careful not to break apart the filets when turning them over. Remove filets from pan when done and place on a warm serving platter. In the same pan over medium heat, add the artichoke, sundried tomatoes, and capers to the pan. Cook for 30 seconds and deglaze pan with the white wine and lemon juice. Reduce the wine by half; then add the stock, bring to a simmer, reduce a bit more and remove from the heat. Swirl the whole butter into the pan until the butter is completely incorporated. Adjust flavor with the salt and pepper. Distribute the crabmeat over the top of the snapper, and immediately drizzle the sauce for the snapper. Garnish with some fresh chopped basil and parsley.

Let's talk about wine: To enhance the flavor of this dish, I have found **Sonoma-Cutrer Les Peirres** and **Markham** chardonnays are nice choices.

Yellow Gazpacho with Poached Rock Shrimp

2 4x5 yellow tomatoes, cored and seeds removed, coarse chop
1small yellow onion, coarse chop
1 English cucumber, peeled and seeds removed, coarse chop
1yellow pepper, stem and seeds removed, coarse chop
1 small chayote, coarse chop
1 garlic clove, chopped
½ ounces olive oil
1 ounce sherry vinegar
1 teaspoon cilantro, chopped
¼ to ½ cup water
½ lb rock shrimp, peeled and deveined, tail-off, poached and cooled
Extra virgin olive oil, for garnish
Sprig of cilantro, for garnish
Sea salt to taste
Ground white pepper to taste

Coarsely chop the tomato, cucumber, pepper, onion, chayote and garlic. Place half the vegetables in a large blender, or food processor with half the water and cilantro and begin to "pulse" the blender to break down the vegetables into a puree. Continue to add the vegetables until all the vegetables are pureed. You may need to add a bit more water to help with the process. Blend until very smooth. Remove the puree from the blender and place in a large mixing bowl. Season the puree with the sherry vinegar, olive oil, salt and pepper. Allow the gazpacho to sit for 30 minutes to allow the flavors to "meld". Garnish each serving with a few poached shrimp in the center of the bowl, a drizzle of extra virgin olive oil and a sprig of cilantro.

Here I recommend a nice *sauvignon Blanc* such as **Honig** or **Sterling Vintner's Collection,** or a *Pinot Grigio* such as **Gabbiano,** or **Barone Fini.**

Chicken Scarpariello

My wife's family first introduced this recipe to me. It was an award-winning dish from their restaurant in Boca Raton. It is a traditional "Peasant Dish". A type of Italian "Pot-Luck". But one thing was certain. This was not luck, this was all love......

6 Italian sausage links, par grilled, cut in 1 inch pieces
3 large Yukon gold potatoes, peeled, cut into 1 inch cubes
1 ounce extra virgin olive oil
Pinch of sea salt
Pinch of ground black pepper
1 teaspoon fresh oregano, chopped
6-8 ounce skinless, boneless, chicken cutlets cut in half
All purpose flour
4 tablespoons extra virgin olive oil
4 garlic cloves, coarse chop
1 cup dry white wine
1 ounce imported balsamic vinegar
1 cup low sodium chicken stock
8 –10 sweet cherry peppers (or hot)
2 teaspoons fresh oregano, chopped
Sea salt to taste
Ground black pepper to taste
2 tablespoons unsalted butter
Chopped Italian parsley for garnish

Par-grill the sausage on the grill or in the oven until cooked through. Allow the sausage to cool. Cut the sausage into 1 inch pieces. Set aside for later use.

Pre heat an oven at 350°. Peel and cube the potatoes. Toss with the olive oil, salt, pepper, and oregano. Place on a baking pan, and roast potatoes in the oven until very crispy. Toss the potatoes in the pan a couple of times during the cooking process to get an even cook on them. Once the potatoes are done, remove the potatoes from the pan and set aside for later use.

Pound the chicken cutlets lightly between sheets of plastic wrap. Season the cutlets with salt and pepper. Dust lightly with flour. Sauté the chicken over medium heat in the olive oil until *almost* done. Add the garlic around the chicken in the pan. Continue to cook 30 seconds, or until garlic starts to become golden in color. Immediate deglaze the pan with the wine; reduce by half, then add the balsamic vinegar and chicken stock. Bring pan to a simmer. Add the sausage to the pan along with the cherry peppers and oregano. Adjust flavor with salt and pepper. Finally, at the last moment, add the roasted potatoes; toss a couple of times, and begin to plate the dish on a large platter. Once all the components of the dish are plated, return the pan with the sauce to the burner. Bring to a simmer; swirl in the butter until completely incorporated. Pour sauce over the entire dish. Garnish the dish with some chopped Italian parsley.

Variation #1: You may substitute a 4-5 pound whole roasting chicken, cut into pieces, tossed with some olive oil, and seasoned with salt, pepper, and oregano, and roasted in the oven, instead of the cutlets for more of a traditional dish.

Let's talk about wine:

What better choice than **Santa Margarita** Pinot Grigio to go with this Tuscan dish; or a personal favorite, **Ruffino Gold Label** if you prefer Chianti.

Mesa Verde Green Chili

I was first exposed to this dish on my trip to Durango, Colorado to visit family. Already a big fan of Southwestern cuisine, I just couldn't get enough.

4 pounds Anaheim or New Mexico chilies, roasted

2 pounds pork butt, cut into 1 inch cubes
2 tablespoons olive oil
2 large yellow onions, chopped
8 garlic cloves, chopped
1 ½ tablespoons toasted cumin
1 teaspoon fresh Mexican oregano
2 tablespoons fresh cilantro, chopped
¼ cup fresh Serrano chile pepper, chopped
4 cups vegetable broth
2 large russet potatoes, 1 inch dice
6 plum tomatoes, coarse dice

Roast in the oven, or "blister" the Anaheim chilies on the BBQ. Cook the chilies until the skin starts to char and pull away from the meat of the Chile. Place the cooked chilies in a brown paper bag and close, allowing the peppers to "steam," and then cool. Once cool, remove the chilies from the bag; remove the charred skin, stems and seeds from the chilies. (Try NOT to rinse the peppers under water. It may compromise to quality of the finished dish.) Cube the pork butt in 1 inch cubes and set aside for later use.

Heat the olive oil in a Dutch oven, or large pot over medium high heat. Add the cubed pork, garlic, onion, cumin and oregano. Cook and stir until the pork has browned. Cook and stir a few more minutes, then add the cilantro and vegetable stock to the pot. Reduce the heat to low, and simmer for about 30 minutes. Add the potatoes to the stew, and simmer for another 45 minutes. Add the roasted chilies to the pot, along with the serrano chilies. You may add a bit more stock if the stew starts to become a bit to dry. Once the pork and potatoes are tender, add the tomatoes. Cook for about 10 more minutes, then remove from heat and serve.

Let's talk about beer:

What better to pair chili with than an ice cold beer? I like **Fat Tire Amber Ale, Arrogant Bastard Ale,** or **Avalanche Ale** from Breckenridge Brewery.

Herb Crusted Rotisserie Pork Loin Cooked Over Lobelville Cedar

A few Thanksgivings ago, my family decided to spend Thanksgiving week in a small town about an hour outside Nashville, Tennessee, named Lobelville. Each day, one family was in charge of one day's cooking. On my day, I built a fire pit, and I decided to cook a pork roast on a rotisserie over an open cedar wood fire with cedar gathered from the forest behind the house. Needless to say, it's now infamous.

1 whole 4-5 pound pork roast, clean of some fat
  and sinew
¼ cup extra virgin olive oil
2 tablespoon fresh basil, chopped
2 tablespoon fresh rosemary, chopped
2 tablespoons Italian parsley, chopped
1 tablespoon fresh thyme, chopped
1 ½ tablespoons "cracked" black peppercorns
1 ½ tablespoons sea salt
Butcher string
Rotisserie skewer attachment

Place the pork tenderloin on a cutting board. Begin to trim some of the fat away from the meat, but not all of it. In a small mixing bowl, combine the fresh chopped basil, rosemary, parsley, thyme, cracked black peppercorns and salt. Blend well.

Rub the pork down, completely with the olive oil. Begin to evenly distribute the herb mix over the entire pork roast. Massage the herbs into the pork. Allow the pork to sit for about an hour before cooking. Take the butcher string and tie the pork loin down the length of the roast, keeping the string about 3" apart from each other. This will allow the pork to cook evenly throughout. Skewer the loin down the center; secure the pork with the "barbs" from the rotisserie so it doesn't move during the cooking process. Place the pork on the rotisserie over a roaring cedar wood fire, about 8-10 inches from the flame. Allow the roast to rotate over the fire for 1-2 hours, or until the internal temperature is 145 to 155°, or however you like your pork. (Don't forget carryover cooking). If you don't have the benefit of a rotisserie, you may cook the pork in the oven at 400° for 30 minutes, then 350° for another 45 minutes, or to desired doneness. Or, you can grill the pork on the BBQ over indirect heat. Allow pork to rest for 15 minutes before carving. Place on warming serving platter.

*Note: Carryover is the continued cooking of an item even though the item has been removed from the direct cooking source.

Let's talk about wine: Because the flavor of the meat is so pronounced, I like to savor the flavor with a *pinot noir* such as **Ken Wright Willamette Valley**, or **Zaca Mesa Santa Barbara**.

Chef Joe's Famous Baby Back Ribs

4-20-24oz Baby Back Rib Racks

BBQ Sauce:

2 cups ketchup
½ cup spicy brown mustard
½ cup brown sugar
¼ cup apple cider vinegar
1 tablespoon onion powder
1 tablespoon chili powder
1 tablespoon ground black pepper
2 teaspoons garlic powder
1 teaspoon cumin
½ teaspoon celery salt
½ teaspoon sea salt
1 tablespoon liquid smoke
3 tablespoons Worcestershire sauce

Braising liquid:

1 quart BBQ Sauce
1 quart water
¼ cup apple cider vinegar
¼ cup honey
¼ cup brown sugar
6-12oz bottles, Yuengling lager
Sea salt to taste
Ground black pepper to taste

To make the BBQ sauce, place all the ingredients in a pot and bring to a simmer. Cook for 30 minutes, stirring occasionally, and allow thickening. Set aside.

Score crosswise on the bone side, (underside) of the rib racks several times with a small knife. Season the ribs with some salt and pepper. Set in a deep roasting pan and set aside.

In a large pot, combine the BBQ sauce, water, cider vinegar, honey, sugar and 4 bottles of the beer. (The other 2 bottles are for the chef.) Bring to a simmer. Place the braising liquid into the pan, submerging the ribs. Wrap the top of the pan with plastic wrap, and then aluminum foil. Place in a preheated 325° oven for 2 ½ to 3 hours. After 2 ½ hours, check the ribs to see if the bones are starting to separate from the meat. If so, they're done, otherwise continue to cook until the desired result.

Remove the ribs from the braising liquid and allow the ribs to cool completely. (May be made a day ahead).

When ready to eat, grill the ribs on the BBQ over a high heat, glazing the ribs as they cook with the BBQ sauce. Serve when heated through.

Let's talk about wine: If in the mood for wine with my ribs, I like **Liberty School**, or **Franciscan** *Cabernet Sauvignon*.

Let's talk about beer: With ribs, some of my preferred choices are **Bass Ale, Corona, Brooklyn Lager,** and **Harpoon IPA.**

Hoisin Ginger Glazed Pork Loin Rib Chops

4-14 ounce pork loin rib chops, 1 ½ inch thick
1 ounce Sesame Oil
1 cup Soy Sauce
2 ounces sweet chili sauce (Mae Ploy)
2 tablespoons fresh ginger, minced
4 garlic cloves, minced
1 cup Hoisin sauce
2 tablespoons brown sugar
2 green onions, minced
1 stalk lemongrass, bottom half crushed and minced
2 tablespoons cilantro, chopped

In a mixing bowl, place all ingredients and mix well. In a separate bowl, place the pork chops and coat each pork chop generously with the glaze. Reserve some of the glaze for later use. Allow the pork to sit for 2-3 hours before cooking. When ready to cook, heat the BBQ to a high heat. Clean the grates well and wipe with a paper towel and a bit of oil. Close the BBQ lid to allow the grates to get very hot. Once hot, place the marinated pork chop on the grates and allow searing.

After about 5 minutes, turn the chops over and continue to cook another 5 minutes. Close the BBQ lid. After another 5 minutes, open the BBQ lid and once again turn the chops over, to assure even cooking. Baste the pork with a bit of the reserved glaze. Close the lid and continue to cook.

Again, after another 5 minutes, turn the chops over. Baste once again, and finish the cooking time. The internal temperature should be 145 to 155, but you cook it how you like it. Glaze the chops one more time before removing from the grill and serve.

Let's talk about wine: I like to complement the sweet and slightly spicy flavor of this dish with a *Riesling* such as **Hugel** and **Domaine Schlumberger**, both from Alsace, and **Hogue Cellars** of Washington State.

Let's talk about beer: Again, to enhance the glaze on the pork, **Shiner Bock Spaetzle, Anchor Steam Ale,** and **Monk in the Trunk Organic Amber** are nice choices.

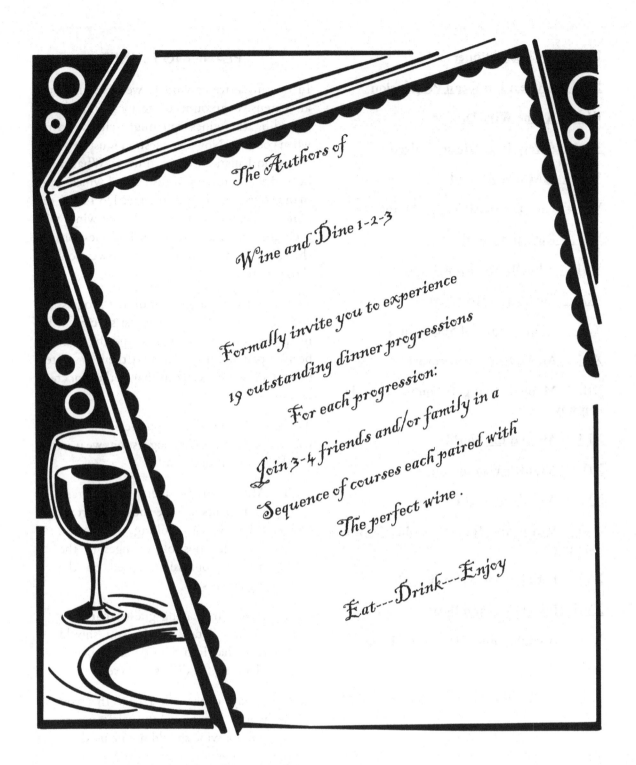

The Authors of

Wine and Dine 1-2-3

Formally invite you to experience

19 outstanding dinner progressions

For each progression:

Join 3-4 friends and/or family in a

Sequence of courses each paired with

The perfect wine.

Eat---Drink---Enjoy

Chapter 15:

Planning a Dinner Progression

PLANNING DINNER

In this inventive cookbook, we have given you an extensive amount of recipes and choices regarding the wines you might choose to use when cooking. Now the question must be asked---how do I plan an entire dinner? What might be a nice progression of dishes and wines? How many courses do I wish to serve? Do I serve one wine throughout dinner, or change wines with each course? These are all fitting questions. In this next chapter, we hope to answer some of those questions.

We will offer you a series of dinner progressions and suggestions. We will suggest specific dishes in specific orders and suggest specific wines or beers to pair. We urge you to try them as written, but as with all else, you can change them or create new ones.

As you begin to use these progressions, or create your own, there are a few suggestions we urge you to take into consideration:

1. Always remember that fresh ingredients are the most important thing when cooking, so always allow for possible changes in the meal's progression, based on the ingredients.

2. If you are having guests that have special dietary needs, you should take that into consideration before planning the dishes to serve.

3. Always cook with a wine that you would like to drink; a leftover or inferior wine should not be used.

4. If using a red that requires "decanting," make sure you build that time into your planning.

5. Whenever possible, think of using the ADD wine as the PAIR wine.

6. Consider how spicy you would like your dinner to be. You may decide

to vary the spice, or maintain it throughout the meal.

7. Consider a similar question about the richness of the dishes you choose.

8. Pair the wines with the courses carefully so that each provides that third layer of taste we spoke about in the introduction. Remember the taste of the food, plus the taste of the wine, should equal a taste that is better than the sum of its parts.

I
A classic dinner

Appetizer:

Classic Chopped Tomato Bruschetta

Cannellini Beans & Pancetta Bruschetta

Moet Imperial Nectar Rose

Soup:

Italian Bread Soup

Amici Sauvignon Blanc

Entrée:

Chicken Cutlets Francese

Spaghetti Garlic and Oil

Barone Fini Pinot Grigio

Dessert:

Oranges in Orange Syrup with fresh whipped cream

Grand Mainer

****

II
A Great Europeans Progression

Appetizer:

Chicken Livers in Sherry Tapas

Mixed Spanish Olives Tapas

Served with crusty French or Italian bread

Osborne Fino Sherry

Pasta:

Red Lentil Stew

Angeline Pinot Noir Rrv

Entrée:

Sautéed Sweetbreads

Paul Hobbs Chardonnay

Dessert:

Cheese & Fruit Platter

Quinta 10 Year Old Tawny Port

****

III
A one wine dinner:

Appetizer:

Crabmeat Spread Bruschetta

Spinach Spread Bruschetta

Served with baked pita wedges

Newton Unfiltered Chardonnay

Pasta:

Rotini with Peas

Continue with the Newton Unfiltered Chardonnay

Entrée:

Roasted Lemon Chicken with 15 Cloves of Garlic, served with cooked basmati rice as a side.

Continue with the Muirwood

Dessert:

Pecan Pie served with fresh whipped cream

Continue with the Newton Unfiltered Chardonnay

****

IV
A very rich dinner indeed

Appetizer:

Coquilles St. Jacques

Chateau de la Tour de l'Ange, Macon-Village

Second Course:

Liver Tyrolesine

Dr. L Riesling

Entrée:

Argentine Rib-Eye Steak with Chimichurri,

Served with Stuffed Tomatoes

Flichman Tupungato

Dessert

Ricotta Cheese Cake

Martini and Rossi Asti

****

V
MMMMM Good

Appetizer:

Mozzarella in Carrozza

Bougrier Vouvray "V"

Soup:

International Chicken Soup

La Crema

Entrée:

Italian Herb Pork Roast and Cold String Bean Salad

Jordon Cabernet

Dessert:

Key Lime Pie with fresh Whipped Cream

Osborne Tawny Port

****

VI
Let's do an all veggie dinner

Appetizer:

Broccoli Rabe Bruschetta

Mashed Cauliflower Bruschetta

Served with slices of toasted Italian bread

Nino Franco Prosecco

Second Course:

Spinach Cannellini in Béchamel Sauce

Newton Unfiltered Chardonnay

Entrée:

Roasted Mushrooms with Shallots and Fresh Herbs with Basmati Rice

Trimbach Pinot Blanc Alsace

Dessert:

Pears Poached in Wine

The port you choose to poach the pears

****

VII
Rich and Royal

Appetizer:

One serving of French Chicken Wings

One serving of Chinese Chicken Wings

La Crema Pinot Noir

Soup:

Italian Bread Soup

Trecciano Chianti Sensi

Entrée:

Crispy Beef in Oyster Sauce with cooked basmati rice

14 Hands Cabernet

Dessert:

Zabaglione with Raspberries & Blueberries

Bellini Vin Santo

****

VIII
A Really Sparkling Dinner

Appetizer:

Quick Liver Pate served with crackers

Martel Prestige Brut or Moet Brut

Fish Course:

Filet of Sole in Parchment

Piper Heidsiech Brut

Entrée:

Chicken Cutlets with Lemon & Capers

Billecart-salmon Brut

Dessert:

Peach Pizza

Veuve Rose

****

IX
This is a Really Offal Dinner

Appetizer:

Pickled Pigs Feet

Asian Style Chicken Feet

Botter Prosecco

Soup Course:

Tripe Soup

Mulderbosch Rose

Entrée:

Liver with Bacon and Onions

Two Hands

Dessert:

Hot Buttered Rum

****

X
A Big Dinner of Small Bites

Here, we present to you, a "small bites" dinner. It is probably best served as a pick up buffet type dinner with drinks. It would make a nice cocktail party selection of small bites. The servings below should serve 4-6 people. You can increase the number of each offering depending on the number of people you are serving. You can add multiples of the dishes listed, or add additional small bite dishes from the recipes provided throughout the book.

(A) Tapas:

a. Stuffed Mushrooms

b. Shrimp and Serrano Ham

c. Warm Mixed Spanish Olives

(B) Bruschetta

a. Balsamic Onions

b. Italian Tuna

c. Hot Peppers

(C) Wings

a. One order of buffalo wings

b. One order of Thai wings

(D) Salads

a. Cold Pasta Salad

b. Fried Eggplant Salad

c. Tuna and Bean Salad

Let's talk about wine/beer: With this type of dinner you should choose a selection of wines and beers to serve. Choose at least one red and one white and at least two types of beers that you feel will compliment the dishes served. Remember if you choose to really spice up the dishes you will have to choose wines that have a bit of sweetness and beers that are crisp and hoppy in nature.

****

XI
An All American Dinner

Appetizer:

Long Island on the Half Shell with various sauces

Amici Sauvignon Blanc Napa

Soup:

Manhattan Clam Chowder

Angeline Chardonnay Rrv

Entrée:

Texas Style Spare Ribs

Cheddar, Bacon and Scallion Biscuits

Gordon Brothers Syrah

Dessert:

New York Cheesecake

Washington Hills Gewürztraminer

****

XII
"Manga! Manga! You're too thin anyway!"

Appetizer:

Potatoes & Eggs Bruschetta

Shrimp Scampi Bruschetta

Served with crostini

Nino Franco Dry Prosecco

Pasta:

Angle Hair with Cauliflower

Barone Fini Pinot Grigio

Fish:

Filet of Sole, Lemon & Capers

Continue with the Barone Fini

Meat:

Veal Marsala with Mushrooms

Kupelwieser Lagrein Alto Adige

Dessert:

Ricotta Cheese Cake

Double Espresso Coffee

Served with lemon zest; anisette, or Sambucca

Martini & Rossi Sweet Vermouth on the Rocks

Please allow at least 3-4 hours to savor this meal.

****

XIII
Around the World

Appetizer:

Herring in Sour Cream

Adler Fels Sauvignon Blanc

Salad:

A Real Greek Salad

Domestica Red

Second Salad:

Nam Sod

Muller Spatlese

Entrée:

Chilean Empanadas

Valserrano Rioja Reserva

Dessert:

Zeppole de San Giuseppe

Freixenet Semi Seco

****

XIV
A quick Visit to France

Appetizer

Mussels Mariniere

Rothschild Blanc

Soup:

Warm Vichyssoise

Domaine St. Martin Macon-Village

Entrée:

Duck with Glaze, Variation #1

Stuffed Tomatoes

Louis Latour Pinot Noir

Dessert:

Crème Brulee

Martel VSOP Cognac

****

XV
A Cool Summer Dinner

Appetizer:

Prosciutto Appetizer

Amici Sauvignon Blanc

Soup:

Golden Gazpacho with Poached Rock Shrimp

Duckhorn Sauvignon Blanc Napa

Entrees:

Maine Lobster Rolls

Cold Pasta Salad

Billecart-Salmon Rose

Dessert:

Carrot Cake

Rosa Regale or Soria Brachetto

****

XVI
Warm-up for a Cold Winter's Evening

Appetizer:

Roasted Peppers, Variation #3

Beringer White Zinfandel

Entrée:

Nick's Chili

Served with raw onion, shaved cheddar cheese and sour cream garnishes

Choose a Dr. Heidemanns Riesling based on hot spicy you choose to make the chili:

MILD: Kabinett

MEDIUM: Spatlese

HOT: Auslese

Dessert:

Warm Pecan Pie

Hot Buttered Rum

****

XVII
Let's Do Salads for Brunch

The following group of salads should serve at least 8 people. Serve with a variety of breads and enjoy:

1. New Jersey Tomato Tart

2. Warm Spanish Olives Tapas

3. Citrus Shrimp and Fennel

4. Cold Pickled Pigs Feet

5. Fried Fingerling Potatoes in Aioli

6. Stuffed Tomatoes

Let's talk about wine: Choose one Brut, one Rose and one Extra Dry sparkling wine to serve: <u>Veuve Clicquot Brut</u>, <u>Montaudon Rose</u>, <u>Martell Extra Dry</u>

****

XVIII
Small Bites and Beers

The following should serve 6-8 people:

1. **French Chicken Wings**

2. **Wings from India**

3. **Chicken Meatballs in Gravy**

4. **Sausage, Potatoes, Onions and Olives**

5. **Cheddar, Bacon and Scallion Biscuits**

6. **Stuffed Small Hot Peppers**

Let's talk about beer: Choose a number of beers to serve: one lager (<u>Yuengling</u>), one ale (<u>Bass</u>) and one stout (<u>Samuel Smith's Oatmeal</u>). For dessert serve a cold <u>Raspberry Lambac</u>.

****

XIX
A Highly Rated (wines) Dinner

Appetizer:

Nam Sod

<u>Dr. Heidemanns Spatlese</u> (95 pts; Wine Spectator)

Pasta:

Gnocchi in Butter Sauce

<u>Montaudon Classe "M"</u> (91pts; Wine Spectator)

Entrée:

T-Bone steak with Chimichurri Sauce

Seville Cauliflower

<u>Caymus Special Select 2006</u> (97pts; Wine Spectator)

Dessert:

Oranges in Orange Syrup served over Toasted Buttered Pound Cake

<u>Chateau Suduirant Sauterne</u> (97pts; Wine Enthusiast)

AND IN CONCLUSION

"And now it's time to say goodbye to all our fam--i--ly". My apologies to you Mickey, I just couldn't resist. As we end our journey together through the world of **Wine and Dine 1-2-3,** we look back and hope that in a way we have created a family.

In this time when the definition of "family" is expanding, and rightly so, we hope we have helped to create a family of individuals who love food and wine and beer and are looking to expand their knowledge and experiment. We hope you too feel that you have joined that family.

What began with my cooking and pairing food for the wine classes we offered at work has expanded into a book with over 500 recipes and over 2,500 wine/beer suggestions. We had to organize the authors of the book----- that was not always easy; establish timelines---even harder. But we have now completed the work and offer it to you hoping you accept it with the same love with which it was produced.

I hope we have touched you in a very special way----there goes my Italian romanticism again. But the book contains much more than just recipes with wine and beer suggestions. True, we have offered many classic recipes from around the world and right here at home in this wonderful country in which we live. In addition, among the pages of this text are many recipes from our personal lives, our backgrounds, our parents, our grandparents, our extender families.

We have given them to you because we want them to live on with you and your families and we hope that they create traditions of your own.

My mother, until her death at 93 years old cooked many of these recipes on a regular basis to take care of her family of 5 children, her grandchildren and great-grandchildren.

You will find these recipes in the Sunday Ragu (you can also call it sauce or gravy); the Christmas Nut Rings; the Pizza Dough; Sausage and Swiss chard and many more. As for the other recipes and ones from other cultures, we have tried to offer you ones that reflect those cultures.

Joseph Coletto, my nephew, has joined me on this journey and has added so much in the way of recipe review and additions. It is exciting to be working with him because he feels the same sense of family that I do; to know that, you need only be at his home on Christmas Eve. It has been wonderful to reconnect with this outstanding person, father, chef.

Joseph Kudla, a lover of food and wine has supported these efforts and has brought knowledge of wine and beer, second to none in the industry. Without him we would not have been able to bring you all the wonderful ADD and PAIR selections that we have.

In future books, we hope to bring you many more and different recipes. Perhaps we will concentrate on one cuisine that we only touched here. Perhaps we will bring spirits into the mixture. Perhaps we will not even speak about alcohol. We look forward to sending you even more "From the Heart."

In any event, as we leave you and with further apologies to Mickey----we hope to **"C"**---**see you real soon "Y"**--- Why? Because we love you

Eat---drink---enjoy!!

Beer/Wine Index

Index